Death in *Winterreise*

MUSICAL MEANING AND INTERPRETATION
Robert S. Hatten, editor

LAURI SUURPÄÄ

Death in *Winterreise*

Musico-Poetic Associations in Schubert's Song Cycle

INDIANA UNIVERSITY PRESS

Bloomington & Indianapolis

This book is a publication of

Indiana University Press
Office of Scholarly Publishing
Herman B Wells Library 350
1320 East 10th Street
Bloomington, Indiana 47405 USA

iupress.indiana.edu

Telephone orders   800–842–6796
Fax orders   812–855–7931

⊖ The paper used in this publication meets the minimum requirements of the American National Standard for Information Sciences—Permanence of Paper for Printed Library Materials, ANSI Z39.48–1992.

Manufactured in the United States of America

Cataloging information is available from the Library of Congress.

ISBN 978-0-253-01100-8 (cloth)
ISBN 978-0-253-01108-4 (ebook)

1 2 3 4 5   19 18 17 16 15 14

To Tiina, Susanna, and Iiris

Contents

Preface

Franz Schubert's *Winterreise* provides a wealth of material for examining inter-actions between words and music. Indeed, the song cycle's deep, many-sided, and often unpredictable quality has produced a wide-ranging body of literature on its text-music relations. Yet the existing literature has far from exhausted *Winterreise;* there is still much that has not been studied or that merits new interpreta-tions. By examining in detail most of the second part of *Winterreise,* songs 14–24, this book attempts to complement the picture, incomplete though it will remain. The choice of songs to be studied is based on the cycle's poetic organization. My intention is to illuminate one narrowly defined area of the musico-poetic aspects of *Winterreise,* namely, how the notion of death occurs in the poems of the cycle's second part and how this theme is reflected in the music. The protagonist's atti-tude to death changes as the cycle proceeds. Initially, in "Der Lindenbaum" (no. 5) he wishes to avoid death, but ultimately, in the songs that I will discuss (nos. 14–24), death becomes a tempting, even longed-for possibility: death would pro-vide the lonely wanderer an escape from his painful life. It is on this positive view of death that I will concentrate, hence, the discussion of songs 14–24 only. In the poems the desire for death is often contrasted with lost love, the starting point of the wanderer's desolate winter journey, and I will also elucidate the relationships between lost love and death.

Past love and future death can be seen as combined into one larger subject: they both represent longing, the *Sehnsucht* characteristic of early German Ro-mantic literature. But to understand the overall unfolding of *Winterreise,* it is important to keep in mind that the wanderer longs for two objects, not just one: the beloved in the cycle's first part and death in the second. That neither yearn-ing can be satisfied makes the cycle all the more tragic. The longing for unobtain-able love and death is directly related, at a more general level, to a theme that per-vades the entire cycle of *Winterreise:* the juxtaposition of illusion and reality. This juxtaposition affects the course of the cycle in numerous ways, so the examina-tion of death (and its relation to lost love) provides a chance to discuss one facet of this broader theme.

The shift from looking back (to the love of the past) to abandoning hope of re-gaining the beloved and beginning to look ahead (to a death ultimately desired) is the foundation on which I base my interpretation of *Winterreise*'s underlying narrative. In short, longing remains the central topic, but the object of the long-ing changes. The change is not instantaneous, however. Rather, it moves through various stages of uncertainty, hope, determination, and frustration. These phases carry the underlying narrative to the cycle's ending, a conclusion, however, that brings no consolation or peace.

In writing this study I have three aims; the first two are directly related to Schubert's cycle, while the third is more general. The first is to provide close readings of songs 14–24 with a concentration on Schenkerian voice leading and expression. In this way, the study attempts to fill a clear void; although there is much general literature on *Winterreise,* there are surprisingly few detailed musical analyses of its individual songs. Second, I discuss the cyclical aspects and underlying narrative in part 2 of *Winterreise* and thereby challenge the quite widely accepted view that there is no goal-oriented trajectory in the cycle. Third, I present new methodological perspectives on the musico-poetic associations both in individual Lieder and in song cycles. Text-music relationships are discussed in separate songs at three levels: imitation, emotions, and structural relationships. Most important, this study introduces one way of examining structural relationships between music and text without suggesting that music directly represents the semantic content of a text. With song cycles, in turn, the study introduces novel methodological ways of elucidating poetic narrative, harmonic unity, and musical cross-references.

* * *

This book is divided into three parts. Part 1 (chapters 1–4) provides background. The first two chapters are mainly historical. Chapter 1 discusses the genesis of both the text and the music of *Winterreise* and provides a tentative view of the cycle's poetic narrative. Chapter 2 briefly charts the historical environment in which the cycle was composed, discussing early nineteenth-century views of the Lied, song cycles, and the notion of death. Chapters 3–4 supply theoretical background for analyzing the music, the text, and musico-poetic aspects. While chapter 3 offers five fundamental propositions on which the discussion of the relationships between music and text will be based, chapter 4 introduces some principles of Greimassian semiotics and Schenkerian analysis that will be applied in examining the poetic and musical structures, respectively. This pairing of Greimassian and Schenkerian theories provides a novel means for discussing structural musico-poetic associations.

Part 2 (chapters 5–11) offers analyses of songs 14–24. Each analysis proceeds in three stages: first, the music and the text are discussed independently; thereafter, the discussion of the musico-poetic associations is based on these. In addition to poetic and musical structures (which are elucidated, as noted above, through Greimassian and Schenkerian theories), the analyses take into account textual and musical expression as well as musical imitation. Each song is studied as a closed entity, with only a few passing references made to the overall course of the cycle.

Part 3 (chapters 12–14) concentrates on the cyclical aspects. Chapter 12 reviews some methodologically oriented literature on song cycles, concluding that the discussions of any cycle's unity are often based on three interrelated and interlinked factors: textual unity (either a narrative or a recurring poetic theme), musical cross-references (often motivic connections), and harmonic relation-ships (associations between the keys of a cycle's individual songs). Furthermore, some studies challenge the very concept of the unity of song cycles. Chapter 13 then discusses these issues vis-à-vis *Winterreise* and suggests a novel approach to all three areas of connections: the discussion of the poetic trajectory draws on narratological ideas of Roland Barthes, musical cross-references are understood to cover a wide variety of musical elements (not only motivic connections), and the large-scale harmonic logic is examined through principles of neo-Rieman-nian theory. Finally, chapter 14, the epilogue, suggests a rather precise meaning for the notion of death in *Winterreise*.

The three parts differ from each other in their orientation. The first and third are quite general, mostly requiring no specific music-theoretical knowledge. The second, by contrast, consists of detailed analyses of songs 14–24, and here the reader should have knowledge of the principles of Schenkerian analysis. At the end of each analytical chapter in part 2, I have added a short paragraph summing up the poetic situation in the song just examined. Those readers who do not want to read the detailed musical analyses may read these paragraphs only, as they should provide sufficient information for following the discussion of the cyclical aspects of *Winterreise* in part 3.

Acknowledgments

This study has been greatly influenced by many people, including colleagues who have commented on various drafts and analyses, as well as scholars whose ideas have influenced my way of thinking. It is not possible to mention all of the individuals who have, either directly or indirectly, molded my musical views generally or my approach to *Winterreise* in particular. Yet there are several people whose influence has been so remarkable that their roles must be acknowledged.

Professor Carl Schachter has had a great impact on my musical thinking. Even though I haven't discussed the songs of *Winterreise* with him (if my memory serves me correctly, "Der Wegweiser" is the only song examined in this study that we ever looked at together), his approach to music can be seen throughout this book both in my musical analyses and in my views on the nature of musico-poetic associations. Professor L. Poundie Burstein read parts of an earlier draft and made valuable comments. Dr. Leena Eilittä read the sections that discuss German Romanticism, and her expertise in this field was extremely helpful. Dr. Olli Väisälä has shared my interest in Schenkerian analysis at the Sibelius Academy, and our countless discussions on specific analytical details, as well as on large principles, have been both fun and thought provoking. At the final stage, Professor Glenda Dawn Goss read the entire manuscript, helping me in countless ways to improve my English language. In addition, she made several perceptive comments on the book's content. My students at the Sibelius Academy, as well as those in the workshops I gave on *Winterreise* at the Graduate Center of the City University of New York, asked thought-provoking questions that forced me to refine my readings. During the New York workshops, Professor William Rothstein made perceptive comments on several of my analyses. Professor Robert S. Hatten has been most supportive throughout the many years I have worked on this project. He read the entire manuscript, making numerous valuable comments. The anonymous readers of the Indiana University Press made me tackle some difficult topics I had been afraid to face, which greatly improved the book. The staff at the Indiana University Press were always ready and willing to help in practical matters, and their professionalism guaranteed a safe end to a long journey. I wish to thank especially Mary M. Hill, Jenna Whittaker, and Raina Polivka for their efforts in bringing this book into print.

Finally, the support of my family and friends and the interest they have shown in my work have been of immeasurable value. I wish to thank especially my wife, Tiina, and our daughters, Susanna and Iiris, to whom I dedicate this work.

Note on the Translations
of the Poems

I have consulted the published translations of the poems of *Winterreise* by George Bird and Richard Stokes (1991), Lois Phillips (1996), Richard Wigmore (1988), and Susan Youens (1991). The translations presented in this book are based in part on these sources but modified so as to convey as clearly as possible those aspects of the poetic meanings that I address in my analyses.

Death in *Winterreise*

Part 1. Background

1 Genesis and Narrative of *Winterreise*

1.1. The Genesis of *Winterreise*

The genesis of both the poems and the music of *Winterreise* is complex and took place in several stages.[1] The poet Wilhelm Müller published the verses used in the cycle in three separate collections (table 1.1). The first twelve poems initially appeared in *Urania: Taschenbuch auf das Jahr 1823*. Susan Youens (1991, 22) has argued that Müller first considered these twelve as a complete and closed whole. Yet Müller published ten more poems, still in 1823, this time in *Deutsche Blätter für Poesie, Litteratur, Kunst und Theatre*. In 1824 these two sets appeared along with two additional poems ("Die Post" and "Täuschung") in a publication called *Gedichte aus den hinterlassenen Papieren eines reisenden Waldhornisten II*. This was the first time the twenty-four poems were published together. In this third publication, Müller drastically changed the order of the poems. Hence, the overall course of the final cycle differs significantly from what would have happened if the first two publications had simply been conjoined and supplemented by the two added poems. Müller's reasons for changing the order or for supplementing the original *Urania* poems in the first place are not known.[2]

Schubert composed *Winterreise* in two stages, and, accordingly, the cycle consists of two parts, first published separately. He apparently intended the first part, songs 1–12, as an independent whole. It is likely that Schubert first discovered only the twelve poems published in *Urania* and set these without knowing the other twelve. As table 1.1 indicates, the order of the first twelve songs of *Winterreise* corresponds exactly to that of the *Urania* poems. Both the manuscript of the first part and the engraver's fair copy have the word *Fine* after the twelfth song, which supports the assertion that part 1 was originally intended as a closed cycle.[3] In the first edition, the word *Fine* has been deleted. The autograph manuscript of part 1 is dated February 1827. As Robert Winter (1982, 241) has shown in his manuscript study, Schubert had the kind of paper used in the autograph of part 1 from September 1826 to May 1827; thus, this autograph must have been finished by May 1827 (an exception being the revision of "Rückblick," which could not have been composed before June 1827).

Schubert apparently discovered the twenty-four poems published in *Waldhornisten* only after having completed part 1. As table 1.1 shows, he did not change the order of the first twelve songs as Müller had done with the poems, thereby keeping part 1 as in Müller's original scheme. Schubert also preserved the order of the new poems as they appear in *Waldhornisten*, only he put them

Table 1.1. Order of the poems in Wilhelm Müller's three publications and in Schubert's cycle

Urania	Deutsche Blätter	Waldhornisten II	Schubert	Key of the autograph → key of the first edition
			PART 1	
1. Gute Nacht (1)		1. Gute Nacht (1)	1. Gute Nacht	
2. Die Wetterfahne (2)		2. Die Wetterfahne (2)	2. Die Wetterfahne	
3. Gefrorne Tränen (3)		3. Gefrorne Tränen (3)	3. Gefrorne Tränen	
4. Erstarrung (4)		4. Erstarrung (4)	4. Erstarrung	
5. Der Lindenbaum (5)		5. Der Lindenbaum (5)	5. Der Lindenbaum	
6. Wasserflut (6)		6. Die Post (13)	6. Wasserflut	f♯ → e
7. Auf dem Flusse (7)		7. Wasserflut (6)	7. Auf dem Flusse	
8. Rückblick (8)		8. Auf dem Flusse (7)	8. Rückblick	
9. Irrlicht (9)		9. Rückblick (8)	9. Irrlicht	
10. Rast (10)		10. Der greise Kopf (14)	10. Rast	d → c
11. Frühlingstraum (11)		11. Die Krähe (15)	11. Frühlingstraum	
12. Einsamkeit (12)		12. Letzte Hoffnung (16)	12. Einsamkeit	d → b
			PART 2	
		13. Im Dorfe (17)	13. Die Post	
	1. Der greise Kopf (14)	14. Der stürmische Morgen (18)	14. Der greise Kopf	
	2. Letzte Hoffnung (16)	15. Täuschung (19)	15. Die Krähe	
	3. Die Krähe (15)	16. Der Wegweiser (20)	16. Letzte Hoffnung	
	4. Im Dorfe (17)	17. Das Wirtshaus (21)	17. Im Dorfe	
	5. Der stürmische Morgen (18)	18. Irrlicht (9)	18. Der stürmische Morgen	
		19. Rast (10)	19. Täuschung	
	6. Die Nebensonnen (23)	20. Die Nebensonnen (23)	20. Der Wegweiser	
	7. Der Wegweiser (20)	21. Frühlingstraum (11)	21. Das Wirtshaus	
	8. Das Wirtshaus (21)	22. Mut (22)	22. Mut	a → g
	9. Mut (22)	23. Einsamkeit (12)	23. Die Nebensonnen	
	10. Der Leiermann (24)	24. Der Leiermann (24)	24. Der Leiermann	b → a

in sequence in part 2 instead of scattering them among the poems of part 1 as Müller had done. There is only one exception to Schubert's adherence to Müller's order: he reversed the positions of "Die Nebensonnen" and "Mut."[4] As a result, the overall narrative formed by Schubert's *Winterreise* differs from that in Müller's complete cycle in *Waldhornisten*.

The autograph manuscript of part 2 is a fair copy dated October 1827. Winter (1982, 248) has demonstrated that the songs were written on paper that Schubert used from October 1827 to April 1828. But since the autograph is a fair copy, Schubert must have composed the songs earlier, and sketches for "Mut" and "Die Nebensonnen" can be dated from June to September 1827, suggesting that Schubert was working on the songs of part 2 at that time (246, 248). The documentary evidence, then, supports the assertion that he began to work on part 2 (sketching it at least as early as June 1827) only after having completed part 1 (which was finished by May 1827).

Five of the songs appear in different keys in the first edition from those found in the autograph manuscript (see the last column of table 1.1). Youens has suggested that these transpositions might have been made at the request of the publisher, Tobias Haslinger, in order to avoid uncomfortably high pitches for the singer. The publisher might have feared that a high tessitura would reduce the market for the cycle (Youens 1991, 95–96).

The above-drafted genesis of *Winterreise* raises two questions important for our present concerns: Should Müller's final ordering of the poems (as found in *Waldhornisten*) be taken into consideration in the overall narrative of *Winterreise*? Should the songs that were transposed be analyzed in the keys found in the manuscript or in the first edition?

As for the first question, since this study deals with Schubert's *Winterreise*, it seems justifiable to discuss the narrative only as it appears in the song cycle. (This does not mean, of course, that the comparison of the two orderings would not be an interesting topic for a separate study.) The second question is more problematic. Scholars have not been unanimous in considering the relative merits of the two transpositions for the overall tonal scheme. Christopher Lewis (1988, 58–66) has an interpretation of the overall dynamic of the cycle that relies on the keys of the autograph, while Kurt von Fischer suggests that the keys in the first edition are better related to the text (Fischer's view is discussed in Lewis 1988, 62). Youens (1991, 95–99), in turn, has suggested that the original keys might have had poetic implications for Schubert but that the transpositions too form an effective, if somewhat different, dramatic tonal plan. Finally, Anthony Newcomb has argued that "the transpositions do not much change the overall effect of tonality in the cycle" (1986, 169).

Here I will examine the songs in the keys of the first edition. Schubert helped to prepare the engraver's copy of part 1, and he proofread part 2, so these are the final keys that he saw and evidently accepted. Moreover, we cannot know for sure what led to the transpositions, and the situation might even be different for different songs. In the autograph manuscript of part 1, Schubert (1989, 33) gave instructions to transpose "Rast." I have not had the opportunity to study the original autograph, but judging from the facsimile edition (Schubert 1989), it appears that the ink in these instructions is the same as in some of the final changes and additions to the song. So it is at least conceivable that the idea of transposition was Schubert's own, born at the same time as other final changes.[5] The other two transposed songs from part 1 ("Wasserflut" and "Einsamkeit") appear in the new keys only in the engraver's copy.[6] But even here the idea of transposition might have originated with Schubert. We know that he worked closely with the copyist when preparing the engraver's copy. In her introduction to the facsimile edition, Youens has observed that "passages that differ markedly from the autograph appear in the *Stichvorlage* with no trace of correction [by Schubert]" (Schubert 1989, xvin18). Thus, these alterations are not mistakes by the copyist but rather changes suggested by Schubert himself. Again, it is at least conceivable that Schubert had second thoughts about the keys and had these changed when the engraver's copy was prepared. The situation is different in part 2. Here the manuscript contains transposition instructions in the hand of Tobias Haslinger, the publisher.

The circumstances are thus complex, and it is not possible to know Schubert's thoughts on the situation. As a result, it is not clear whether the new keys should be handled the same in every case. For example, should the new key for "Rast" be used (since it has Schubert's own instructions for transposition, possibly made during the final changes) while analyzing the other songs in the original keys? Or should the new keys be used in analyzing part 1 while opting for the original ones in part 2, since the instructions to transpose the songs are in the publisher's hand? To avoid such questions, which are unanswerable given the current knowledge of *Winterreise*'s compositional history, I will use the keys in the first edition, which we know Schubert accepted, or at least knew about, as he prepared his work for publication.

Some associations among the songs will certainly be lost.[7] For example, if "Einsamkeit" remains in the original D minor, it provides a firmer conclusion for part 1: the music returns to the key of the opening song, so that D minor frames part 1 and hence underlines its unity.[8] But the transpositions also create new connections. For example, if "Wasserflut" is transposed into E minor, then songs 5, 6, and 7 form a tonally unified whole (all in E major or minor). In spite of such fluctuating connections, I do not believe that the keys of the five transposed songs are of primary importance for the overall course and unity of *Winterreise*. I will return to this issue in section 13.2, which discusses the large-scale harmonic organization of the second part of *Winterreise*.

1.2. Underlying Narrative in the Poems of *Winterreise*

Many scholars dealing with *Winterreise* have discussed the degree to which the poems form a unified plot or a thoroughgoing underlying narrative. The cycle is often compared to *Die schöne Müllerin,* and, by comparison, the poems of the earlier cycle seem to form a much clearer plot. There are also studies

Table 1.2. Underlying narrative of *Winterreise*

state 1		state 2
looking backward		looking ahead
love	⇒	death

that completely deny any overarching trajectory in *Winterreise*. Cyrus Hamlin, for example, has suggested that "the twenty four poems published by Wilhelm Müller that make up this cycle categorically resist and oppose any sense of narrative" (1999, 116), while Charles Rosen has spoken about the "reduction of narrative almost to zero" (1995, 196). The commentators who deny any plotlike trajectory do not necessarily argue, however, that the cycle lacks unity. But this unity is seen to grow out of the inner sentiments of the protagonist rather than from outward actions.[9] Thrasybulos G. Georgiades, for example, has suggested that *Winterreise* "is governed throughout by only one theme, varied in different ways: the unhappy me, which is mirrored in nature (or some other factor: 'Die Post,' 'Der Leiermann'); the innermost being, whose state is defined through its reflection in the outer: 'My heart, in this brook do you now recognize your own image' ('Auf dem Flusse'), 'My heart sees its own image painted in the sky' ('Der stürmische Morgen')" (1967, 359). Youens, in turn, has argued that *Winterreise* "is a monodrama, a predecessor of Expressionist interior monologues. In such works as . . . Arnold Schoenberg's *Erwartung*, a single character investigates the labyrinth of her or his own psyche in search of self-knowledge, escape, or surcease from pain, a flight inward into the hothouse of imagination rather than outward into the real world" (1991, 51).

Despite the sparseness of concrete goal-directed action, I suggest that the poetic cycle does have a kind of plot, albeit a vague one. This narrative consists only partly of actual events. The main unifying features occur in the protagonist's inner world, as is also suggested in the comments quoted from Georgiades and Youens above. But I would argue that this inner world is not invariable throughout *Winterreise*. Rather, it changes during the cycle, and this change is related to one of the most pervasive features of the wanderer's inner thoughts: the juxtaposition of reality and illusion. There are two fundamental forms of illusion in the poems: one is associated with the love that has been lost, while the other is associated with a longing for death. (Death may also be understood more generally to symbolize a state of peace wherein misery is no longer felt. I will return to this issue in section 2.3 and chapter 14.) The first illusion looks back to the past, while the second looks ahead to something the protagonist hopes to attain in the future. The cycle moves from the first illusion, which governs part 1, to the second illusion, which governs part 2.

Since there is a transformation from the first illusion to the second, there is also narrative activity, clarified in table 1.2. This underlying narrative consists of two states and a movement from the first state to the second. In both, the protagonist tries to reach something that he ultimately cannot attain and that therefore remains an illusion; in the first state, he looks back to the lost beloved, while in the second state, he looks ahead to death, for which he longs. Both states portray a situation that is unpleasant for the narrator, since he cannot have the object for which he yearns. The protagonist's temporal perspective on these two forms of illusion (love and death) is always the present moment in his journey. With some brief and fleeting exceptions, the wanderer knows that the illusion he contemplates and longs for is not, and cannot be, real. This knowledge makes his longing even more desperate.

Individual poems by no means elaborate on this underlying narrative (a shift from looking back to the lost love to looking ahead to the hoped-for death) consistently enough to form an unequivocal, linear trajectory that spans the cycle. In this sense I agree with the scholars referred to above who state that *Winterreise* has no clear narrative. Yet I would like to suggest that the cycle can be loosely divided into connected groups of poems and that these groups consistently elaborate on the underlying narrative shown in table 1.2. Here I offer a tentative division of the poems into thematic groups, based on the texts alone, without taking the music into consideration. In chapter 13, which examines cyclical aspects of part 2 of *Winterreise*, I will also discuss the overall organization from the musico-poetic perspective and, more formally, the foundations of my proposed textual narrative.

I divide the poems into nine units, based on thematic factors. The units are not equal in length: some include as many as five poems, while others consist of only one. Several of the units include poems that contrast with others in their group, thereby challenging the cohesion of the units. In such instances the unity is suggested by the larger context: the thematic contrast among contiguous units speaks for the unity within the intervening group. Occasionally, some poems that contrast with their own unit might, from the perspective of content alone, be better suited to some other group. I will not, however, assemble nonadjacent poems belonging to different units. In other words, my division is based only on thematic links between contiguous poems, or groups of poems (a syntagmatic perspective), rather than on general thematic associations that do not take the poems' location in the cycle into account (a paradigmatic perspective).[10] Since here my aim is to indicate how the underlying narrative shown in table 1.2 is elaborated upon in individual poems, the syntagmatic perspective seems justified. I will, however, comment on associations among the groups, since these, of course, form an important strand in the cycle.[11]

1. Departure (Poems 1–5)

In this group, the wanderer begins his journey. He leaves the town where his beloved lives, explaining the reasons for his departure. This group is unified by references to places and objects associated with the beloved: in "Gute Nacht" the speaker leaves her house and walks past its gate; in "Die Wetterfahne" he looks at the weather vane on the roof of the beloved's house; in "Erstarrung" he looks at the meadow where they walked in the summer; and in "Der Lindenbaum" he walks past a linden tree in whose shade he spent happy times in the past. In each of these poems, the concrete references are juxtaposed with comments on the speaker's present inner state, the misery resulting from the loss of love. The recollection of past happiness represents illusion; the present misery is reality.

Two poems of this first group deserve further comment. The third poem, "Gefrorne Tränen," differs from the others in this group because there are no references to concrete factors associated with the beloved. Rather, the narrator emphasizes his emotions and the strong contrast between his intense feelings and the cold winter. "Gefrorne Tränen" can thus be understood as an outpouring of the wanderer's inner sentiments, irrespective of the concrete associations in the surrounding poems. This poem stresses underlying unhappiness rather than the act of departing. The other poem deserving special mention is "Der Lindenbaum." Here the narrator makes the first choice in the cycle (the decision to depart had been made before the opening poem): he chooses to continue the journey instead of seeking rest, or death, in the shadow of the linden tree. Thus, the protagonist consciously chooses his journey with all of its miseries.

2. The Continuation of the Journey and the Outpouring of Misery (Poems 6–9)

Once the choice to continue the journey has been made in "Der Lindenbaum," references to specific things associated with the beloved cease. The narrator is already far from the town (as suggested at the end of "Der Lindenbaum" and in the final stanza of "Wasserflut"). Now that he has left his beloved and the town behind and is without tangible reminders of the past, he can concentrate on his feelings, the misery resulting from losing the beloved. He compares these sentiments with the outer reality and nature, a comparison already made in "Gefrorne Tränen." Thus, there is a thematic association between the first two groups. In "Irrlicht" the wanderer has lost his way while following the will-o'-the-wisp. But he cares little whether or not he finds the way, stating that his only consolation is that all misery will end in death. This poem could be understood as a description of fatigue, primarily mental (following the depressing emotions of the previous poems) but also physical (the long journey without interruption): the wanderer is too tired to grasp reality and instead follows the will-o'-the-wisp—an illusion.

The eighth poem, "Rückblick," differs from the others in this group, thematically being associated with the poems of the first group. Here the speaker again makes clear associations with things connected to his beloved, specifically, the town where she lives. The poem would seem to contradict the chronology of events. But this contradiction is justified by the song's title, "Backward Glance." Moreover, "Rückblick" has a clear function in this second group. On the one hand, the poem's final stanza shows that the option of turning back is still in the narrator's mind; at least implicitly, his love and the vain hope of regaining it linger on. The cycle's first form of illusion, the lost love, is again stressed. On the other hand, the rush away from town sets up the fatigue in the subsequent "Irrlicht."

3. Rest and Dreams (Poems 10–11)

The fatigue intimated in "Irrlicht" is made explicit in "Rast" when the speaker says that he realizes how tired he is only when he stops to rest. The weariness of "Irrlicht" was indeed only implied: the protagonist was too tired even to notice, and hence, "Rast" retrospectively justifies the above interpretation of "Irrlicht." In "Frühlingstraum" the protagonist falls asleep, dreaming of spring and love, the illusions that prevail in the preceding poems. When he awakens, these dreams are abruptly juxtaposed with reality. This direct juxtaposition of loss of love and past happiness, or winter and spring, sums up the opposition of reality and illusion expressed in the preceding poems.

4. The Journey Continues: Deep Depression (Poem 12)

After the remainder of the third thematic group, the journey continues. The narrator sees no consolation and simply goes on walking. Part 1 of *Winterreise* thus ends in deep depression whose reasons are clearly recalled and encapsulated in the preceding poem, "Frühlingstraum." It seems that the protagonist no longer contemplates regaining lost happiness, which was abandoned for good in "Frühlingstraum." Rather, he simply wants to feel less miserable, to arrive at a more peaceful state of mind.

Part 1 of *Winterreise* thus forms a clear narrative, which stems from the chronology, the events, the environment, and the protagonist's emotions. The situation is different in part 2. Here the narrative is somewhat more abstract, based less on chronology and actual events. Moreover, the cohesion of the poems is not as strong as in part 1. Yet I believe that an overarching course can also be described for part 2.

5. Continuation and Back References (Poem 13)

The function of "Die Post" in the overall course of *Winterreise* is quite problematic. As discussed in section 1.1, the poem was added only in the third of Müller's publications; it did not appear in the *Deutsche Blätter,* which includes ten of the twelve poems of *Winterreise*'s part 2 in almost the same order as in Schubert's cycle. In *Waldhornisten* "Die Post" is the sixth poem. In this position it clearly seems to underline the distance from the town mentioned at the end of the preceding poem, "Der Lindenbaum." As the beginning of part 2, however, "Die Post" could be understood as having a different function. After the hopeless "Einsamkeit," "Die Post" recalls elements mentioned in the earlier poems, which led to the depressing ending of part 1: the beloved (directly mentioned, incidentally, only once more after this, in "Täuschung"); the town where the beloved lives and its surroundings; and finally, the impossibility of regaining the past, symbolized in "Die Post" by the fact that the narrator receives no letter. In addition to recalling the previous events, this poem is the cycle's last to represent clearly the first state of the underlying narrative, the one recalling lost love. Thus, it functions as a kind of mediator between the two states shown in table 1.2.

6. Death as a Positive Option (Poems 14–15)

With "Der greise Kopf" and "Die Krähe," attention turns from meditation on the past to contemplation of the future (see table 1.2). Now death is mentioned as a positive option, something hoped for but not yet at hand. In "Der greise Kopf" the narrator wishes that he were old (death would be near), but this turns out to be an illusion. In "Die Krähe" a crow has been the protagonist's companion throughout his journey, and he hopes that it is a symbol of death, accompanying him to the grave. These two poems are an important turning point in the cycle, transferring the emphasis on the first state, shown in table 1.2, to the second state. The protagonist now sees signs (his graying hair and the crow) that he interprets as being, or rather hopes them to be, references to death. Furthermore, "Der greise Kopf" and "Die Krähe" continue on from the state suggested at the end of the fourth unit, the last song of part 1 ("Einsamkeit"). There the protagonist wishes that he no longer would feel so miserable. The death mentioned in "Der greise Kopf" and "Die Krähe" can be understood as a state where such sadness is not felt.

7. Reflecting on the Idea of Death and Renouncing Love (Poems 16–19)

The seventh group is perhaps the most loosely connected in the cycle, and its interpretation as a unit is justified primarily by the larger context, the fact that it is framed by the first contemplation of death in the sixth group and the ultimate choice of death in the eighth. Before the protagonist can hope to reach the second state of the underlying narrative shown in table 1.2, he must abandon the first state altogether: he cannot hope to get the beloved back and at the same time want to die. As a result, he must stop yearning for past happiness. I argue that the seventh group describes this process of giving up these initial hopes. It gradually moves toward an acceptance of death, with the wanderer admitting that it is impossible for him to attain love. Accordingly, this group provides a context for the notion of death that emerged in the sixth group of poems.

"Letzte Hoffnung," the first poem in the seventh group, supports this somewhat speculative reading. Here the protagonist must accept that all hope is gone, and at this point in *Winterreise*, lost hope would seem to refer clearly to past happiness. The same impression is conveyed by the next poem, "Im Dorfe," where the narrator says that he is through with all dreams. In effect, there is no hope of regaining lost happiness; it is only an illusion. "Täuschung" underlines this idea by emphasizing that the beloved and her warm house are the wanderer's delusions.

The intervening "Der stürmische Morgen" may be interpreted as describing the wintry emotional coldness and the rather broken quality of the self that follow from giving up hope of love; the speaker would lose something fundamental to humanity, the capacity to love. Yet this unsettled coldness is ultimately preferable to misery. This reading of "Der stürmische Morgen" is supported by two direct references to poems in part 1: the emotional coldness in the last two stanzas of "Erstarrung" and the wildness of the storm as a kind of consolation in "Einsamkeit."

8. The Choice of Death (Poem 20)

"Der Wegweiser" is one of the key poems in *Winterreise*. The sixth group presents death as a positive option, while in the seventh there is a gradual acceptance that loss of love is necessary for finding death or, more generally, peace of mind. In "Der Wegweiser" the narrator consciously chooses to seek death: he says that he must travel a road from which no one has returned.

9. The Inability to Find Death (Poems 21–24)

In the ninth and final group the protagonist would like to find the death he has chosen in "Der Wegweiser," but this turns out to be impossible. In "Das Wirtshaus" he has arrived at a cemetery, but there is no place for him; in "Die Nebensonnen" he waits for the last of his three suns to set, as darkness will only arrive thereafter; and in "Der Leiermann" he would like to join the hurdy-gurdy man, who has lost all emotions and may be understood as a symbol of death, a state in which misery and pain—or any emotions—are no longer felt. The frustration of not being able to find the peaceful state spoken about in these poems is illustrated in "Mut," a poem that follows the first unsuccessful attempt to find peace in "Das Wirtshaus."

The ninth group represents the second state shown in table 1.2. Now the object of the protagonist's hopes is death, but it eludes his grasp. Hence, death, like love, remains an illusion, providing a desperate end to a desperate journey.

To summarize the underlying narrative: first, the protagonist leaves town, noticing its tangible features and surroundings (poems 1–5). Once the town has been left behind, he contemplates his misery (poems 6–8). He grows weary (poem 9), a state he becomes aware of only when he stops to rest (poem 10), and he falls asleep (poem 11). On waking up, he again sees the reality that displaces his dreams (poem 11) and so continues on his hopeless journey (poem 12).[12] There are two poems that interfere with this narrative flow ("Gefrorne Tränen" and "Rückblick"), but these can be seen as having important functions in the overall narrative course, as suggested above. Part 1 then represents in its entirety the first state of table 1.2.

Part 2 opens by briefly recalling (in poem 13) this first state. Death is then mentioned as a positive option (poems 14–15). But in order to find death, the wanderer must first abandon the hope of regaining love (the first state in table 1.2), a question he now contemplates (poems 16–19). The choice of death, and as a result the abandonment of hope, is then made (poem 20). Poems 14–20 can be understood as representing the transformation (the double-lined arrow) shown in table 1.2. The protagonist is about to abandon his initial illusion, the hope of regaining love. The choice is difficult but is ultimately made in "Der Wegweiser." (This choice can be understood as a counterpart to the wanderer's decision not to seek death, which he makes in "Der Lindenbaum.") The choice in "Der Wegweiser" is to leave love behind and opt for death, the second form of illusion. The choice leads to poems in which the narrator tries to find death or peace (poems 21–24). He is not successful, and even at the end, death too remains an illusion.

1.3. Death in the Overall Narrative of *Winterreise*

Because this study examines the function of death in *Winterreise*, the detailed analyses concentrate on songs 14–24, the settings in which the protagonist deals with his relationship to death. Accordingly, the emphasis is on the second part of the cycle, in which the wanderer looks ahead to his coming demise, rather than on songs in which he recalls the love he has lost. (In many instances, thoughts of both love and death are present, so a distinction is not always possible.) However, I will not examine all the songs in *Winterreise* referring to death. Before "Der greise Kopf," the first song to be analyzed here, death is mentioned in two poems. In "Der Lindenbaum" (no. 5) the speaker hears the linden tree calling to him, promising peace, apparently in death. But the wanderer refuses to follow the call, instead continuing his journey through the cold and wind. In "Irrlicht" (no. 9) the protagonist observes that, just as every stream ultimately finds its way to the sea, so all sorrows will end in the grave. The song clearly expresses the idea of death as a peaceful state that relieves the sufferer of all pain, a theme that will govern the second part of the cycle.

Death is thus depicted in a very different light in "Der Lindenbaum" than in "Irrlicht." It is something to be shunned in "Der Lindenbaum" (in which the protagonist walks on, refusing to heed its call), while in "Irrlicht" death is the almost fatalistic destiny of all mankind and all emotions. Both views differ from the perspective of the cycle's second part, wherein death is seen in a positive light. The difference is clear in "Der Lindenbaum," where death is negative and something to be avoided, whereas in "Irrlicht" death is viewed as a state in which there is no more misery, a position much closer to that of part 2. But although in "Irrlicht" death is ultimately human destiny, the end of our path, in the part 2 poems death is increasingly viewed as an option that can be consciously chosen. In other words, death is not only the end point passively reached at a certain moment but also something that can be actively pursued.

The narrative function played by the theme of death in these two poems, which is clearly secondary to the local narrative, also differs significantly from the poems of part 2. In "Der Lindenbaum" the thought of death occurs when the protagonist leaves the town in which his beloved lives; he is only beginning his journey. By contrast, in "Irrlicht" the thought comes when the speaker is pouring out his misery. Furthermore, death remains an isolated topic in each poem: it has no points of connection with the surrounding poems. In part 2, however, death is a constant presence; it is no longer a theme that occurs only in a few poems (as discussed in the preceding section). The wanderer begins to see death as something positive that can (and should) be actively sought. This trajectory is consistently elaborated on as the second part unfolds, as will be explained in more detail in chapter 13.[13]

These differences of perspective justify the exclusion of "Der Lindenbaum" and "Irrlicht" from the songs to be analyzed in detail here. Yet it is not insignificant that death is introduced in part 1. When it becomes a primary theme in the cycle's second part, it does not appear out of nowhere. Rather, death has been considered previously, although the attitude is different from the stance in part 2. First, death is seen as something to be avoided ("Der Lindenbaum"); then it is considered the ultimate destiny, lying somewhere in an indistinct future ("Irrlicht"). From "Der greise Kopf" onward, death is viewed as something positive, a state the protagonist hopes to find soon, and it is this view on which the analyses in this study concentrate.

2   *Winterreise* in Context

2.1. Lied and Song Cycle in the Early Nineteenth Century

The moment when the Lied was born has sometimes been pinpointed precisely: October 19, 1814, the day Schubert composed "Gretchen am Spinnrade," his first great Goethe setting.[1] The early history of the genre is, of course, more complex than this. Lieder had been composed before 1814, and the genre had been discussed in literature. Yet the claim is not without foundation. Schubert's through-composed "Gretchen am Spinnrade" hardly meets the requirement that contemporaneous commentators demanded of Lieder. More generally, the novel features of Schubert's Lied output (of which "Gretchen am Spinnrade" is an early example) had an enormous impact on the genre, expanding the conventions that had hitherto been associated with it. Moreover, the contrast that many of Schubert's Lieder had with their predecessors (as well as with contemporaneous songs) indicates that in Schubert's time, there were significant differences among the various types of Lieder. Indeed, Carl Dahlhaus has suggested that we should not approach Lieder with the assumption that there is a unified Lied genre: "Strictly speaking, 'the' lied is no more a genre than 'the' piece of instrumental music. . . . To grasp the historical character of the Schubert lied, as well as the European context from which it stood out, we will have to proceed from the wide array of lied traditions rather than the unity of the lied as an ideal" (1989, 96).[2]

The emergence of the Lied as a significant genre in the early nineteenth century was greatly influenced by the changes in German poetry wrought by the young Goethe and his generation; for decades Goethe's texts remained primary among the poets whose verses were set to music.[3] Goethe's poems established the lyrical mode as the central mode of poetry, and the principles found in his poems were followed (and imitated) by numerous writers, among them Wilhelm Müller, the poet of *Winterreise*. Cyrus Hamlin has noted that "Goethe's supreme achievement as a poet resides in the simplicity and seeming spontaneity and authenticity of his songs (*Lieder*)" (2005, 171). Formally, the lyrical poems by Goethe, as well as those by other writers of the time, were often simple and folklike in character.[4] Usually, but by no means always, the texts consisted of several stanzas of four lines each. Thematically, they frequently featured an outpouring of personal emotions, clearly centering on the speaking self. The poems often presented love and longing in one form or another or used nature as a metaphor for personal sentiments. Alongside the lyrical poems there were more dramatic poems, which included a clearer narrative trajectory. These might describe supernatural events, for example, or heroic deeds. Again, Goethe was a significant figure here, evident from his ballad "Erlkönig," which was set to music by Schubert and several other composers in the first decades of the nineteenth century.

This new poetry provided composers with texts that exhibited immediate and personally felt emotions. The Lied as a musical genre was thus intimately entwined with the poetry written in the last decades of the eighteenth century and the first decades of the nineteenth, a connection stressed by Steven Paul Scher:

> The decisive impetus came in the guise of a veritable poetic revolution, without which the lied as we know it today would be inconceivable. Beginning in the early 1770s, the stagnating German lyric—its language, form, tone, and expressive content—underwent an unprecedented rejuvenation. . . . Radically new in this poetry was its primary emphasis on the self, on personally experienced emotion, expressed in a language of fresh immediacy, youthful impetuosity, and lyrical exuberance. (1990, 131–32)

The poetry gave the composer the starting point, and contemporaneous commentaries accordingly emphasized the primacy of text over music—text was indeed understood as the defining factor of a Lied.[5] The early definitions of the Lied, which precede *Winterreise,* often stress several recurring features: The Lied should be simple, strophic, and governed by one emotion (which stems from the text). The characteristic features of lyrical poetry (simplicity, strophic structure, and singular emotions, in particular) should be present in the musical settings as well. In addition, Lieder should not be too difficult to sing; the bourgeoisie was actively engaged in singing, and the repertoire should be easy enough for such amateur singers to perform.[6] These qualities of the Lied are clearly stated in Heinrich Christoph Koch's *Musikalisches Lexikon* (1802): "A Lied is essentially any lyrical poem of several strophes which is intended to be sung, and which has a melody that will be repeated with every strophe, and which has the property of being able to be sung by any person who is equipped with healthy and not entirely inflexible singing-organs, and that can be sung without prior artistic training" (translated in Perrey 2002, 47).

It is noteworthy, and usual for the time, that Koch considered the Lied primarily a poetic genre. This has consequences for the musical settings. Because the poem consists of several strophes, the music must follow the same formal layout; that is, a Lied should be strophic, not through-composed. Yet Koch did concede that there are different kinds of Lieder: "The Lied includes various characters and categories whose differences result partly from content, partly from form" (Koch 1802, col. 902). But in discussing such differences, Koch referred solely to textual qualities; for him, the poem was the defining aspect of a Lied.

The poem, and its emotion in particular, is also the Lied's starting point in E. T. A. Hoffmann's review of Wilhelm Friedrich Riem's *Zwölf Lieder,* op. 27, published in *Allgemeine musikalische Zeitung* in 1814 (the year Schubert composed "Gretchen am Spinnrade"). In his essay, Hoffmann describes what "a true Lied" is like: "The poet's proper object is to enunciate his inner experience purely in words, so that frequently many stanzas are needed to give full expression to every emotional impulse" (1989, 378). The poem and its emotion must then guide the composer.

> In the Lied, therefore, all forms of broader development obscure the poet's intention, and the alien spirit appearing unannounced upon the scene destroys the magic of the words. The composer, stirred by the deep meaning of the Lied, must bring all the emotional impulses into a single focus. . . . In order, therefore, to compose a Lied that fully matches the poet's intention, it is necessary for the composer not only to grasp its deeper meaning but rather to become the poet himself. The spark that kindled the Lied within the poet must glow again with renewed vigour within the composer. (Hoffmann 1989, 379)

Even though Hoffmann's early Romantic language differs considerably from Koch's writing (whose clarity derives from Enlightenment ideals), Hoffmann's basic view of the Lied closely resembles that of the earlier commentator. Hoffmann emphasizes the emotional quality of the poem as the springboard for composing a Lied, while Koch states, rather similarly, that the content of the poem should affect the character of the Lied. Thus, for both writers, the poetic quality defines the nature of the Lied.

Like Koch, Hoffmann also emphasized simplicity in composing Lieder.

> It is supremely [sic] in composing Lieder that nothing can be ruminated upon or artificially contrived; the best command of counterpoint is useless here. . . . Lieder of earlier composers were extremely simple[,] . . . compact in scale, usually with no ritornello and only accommodating one stanza; singable, that is to say without wide leaps and only covering a limited compass. But it should be obvious from what has already been said that all these characteristics proceed from the very nature of the Lied. To stir the innermost soul by means of the simplest melody and the simplest modulation, without affectation or straining for effect and originality; therein lies the mysterious power of true genius. (1989, 379)

Hoffmann does note, however, that in vocal music there are instances in which the music may be more complex, thus playing a more defining role in the musico-poetic whole; indeed, he suggests that such instances can be found in Riem's Lieder, which he is reviewing. But in his view such works should not be called Lieder: "With the possible exception of numbers 2, 4, and 5 [of Riem's op. 27], there is no composition in the collection that could lay claim to the title of a true Lied; they more or less resemble musically developed arias, or seem like a free fantasy spontaneously arising in the musician's fingers and throat as he reads the poem" (Hoffmann 1989, 378). These "free fantasies" fell outside the genre of the Lied, although Hoffmann did not oppose such fantasies from a general aesthetic perspective.[7]

In the first decades of the nineteenth century there were also commentaries that gave more independence to music while retaining the basic approach of Koch and Hoffmann. In 1817, in an essay entitled "Die Liederkunst" (The art of

Lieder) published in *Allgemeine musikalische Zeitung,* Hans Georg Nägeli discussed a phenomenon he termed "polyrhythm" (*Polyrhythmie*): "A higher Lied style will emerge . . . whose characteristic feature is the hitherto unknown polyrhythm, which unites the rhythms of language, singing, and the instrumental part [*Sprach-, Sang-, und Spiel-Rhythmus*] into a higher artistic unity—a polyrhythm that is as significant for the vocal art as polyphony is for the instrumental art" (1817, cols. 765–66). There are two aspects here worth noting: first, music is referred to as an independent component of the Lied; second, the musical material is divided between the voice and the instrumental part. So Nägeli suggests that text and music in the Lied are mutually supportive elements and that both have great importance. Furthermore, the instrumental part, which is only indirectly related to the text, is considered significant. Yet Nägeli avoids any radical departures from the aesthetic of Lieder as described by Koch and Hoffmann; like them, he says that the text is the starting point that defines the musical material: "If correctly applied, all these artistic means serve to heighten the expression of the words . . . to make the text live" (col. 766).

Many songs by Schubert (including those in *Winterreise*) depart radically from these and similar views of the Lied. First of all, Schubert's songs are often through-composed, yet strophic form was considered the norm. Furthermore, many of Schubert's songs depart from the requirement of simplicity that Koch and Hoffmann stress. Contemporaries commented on this departure from the Lied conventions; in a review published in *Allgemeine musikalische Zeitung* in 1824, the author wrote: "Herr F. S. does not write lieder in the accepted sense, nor does he wish to. . . . Instead, he composes free songs [*Gesänge*], sometimes so free that we were better advised to call them capriccios or fantasias" (translated in Dahlhaus 1989, 98). It was also observed that Schubert not only provided music to accompany the poem but also added layers to the text with his music. A review of *Winterreise* in *Allgemeiner musikalischer Anzeiger,* published in 1829, commented that "it often happened, too, that he [Schubert] felt more deeply and more powerfully than the poet himself and rendered the meaning of the words not entirely without exaggeration" (translated in Turchin 1981, 150). Such a strong musical interpretation would seem to exceed the requirements of a composer of Lieder as defined by Koch and Hoffmann and, indirectly, Nägeli. Schubert's songs—with their strong expression, daring harmony, and subtle musico-poetic associations—transcended the norms that contemporary writers expected.

If the Lied was a heterogeneous genre at the beginning of the nineteenth century, so was the song cycle, which became quite popular in the first half of the century. Songs were often performed in different kinds of informal social gatherings, with individual members taking turns singing. The songs performed might form larger units, cycles.[8] Various terms were associated with song cycles: *Liederkreis* and *Liederzyklus* were the most common, but *Liederreihe, Liederkranz,* and *Liederroman* were also used. In practice, these terms did not usually differ in any consistent way from one another.[9] Moreover, contemporary reviewers occasionally saw coherence in song publications, which were simply called collections of Lieder (Turchin 1981, 9). Taken together, all of this suggests that the early phases of the song cycle included many kinds of collections as well as various associated terms.

Despite its popularity, "song cycle" was defined in musical dictionaries only in 1865, well after the genre was firmly established, when Arrey von Dommer published his edition of H. C. Koch's *Musikalisches Lexikon*.[10] Von Dommer takes text as the starting point, referring to a poetic idea recurring in the cycle's poems and creating inner relationships among them. Individual poems then present different expressions of this idea, and the music should mirror these poetic nuances. Even though this definition of song cycle appeared several decades after the genre was established, it includes some features that had often appeared in earlier reviews. Thus, it can serve as a starting point for examining certain aspects associated with song cycles in the early nineteenth century. Most importantly, von Dommer begins his definition by referring to poems. The text was seen as the starting point of a song cycle just as it was considered the springboard for individual Lieder (as discussed above). In addition, von Dommer suggests that a cycle should form a unified whole, but again the poems form the primary source of unity, whereas music has only a secondary role to play in establishing coherence. These same trends can be seen in reviews of song cycles from the century's first decades. When summarizing early nineteenth-century commentaries on song cycles, Barbara Turchin has noted that "the source of unity and coherence resided, primarily, in the poetic content of the works. Indeed, the lion's share of contemporary commentary was directed to the poetic make-up of a song cycle. Among music critics of the time, a sequence of events, a series of emotional states, variations on a theme, and a dialogue between characters were all considered to be viable format capable of lending coherence to a chain of poems" (1981, 220).

Although poetic unity was considered significant, before the 1840s musical coherence was only sporadically commented upon. As Turchin observes, "the question of musical coherence and unity in a song cycle is all but ignored by the majority of the music critics" (1981, 222). On those rare occasions when music was discussed, the ideal of unity at times differed considerably from our present-day views. For example, musical cross-references, often seen today as creating musical coherence, are not necessarily considered a unifying factor by the early critics. On the contrary, if used to excess, such cross-references might be viewed as a fault, preventing a sense of wholeness. In a review of Friedrich Heinrich Himmel's *Liederspiel Alexis und Ida, ein Schäferroman*, published in *Allgemeine musikalische Zeitung* in 1815, the critic wrote that "the collection is published as a whole—indeed, like a novel. But one does not see how it can or could amount to a musical [whole]. It contains far too much that is similar, not only in expression, for which the poet alone can [be blamed], but also in melody, accompaniment, as well as in form, in general. . . . Certain favorite turns of melody and, still more, harmony reappear entirely too often" (translated in Turchin 1981, 22). All writers were not so strict, however, and fewer repetitions were considered acceptable (39).

When musical unity was commented on more favorably, the source of unity was often seen in variety, on the one hand, and in the coherent progression of emotions and expression, on the other, in other words, issues stemming directly from the unfolding poems of a cycle. The association among the keys of individual songs, a source of unity often commented on today, was not discussed before the 1840s. The significance of musical variety and expressive progression is clearly articulated in a review of Friedrich Methfessel's *Des Sängers Liebe, ein kleiner Roman in Liedern* published in *Allgemeine musikalische Zeitung* in 1807. The reviewer compares the poetic and musical curves of the cycle: "One can easily notice that M[ethfessel] has entered totally into the idea of the poet. The series of seven small love songs represents so many situations of a singer in relation to his beloved. . . . The composer likewise offers such a united series according to the musical thoughts and to the expression. It begins very lightly . . . and then gradually is elevated to the most serious" (translated in Turchin 1981, 41). If such a unity existed, then a cycle could be considered a unified entity. This is stated clearly in a review of Heinrich Marschner's *Wanderlieder,* published in *Allgemeine musikalische Zeitung* in 1826, a year before the composition of *Winterreise:* "Although each of these six songs exists on its own and represents a specific feeling sufficiently different from the others, and therefore an individual song can be sung alone very well without damage to the rest, yet again they also have such an exact connection among themselves that they form a sort of tragic *Liederroman*" (141).

The textual origins of the song cycle's unity were seen to be many, ranging from a governing theme without any coherent narrative to novel-like plots, tightly constructed. Ruth O. Bingham (1993, 2004) has distinguished three categories of early nineteenth-century song cycles based on the nature of their poetic unity, although the division does not strictly follow the information provided by historical sources.[11] First, in "topical cycles" the poems are connected by a governing theme, such as wandering, love, spring, flowers, or tragic death. These cycles do not feature a goal-directed narrative but rather circle around a recurring topic. Second, "external-plot cycles" set poems extracted from a narrative prose work, usually a novel, such as Goethe's *Wilhelm Meister.* These cycles exhibit a linear narrative, usually stemming from the plot of the original novel. Furthermore, the listeners might be expected to know the original literary work, which provided a context for the reception of these song cycles. Third, "internal-plot cycles" consist of poems that constitute a narrative but, unlike those of an external-plot cycle, are not extracted from poems occurring in a work of prose. A coherent narrative in such cycles was clearly understood in the early nineteenth century; the reviewers often used the term *Roman* (novel) when referring to cycles with an underlying plot.[12]

Bingham's distinction introduces a division between cycles without linear, narrative activity (topical cycles), on the one hand, and those with some kind of plot (external- and internal-plot cycles), on the other. In practice the division was not always clear-cut. As Bingham herself observed, "there are anomalies in both groups: variation cycles [that is, topical cycles] with linear links . . . and aimless narratives with few or no 'events,' linked primarily through general mood or setting" (1993, 37).

In the early nineteenth century, the performance practice of song cycles differed from today's, and it was by no means a rule that song cycles would be performed in their entirety. On the contrary, performances of Lieder mostly took place on private occasions, and it was far more common to sing individual songs from cycles than to sing entire cycles (Daverio 2010, 364; Tunbridge 2010, 41–45). Yet it appears that Schubert himself considered *Winterreise* as an entity that should (or at least could) be performed in its entirety, contrary to the custom of the time; this is indicated by a recollection of Joseph Spaun, a friend of Schubert who writes about an occasion on which the composer himself performed the entire cycle.

> For some time Schubert appeared very upset and melancholy. When I asked him what was troubling him, he would say only, "Soon you will hear and understand." One day he said to me, "Come over to Schober's today, and I will sing you a cycle of horrifying [*schauerlicher*] songs. I am anxious to know what you will say about them. They have cost me more effort than any of my other songs." So he sang the entire *Winterreise* through to us in a voice full of emotion. We were utterly dumbfounded by the mournful, gloomy tone of these songs, and Schober said that only one, "Der Lindenbaum," had appealed to him. To this Schubert replied, "I like them more than all the rest, and you will come to like them as well." (translated in Youens 1991, 27)

2.2. Relationships between Love and Death in Early Nineteenth-Century Literature

In Germany, the early nineteenth century signified a huge aesthetic and poetic change that affected how death was understood (or could be understood). In the first half of the eighteenth century, aesthetic thinking had drawn on Classical ideals of imitation, which maintained that art should endeavor to represent the external world. Later in the eighteenth century, such a strict view of art as imitation was displaced, or complemented, by ideas about the effect works of art have on an audience. It was now emphasized that one significant task of art is to express emotions and make the audience feel those emotions. By the last decades of the eighteenth century, it was argued that the mind's capacities (often called "imagination" [*Einbildungskraft*]) had a significant role to play in artistic creation. Accordingly, art was no longer considered an imitation of the external world but rather a reflection of the artist's inner sentiments and fantasies.

In his influential study *The Mirror and the Lamp*, M. H. Abrams calls these three, roughly successive stages (1) "mimetic theories" (imitation of the external world), (2) "pragmatic theories" (the effect on the audience), and (3) "expressive theories" (the expression of the poet's sentiments) (1953, 8–26). In poetry, the last stage—expression—is the fundamental representation of the poet's affections, feelings, and inner images. Contemporary writers also commented on this idea. In the 1770s, in connection with poetic expression, Johann Georg Sulzer spoke of a poetic aspect of the imagination (*Dichtungskraft*), which has "the power to create images from objects of the sense and of internal sensations, that have never been immediately perceived before" (translated in Keach 1997, 160). When imagination extends the poet's imagery in this way, Sulzer suggested that "the spiritual being of things becomes visible to us" (161); the poet's inner images and feelings thus become the foundation of poetry. As we saw in the preceding section, this kind of expressive poetry, centering on the self, greatly influenced the emergence of the Lied. Despite such expression of the poet's inner sentiments, the concepts, images, and affections communicated in poetry were to be associated with experiences and therefore should have clear references; the "signifiers" were directly associated with the "signified," to use modern, Saussurean terminology. Language, in effect, was expected to be precise.[13] In a line of thought descending from John Locke's important *Essay Concerning Human Understanding* (1690), eighteenth-century writers saw language as the foundation on which our understanding is based. Language therefore had an epistemological function. Words were understood as signs (fundamentally arbitrary), which significantly influence the way in which we understand our environment, and language provides a kind of syntax that helps us to organize our diverse impressions. As a result, there was a direct connection between language and reason. If reason was to be precise, then language too should be specific.

In late eighteenth-century Germany, this view of language was reflected, for example, in the influential *Abhandlung über den Ursprung der Sprache* (1772) by Johann Gottfried Herder, a theorist who greatly influenced Goethe and for whom language played a significant role in the formation of our understanding. "For Herder . . . language and reason had originated simultaneously, for it was language that imposed a regular 'syntax' on our impressions, reducing them to order" (Hudson 1997, 338). Such a view, which stresses the precise nature of language, still appears in Johann Gottlieb Fichte's *Von der Sprachfähigkeit und dem Ursprung der Sprache* (1795), in which Fichte argued that language is an entirely rational system. For him, language has, in Ernst Behler's words, "the function of expressing thoughts of reason and serves to communicate ideas" (1993, 268). In order to communicate ideas, language must be precise. Despite such striving for linguistic specificity, verbal utterances in late eighteenth-century poetical practice did not necessarily refer to the outside world in a directly imitative manner. Because expression was now the aim of poetry, the language often reflected the poet's internal world. Moreover, language might be used metaphorically, for instance, to personify abstract ideas.

The early Romantic generation, active mainly in Jena as the eighteenth century turned to the nineteenth, suggested a new role and foundation for art. Art and poetry were now considered all-encompassing, having a totalizing, even metaphysical function. The writers began referring to the "infinite," something beyond our direct comprehension and not describable with specific concepts, making it clear that art does not necessarily reflect something concrete that we may perceive (either external, as in imitation, or internal, as in expression). This new view of art can be seen in what Friedrich Schlegel, one of the most important theorists of the first Romantic generation, writes on "Romantic poetry" in *Athenaeum Fragment*, no. 116:

Romantic poetry is progressive, universal poetry. Its aim isn't merely to reunite all the separate species of poetry and put poetry in touch with philosophy and rhetoric. It tries to and should mix and fuse poetry and prose, inspiration and criticism, the poetry of art and the poetry of nature; and make poetry lively and sociable, and life and society poetical. . . . The romantic kind of poetry is in the arts what wit is in philosophy, and what society and sociability, friendship and love are in life. Other kinds of poetry are finished and are now capable of being fully analyzed. The romantic kind of poetry is still in the state of becoming; that, in fact, is its real essence: that it should forever be becoming and never be perfected. It can be exhausted by no theory and only a divinatory criticism would dare try to characterize its ideal. It alone is infinite, just as it alone is free. (Schlegel 1971, 175)

This view of poetry differs from the earlier aesthetics of the eighteenth century. For Schlegel, Romantic poetry is not restricted to poems or even to literature more generally. Rather, it encompasses the entirety of human life (art, society, love) as well as nature. It extends to layers that are beyond our knowledge; it is infinite and free, constantly becoming, and never finished. Schlegel's description is close to the philosophical ideas prevailing at the beginning of the nineteenth century. Indeed, poetry (understood in this wide sense) was seen as a branch of philosophy. Frederick C. Beiser has formulated two theses that clearly state the breadth of the notion of Romantic poetry: "First, it refers to not only literature, but also all the arts and sciences; there is indeed no reason to limit its meaning to literary works, since it also applies to sculpture, music, and painting. Second, it designates not only the arts and sciences but also human beings, nature, and the state" (2003, 8).

Because its foundation is fundamentally elusive, Romantic poetry, as defined by Schlegel, no longer retains an unequivocal, universally recognized association between language (individual words, a "signifier") and the world (the universally acknowledged reference of the words, the "signified"). As Bernadette Malinowski has observed, there was "a linguistic-philosophical conception that is not directed at the mimetic simulation of the poetic object; rather, the poet aims to overcome the conventional paradigms of meaning and thus to dissolve semantically standardized relations of signs and designations. . . . In the final instance, Romantic poetic theory aims to transform language into the unending flow of inconsistent signifiers" (2004, 150–51).

The new view on language can be seen in Novalis's brief essay "Monolog" (Monologue, date unknown), which argues that language is a closed system, ideally detached from the outside world. Thus, the foundation of language is not to be found in the references it makes to outside reality. Novalis implies (but characteristically does not explicitly state) that we can hope to make statements of value only if we do not try to express anything specific. Language thus becomes a medium of Romantic poetry.

If one could only make people understand that it is the same with language as with mathematical formulae. These constitute a world of their own. They play only with themselves, express nothing but their own marvelous nature, and just for this reason they are so expressive—just for this reason the strange play of relations between things is mirrored in them. Only through their freedom are they elements of nature and only in their free movements does the world soul manifest itself in them and make them a sensitive measure and a ground plan of things. So it is too with language—on the one hand, anyone who is sensitive to its fingerings, its rhythm, its musical spirit, who perceives within himself the delicate working of its inner nature, and moves his tongue or his hand accordingly, will be a prophet; on the other hand, anyone who knows how to write truths like these but does not have the ear and the sense enough for it will be outwitted by language itself and mocked by people as Cassandra was by the Trojans. (Novalis 1997, 83–84)

This changing aesthetic environment (and, most important, the abandonment of the particularity of reference, which, earlier, language had been expected to possess) also had its impact on how death and its relationship to love were dealt with in literature. To clarify this change, as well as to demonstrate the range of meanings associated with the death-love connection in the decades preceding the composition of *Winterreise*, I will present two examples that show this relationship differently.[14] The first is Johann Wolfgang von Goethe's *Die Leiden des jungen Werthers* (*The Sorrows of Young Werther*), published in 1774 (Goethe 1989). Here we do not find the image of Romantic ideology as described by Schlegel and Novalis. Rather, Goethe's novel belongs to the tradition of Sturm und Drang, part of the "expressive" phase in Abrams's distinction discussed above. More generally speaking, Goethe himself made it clear that he did not belong to the Romantic school; in an oft-quoted comment from the late 1820s, he noted that "that which is Classic I call healthy and the Romantic that which is sick" (translated in Bohm 2004, 42). *Werther* thus precedes the emergence of Romantic aesthetics and is tied to an era that retained a close connection to concrete concepts and images. The second example is Friedrich Schlegel's *Lucinde*, published in 1799 (Schlegel 1971). In this work, death is no longer understood only as a concrete, physical event. Rather, it has subtle (and characteristically unspecific) symbolic meaning that refers to something beyond our direct comprehension. Accordingly, "death" no longer has an unequivocal reference.

Goethe's *Die Leiden des jungen Werthers* was arguably the most influential and widely read German literary work in the closing decades of the eighteenth century.[15] It epitomizes the ideals of Sturm und Drang as well as the expression of personally felt emotions more generally. The novel stresses the individuality and liberty of its protagonist, free will, and the overwhelming emotions of the self, thus challenging the social conventions of the time and emphasizing the primacy of the individual over society and its rules.[16] The work therefore represents the kind of concentration on the self that is also evident in the lyric poetry of the time, as discussed in section 2.1.

Werther is a nervous, overly sensitive character who responds powerfully to his emotions, particularly to love. The expression of deeply felt emotion is underlined by the novel's form, which consists mostly of Werther's letters. He thus articulates his feelings verbally. The plot is straightforward, consisting of Werther recounting his unhappy love for Lotte, a girl who, at the beginning of the novel, is engaged to Albert, a man she later marries. It is clear throughout the narrative that Werther cannot have Lotte. Werther is desperate over the situation, and the book ends in his suicide, an escape from the misery of his unhappy love. The final pages, which first anticipate and then describe Werther's death, alternate between excerpts from his final letter to Lotte (with extreme outpourings of emotion) and the editor's recounting of Werther's final days. Deeply felt emotions (expressed in Werther's letter) are juxtaposed with more neutral, albeit sympathetic, commentary. The book closes with a description of Werther's end: "Werther had been laid on his bed, his head bandaged, his face already deathlike; he could not move his limbs. His lungs still produced a fearful death-rattle, one moment feebly, the next louder; his end was expected soon. . . . It was twelve midday when he died" (Goethe 1989, 134). The observant, almost clinical quality of this description emphasizes the concreteness of Werther's death—a physical, unambiguous event. Death, as described here, represents late eighteenth-century principles of precise language and concepts, an idea mentioned above. Put another way, the signifier (death) has an unequivocally understood signified.

Contemporaries reacted powerfully to Werther's suicide. In general, more conservative readers were against the novel's justification of self-murder, arguing that it defied social conventions as well as provided a dangerous model for sensitive youth. There was even a rewriting of the book by Friedrich Nicolai, *Freuden des jungen Werthers* (The joys of young Werther), published in 1775, in which a happy ending replaces Werther's suicide, with Werther and Lotte getting married. By contrast, younger commentators understood Werther's emotional reactions very well—his frustration and final decision. Indeed, Werther became a fashionable character among the youth. Yet common to all early responses to Werther's suicide was an understanding that it was a concrete deed leading to a physical death.[17]

In the literature of the first Romantic generation, those writers active in Jena as the eighteenth century turned into the nineteenth, death was no longer necessarily understood as an unequivocal physical event. Since language and individual words ("signifiers") were no longer to be related to a universally understood reference (the "signified"), as we saw above, the notion of death might also have symbolic (and even rather unspecified) meaning. Friedrich Schlegel's *Lucinde* discusses love and its relation to death, characteristically often avoiding specific assessment of precisely what these concepts refer to. The form of Schlegel's novel is also unconventional, and the work cannot be said to have a plot in a traditional sense. These features too reflect the new poetic ideals of the first generation of Romantics (who particularly valued the fragment). *Lucinde* consists of three units, which can be further divided into thirteen sections that do not constitute any clear linear narrative. By far the longest section, the central one, entitled "Apprenticeship for Manhood," precedes all the others chronologically and is the only section with a sense of narrative. It recounts the life of the protagonist, Julius, before he met his great love, Lucinde. The framing sections, six before and six after, can all be understood as impressions, many of them referring to specific literary conventions of the time.[18]

Death is discussed throughout Schlegel's novel; indeed, along with love, it functions as the book's main topic. However, the attitude to death varies considerably in the book's different sections, so the novel as a whole does not provide a unified view of this notion. Such variation is in accordance with Schlegel's ideas about Romantic poetry, discussed above: just as poetry is in a constant state of becoming, Schlegel's novel does not conclusively establish a precise meaning for death. One signifier (death) is thus divorced from an unequivocally defined signified.[19] In the novel's central, more traditionally narrative section, there is a description of death in a clearly physical sense. The text here describes how the young Julius's mistress, a prostitute with whom he had an affair before meeting Lucinde, commits suicide after Julius abandoned her (Schlegel 1971, 86–87). This view of death and suicide as an escape from unfulfilled love is close to that encountered in *Werther*. However, the two deaths have very different implications. While death in *Werther* signifies the end point of the narrative, in *Lucinde* death temporally precedes the main "present" of the book (if one can say that there is a present).

Here I will concentrate on another view of suicide and death found in *Lucinde*, in which these concepts are understood as a means of transcending the boundaries of the finite world and being united with the beloved for all eternity. The idea is a kind of pantheistic union of the self with the beloved, as well as with nature, so that the associations with dying are now positive.[20] This view is most clearly presented in *Lucinde*'s second section, "A Dithyrambic Fantasy on the Loveliest Situation in the World." Here Julius reflects on the eternal and all-encompassing nature of his and Lucinde's love. He charts three phases of their affection, the last of which is related to infinity. The first was the knowledge of love without an object, a phase that consisted of yearning: "And then I think suddenly and movingly again of that dark time when I was always waiting without hope, when I loved intensely without knowing it, when my inmost being was completely filled with an indeterminate yearning that was only seldom expressed in half-suppressed sighs" (Schlegel 1971, 47). The second phase is the present happiness, the union with Lucinde: "I would have thought it a fairy tale that there could be such happiness and such love as I feel now—and such a woman, at once the most delicate lover, the most wonderful companion, and the most perfect friend" (47). In the third phase, Julius has come to believe that a complete union will be attained in death.

Therefore, if I thought the time had come, I'd drink a cup of poison with you just as gladly and easily as the last glass of champagne we drank together. . . . I know that you wouldn't want to outlive me either. You too would follow your rash husband into the grave, and willingly and lovingly descend into the flaming abyss. . . . Perhaps yearning will be satisfied more fully there. . . . What we call life is for the complete, timeless, inner human being only a single idea, an indivisible feeling. For him too there are such moments of the deepest and most complete consciousness when all lives occur to him, combine in various ways, and then separate again. There will come a time when the two of us will perceive in a single spirit that we are blossoms of a single plant or petals of a single flower, and then we will know with a smile that what we now call merely hope is really remembrance. (48–49)

Although hardly making an unequivocal statement, Schlegel nevertheless clearly suggests here that dying together, through suicide, leads to a higher, eternal consciousness and the unity of the lovers. Death is no longer understood as the end of life, as in *Werther,* but rather as a beginning of the kind of union not attainable in this finite world. Thus, death leads to a higher form of love, as it were. Nicholas Saul has aptly described this idea, arguing that Julius's love would become complete with Lucinde's suicide: "Friedrich Schlegel's *Lucinde* gives the definitive theoretical account of Romantic suicide. . . . This act does not so much deny life as aestheticise it: transforms her [Lucinde's] earthly existence into the ultimate Romantic *Fragment.* As such it symbolizes the subject's paradoxical encapsulation of the infinite in the finite, performs the sovereign triumph of love over death, and affirms the absoluteness of her love" (2009, 168).[21]

Death and suicide are thus seen as means of reaching something higher, related to eternity and the absolute, which were such significant ideals in Romantic aesthetics. But this eternity was not understood in the traditional theological way as the Christian afterlife. Rather, the Romantic writers argued, death provides a means to experience the boundless and the infinite, paradoxically, within life. Death is therefore not the end point; instead, it is in the service of life. As Novalis put it in one of his fragments, "Death is the Romanticizing principle of our life. . . . Life is strengthened through death" (1997, 154). Death is not a physical but a symbolic event, not a termination but a continuation of life.

Even this brief comparison of death as portrayed in Goethe's *Werther* and Schlegel's *Lucinde* indicates that the notion assumed various guises at the beginning of the nineteenth century, the decades preceding Müller's poetic cycle and Schubert's *Winterreise.* Although offering only a superficial view of the topic, the comparison suggests that death could be understood either in a concrete manner (as a reference to a physical event) or in a symbolic way (for example, as the kind of pantheistic union implied in Schlegel's quotation above). In the one case, death signifies the end, while in the other, existence continues, albeit in a changed form. This difference mirrored the linguistic change taking place in Romantic ideology, where the concrete use of language was displaced by a more imprecise application of words, an application in which a given "signifier" does not necessarily refer to a universally understood "signified."

2.3. Death in *Winterreise*

Many writers have observed that the phenomenon of death features prominently in Schubert's *Winterreise.* Barbara R. Barry, for example, has spoken about the growing significance of death toward the end of the cycle: "In part 2, after the fruitless hope for a letter [in "Die Post"], he [the protagonist] increasingly dissociates himself from life, human company and reality. Even the perspective of memory fades as he becomes totally isolated and immersed in a locked introspection which draws him slowly but inexorably towards death" (2000, 183). Barry thus notes the significance of death but does not analyze it further or show whether it ultimately arrives. Charles Rosen is equally unspecific, emphasizing that here, death is not even an act. He argues that in *Winterreise* "all events take place before the cycle begins, and we are not even sure what they were. . . . Twenty-four landscapes awaken memories and lead the poet to an acceptance of death. In this cycle not even death is an event. It is an image in the last song, the organ-grinder who mechanically and monotonously turns the handle of his instrument in the frozen winter landscape. . . . With this song the poet welcomes his death" (1995, 194–95). But welcoming death is not the same as dying, so in Rosen's interpretation the situation remains open. Susan Youens is more specific, suggesting that death does not arrive, even though the speaker wants it to: "The cycle has as one essential theme the difficulty of dying when one wishes. . . . No matter how fervently and repeatedly he [the protagonist] wishes for death later in the journey, it is denied him" (1991, 64).

The ambiguous view of whether death ultimately arrives, reflected in the quotations from Barry and Rosen, is understandable, and Müller seems not to have provided unequivocal information on this matter. Youens, on the other hand, suggests that the cycle's end does have a definable poetic closure, and she concludes that, in the end, the wanderer actually stops longing for death. She bases this reading on a contradiction that she sees in the pairing of "Der Wegweiser" and "Das Wirtshaus": "Der Wegweiser" refers to a "road from which no one has returned" (an apparent reference to death), while in "Das Wirtshaus" the speaker does not die. She concludes that death cannot be a longed-for goal in both poems "unless one imputes confusion of purpose to the poet" (Youens 1991, 66).[22] Instead of accepting the contradiction, Youens refers to the iconographic tradition of "Death as musician," suggesting that becoming a musician provides the wanderer, at the cycle's end, an escape from his misery. The protagonist thus gives up at the very end, hoping to die. "For Müller's wanderer, the signpost at the crossroads [in "Der Wegweiser"] is a revelation of destiny: not the death he has desired so fervently but continued life, furthermore, life as a musician, a singer-poet irrevocably set apart from society and condemned to an existence without the 'beloved soul' for whom he longs" (67).

In addition to this uncertainty over whether death comes, there is another, related layer that remains unspecified in Müller's poems, a layer ultimately more important for the topic of this chapter, namely, the very question of whether death should be understood as a concrete, physical event or in a symbolic (or metaphorical) way. In spite of the significance of this question for understanding Müller's poems (and Schubert's *Winterreise*), I am not aware of studies that directly address the issue. In this book I argue that in *Winterreise* death has a symbolic or metaphorical meaning; death is not a concrete, physical event. In the cycle's second part, the protagonist repeatedly expresses his wish to die, but this wish turns out to be impossible to fulfill. If death were understood as an unambiguous physical occurrence, then the desolate wanderer could have died by suicide. As the discussion on Goethe's *Werther* indicated, such an option was readily available in early nineteenth-century literature. Indeed, Müller's earlier poetic cycle set by Schubert, *Die schöne Müllerin*, ends in the protagonist's death, an apparent suicide. But the wanderer's inability to die in *Winterreise* suggests that here Müller gives a more metaphorical meaning to death. It is likely that the poet was fully aware of the symbolic references associated with death in the Romantic era and the variety of meanings it had in the literature of his time. He was a well-educated man and an avid reader who was also a literary critic and editor, so he followed keenly the literary currents of the day.[23]

But to say that death has a symbolic or metaphorical meaning rather than concrete significance in *Winterreise* does not bring us very far in determining precisely how the notion is applied in the cycle. The symbolism here departs radically from Schlegel's view in *Lucinde,* for example. While both works place a fundamentally positive value on death, Schlegel's view leads to a pantheistic union (Julius becoming one with Lucinde and nature), whereas the view presented in *Winterreise* only aspires to peace in order to release the protagonist from his misery. *Winterreise* thus has undertones of tragic renunciation, which merge with the calm that death would provide. Yet Müller's poems do not make clear what such a state of peace would be like; it is a state the wanderer contemplates thoroughly but never fully clarifies.

At the moment it is impossible to specify the exact symbolic meaning of death in *Winterreise,* so for now we must leave it unspecified. Suffice it to say that I do not believe that death should be understood here as a physical event but rather in a symbolic manner. Furthermore, if we follow the ideas of Schlegel and Novalis, death should not be seen as the end point of our lives but rather as a change in our continuing existence; as Novalis observed in the fragment quoted earlier, "life is strengthened through death." In a similar way, death might also be understood in *Winterreise* not as the end of the protagonist's existence but as a change in the mode of his existence.

I will return to these matters in chapter 14 after having analyzed the cycle's songs 14–24. I believe that a rather precise meaning for the notion of death emerges in these songs, but this view is enhanced, at times even clearly suggested, by Schubert's music. Therefore, we will return to this question after a discussion of the poems, their music, and the musico-poetic factors.

3 Text-Music Relationships: Five Propositions

I examined the mainly historical context of Schubert's *Winterreise* in the first two chapters. I now turn to the analytical issues and identify in this chapter some essential questions concerning text-music relationships. If one argues that words and music are related in songs, as one obviously should, then one must also define the nature of this relationship. This in turn raises two questions: Can music be associated with something from the external world? If it can, then what is the character of that association? In this chapter I offer five propositions that I believe a viable interpretation of text-music relationships should take into consideration. These propositions form the basis of my musico-poetic interpretations. Each proposition is contextualized by ideas that associate music with the external world, as suggested by music scholars and philosophers.

3.1. Proposition 1: The Music in Lieder Is Not Representational

The term *representation* has been used in various ways in connection with music. I will follow Roger Scruton's (1997, 118–39) definition in *The Aesthetics of Music,* a useful starting point for discussing musico-poetic associations. For Scruton, representation requires more than word painting and imitation of external sounds; merely copying something in the outside world does not suffice. Integral to his view of representation in the arts is a "fictional world," an idea he uses to describe thoughts and associations (based on semantic content) that a representational work of art arouses in the person perceiving it—thoughts that extend beyond the work or its resemblance to features of the external world. According to Scruton, such a fictional world can emerge in literature or the visual arts but not in music.

Scruton sees music as a purely abstract phenomenon consisting of "forms and organizations that seem interesting in themselves, regardless of any 'fictional world' which this or that listener may try to attach to them" (1997, 122).[1] Because he argues that representation requires understanding what is being represented (an understanding shared by those individuals receiving the work of art), there can be no representation in music: "While the aspect of a painting and the meaning of a sentence are publicly recognized facts, which make possible the intention of representing things, there is no such basis for representation in music" (130).[2]

If a "fictional world" based on thoughts and semantic content is taken as the prerequisite for musical presentation, then I would argue that the music of a Lied is not representational. Music and text can interact in several ways, and I will examine some of these in the propositions offered in this chapter. However, in none of these instances does the music of the Lied meet Scruton's requirements for representation: music as such does not produce a fictional world. The text of a Lied can do this, but the fictional world thus awakened is an outcome of the text alone. For example, the music of a given Lied can, owing to its emotional quality, underline or strengthen the fictional world of the text or even contradict it, but the music cannot make that world arise.

Let us clarify this idea with the opening of the third song in *Winterreise*, "Gefrorne Tränen" (Frozen tears), whose first stanza is as follows:

> Gefrorne Tropfen fallen
> Von meinen Wangen ab;
> Ob es mir denn entgangen
> Daß ich geweinet hab'?
>
> Frozen drops fall from my cheeks; have I then not noticed that I have been weeping?

The beginning of the poem describes the narrator's cheerless state of mind: he has wept without having noticed. The beginning of the poem thus brings about a fictional world: we can imagine the lonely wanderer in the cold, feel his desperation, and envisage his lost love. Music can support and strengthen this fictional world through its emotional quality, for example. But it cannot by itself activate this or comparable fictional worlds. Schubert's music to these words could well accompany another poem with a similar emotional quality. Direct references to semantic content in a Lied and the thoughts arising from it (the fictional world as defined by Scruton) should be understood as based on the text alone, not on the music (with the exception of imitation, to be discussed in the next proposition). Yet, as we will see later in this chapter, there are various ways in which the music of the Lied can refer indirectly to the content of its text, as well as to the fictional world of that text.

3.2. Proposition 2: The Music in Lieder Can Include Imitation

Scruton (1997, 118–39) makes a distinction between representation, the phenomenon discussed above, and imitation. Imitation, he says, refers to instances in which music copies sounds from the outside world, such as the birdsong in Beethoven's Sixth Symphony. Unlike representation, such imitation forms a viable basis for music's reference to the external world—the similarity of sound associates the music with something from the outside. The pure likeness in sound thus creates the association, and no fictional world emerges. For our purposes, it is important to consider whether the words in Lieder change the musical imitation; put another way, do the words and the concrete concepts they embody essentially alter the manner in which music can imitate sounds from the external world?

I believe that the basis for musical imitation is fundamentally similar in instrumental and in vocal music. A certain musical passage either resembles sounds in the external world or it does not; the words do not change the way the music sounds.[3] Nevertheless, words can clarify the imitation considerably or even suggest it in the first place. That is to say, if imitation is to occur in instrumental music, then the resemblance between the music and the external sound that it imitates must be unequivocal, like the birdsong in Beethoven's Sixth Symphony. In vocal music, by contrast, the resemblance can be less specific: the text provides the reference for the imitation, so the similarity between the music and the external sound can be more equivocal.[4]

In vocal music as well as in programmatic music, we occasionally encounter another kind of less specific imitation that is not associated with external sounds; the underlying text or program can lead to imitation of gestures—instead of sounds—in a manner that is not possible in pure instrumental music. Let us take an admittedly macabre example from the ending of Johann Jacob Froberger's *Tombeau de M. Blancrocher,* written to the memory of the lutenist who died from a fall. The piece ends in a long descending scale that can be heard as loosely imitating the lutenist falling down a flight of stairs. Without the title (and the knowledge of the way Blancrocher died) we could not infer any imitation at the end of the piece.

I shall further clarify such less specific imitation in vocal music by referring to the beginning of "Gefrorne Tränen." Taken alone, the piano introduction (mm. 1–7) would not seem to include imitation: it does not copy any sounds from the external world in an unequivocal manner. Yet the words in mm. 7–11 provide a reference for the imitation. When the teardrops are mentioned in the poem, one can interpret the music as an imitation of them. The upbeat figure and syncopation (mm. 1–3 and 8–11), as well as the ♩♫ rhythm, combined with a descending third (mm. 5–6, 8, and 10), resemble—vaguely, yet recognizably—the sound or gesture of teardrops falling. This imitation can only be based on the text, however; the association is too vague to be drawn without the aid of the song's words.

Imitation is a highly important means of making associations between music and text. Yet imitation can only occur in the foreground, so it forms just one layer of the possible word-music associations.

3.3. Proposition 3: Music and Text in Lieder Can Include Similar (or Contrasting) Emotions

Even though many philosophers deny music's ability to represent anything from the outside world literally (as we saw above), they often concede that music can be associated, in some sense, with emotions. Many writers argue, however, that such emotions should not be understood as purely subjective feelings, either as felt by the composer in creating the work or as emotions aroused in the listener by the work. Rather, the emotions are to be conceived as somewhat different, internal properties of a composition. This view is clearly illustrated in Stephen Davies's *Musical Meaning and Expression* (1994, esp. 201–77).

What is essential to Davies's view of the relationship between music and emotions is the role that the object of the sentiments plays in defining individual emotions. If we say that someone is angry, we suggest that he or she is angry at something or someone. This something or someone is the object of the emotion. Davies then argues that, because music cannot represent thoughts, it cannot have such an object. Furthermore, since emotions associated with music do not involve anyone actually feeling these emotions, the emotions expressed in music should be of a kind that need not be felt. In Davies's opinion such emotions do exist, but in order to be able to speak about them in connection with music, one should be acquainted with them outside of their musical context: "The account of musical expressiveness is plausible only if the relevant sort of expressiveness is familiar from mundane, nonmusical contexts. Only if we are comfortably acquainted with unfelt, objectless emotions in ordinary contexts is it plausible to argue that (similar) emotions are expressed in music" (1994, 221). Davies describes such emotions with the phrase "emotion characteristics in appearances": these are emotions that we can recognize, even though no one necessarily really feels them. If, for example, we say that someone looks sad, it does not inevitably mean that the person feels sad. All we can say is that the person has a sad-looking face.

According to Davies, all emotions cannot have such emotion characteristics. This is the case, for example, with the so-called higher emotions, such as hope, embarrassment, and puzzlement, which require an object in order to be defined; one hopes for something and is embarrassed or puzzled by something. In Davies's view, "such feelings or emotions lack natural, primary expressions. The behavior through which they are expressed is behavior of a kind that points to the beliefs, desires, and objects which, in these cases, are so central to their nature" (1994, 226). The emotions that can have characteristics in appearances are of a very general kind, such as sadness and happiness. It is the appearance of these general emotions, Davies argues, that music can express.[5]

Davies thus sees expressed emotions as music's internal properties rather than as feelings experienced by any given person. Somewhat similar conclusions, which stress the role of musical works and their structure when expression and emotions are dealt with, have been suggested by philosophers whose arguments may differ from those of Davies in their details, even considerably. Peter Kivy, for example, writes that "the theory of musical expression I intend to outline here is an account of how it is that music can be *expressive of* the emotions; it is not a theory of how music can *express* them. That is because music does not, I think, ordinarily express them. . . . I want to present a theory of what is going on when we describe music with emotive terms, in the absence of any suggestion that it is expressing the composer's emotions, or anyone else's" (1989, 14; emphasis in the original).[6] Kivy's starting point is the music and its structure. The listener may recognize that music is expressive of a given emotion, even when no one is actually feeling or has felt that emotion. The emotion recognized by the listener, then, is a property of the music, not an experience felt by someone. For his part, Scruton does not speak directly about emotions but rather about expression more generally. Again, the musical structure provides the basis for expression: "The expressive quality of a musical work is developed through the music, and the elaboration of the musical line is at the same time an elaboration of the content. Expression does not reside in some passing resemblance or aspect: it is brought into being through the musical argument, and worked into the musical structure" (Scruton 1997, 345).

Davies's idea of emotion in connection with music, as well as his view that music can express the appearance of only a general emotion (such as sadness or happiness), finds significant musico-poetic links in the Lied. It is, of course, a truism to say that the emotions of music and text are often associated in Lieder. But if we follow Davies's ideas, then we must emphasize that the emotions expressed in music and text are not identical. Owing to its semantic level, text can express individuated emotions with an object, whereas music expresses general appearances. So we should not say that music directly expresses the precisely defined emotions encountered in the text.

The opening of "Gefrorne Tränen" can also illuminate this point. Few would disagree, I think, that the music of the first eleven measures is expressive of sadness. The opening words of the poem, and the emotion they convey, correspond to the character of the music well. Falling tears are clearly signs of sadness, and at this point in *Winterreise*, we know that this emotion is the result of lost love. Yet I would not say that the emotions expressed in the music and the text are identical. The sadness of the music is very general—the same music could just as well set the opening of another sad poem, whereas the sadness in the text is clearly individuated.

Davies speaks about emotions in music at an abstract level, so his ideas present no actual music-analytical tools. In his *Musical Meaning in Beethoven*, Robert Hatten (1994) has provided such tools, in particular for clarifying how to describe the large-scale expressive unfolding of musical works. In discussing relationships between music and expression, Hatten has coined the term *expressive genre* to describe the overarching expressive course of a composition (67–90). This expressive genre provides a framework against which all local emotional and expressive events can be mirrored: "All the outstanding or salient structural events have been related to an overarching hypothesis, the *expressive genre*" (28; emphasis in the original). The expressive genre then functions as a large-scale schema controlling the unfolding of the musical expression. Like Davies, Hatten argues that music's emotional layer, described by an expressive genre, is an intramusical phenomenon: "I maintain that expressive meanings are as purely musical as the forms and structures that serve to distinguish them. And since I believe that such meaning can often be inferred consistently . . . it should be clear that my quarry is not an overdetermined or overly specific program but rather frameworks of conventionally encoded expressive states and processes" (2).

Hatten's expressive genre gives us a valuable tool for describing musico-poetic associations in Lieder: a view of the global emotional trajectory of a Lied's music can provide a counterpart to the overarching emotional course of its text. The expressive genre can either be dominated by one expressive state, possibly with digressions to other states, or move from the opening state to another one at the end. Likewise, the poem of the Lied can be dominated by one emotion, with possible digressions, or move from the emotion governing the beginning to some other emotion at the end. Hence, the large-scale emotional events can be similar in the music and text of a Lied, but the emotions expressed in the music are general, whereas those of the text are individuated.

In considering the course of the emotional events of a work, we can complement the picture given by the global expressive genre by referring to a dramatic curve that consists of the more local intensities of the music's emotions. In other words, the successive intensities of emotional states may form temporal trajectories. In *Music as Discourse,* Kofi Agawu (2009) has discussed the concept of a "high point" that is closely associated with the notion of the dramatic curve. Agawu argues that pieces of music can often be understood as consisting of a dynamic curve that "rises gradually from a relatively low point, reaches a high point[,] . . . then subsides rapidly thereafter" (62). Such dramatic curves and high points can help to elucidate the shifting emotional intensities in a musical work's expressive genre. Agawu argues further that in addition to the global high point, a piece of music may include more local, subordinate high points. "Psychologically, a single high point typically dominates a single composition, but given the fact that a larger whole is often constituted by smaller parts, each of which might have its own intensity curve, the global high point may be understood as a product of successive local high points" (61).

Regarding the concept of a high point, it should be emphasized that in individual compositions, the high point can be constituted by various kinds of musical elements. Most often it is marked by an increase in the dynamic level and rhythmic activity or by dissonances and a fuller texture. But it might just as well consist of, say, softer dynamics and more leisurely motion or remote tonal areas.[7] Owing to this variety, there is no methodology that would enable us to trace unequivocally the location of a high point; we cannot say that by paying attention to some musical parameter (say, texture), we could find the "correct" high point. Rather, in some individual cases, it may seem plausible to refer to one musical parameter (or a combination of parameters) as the foundation of a high point, while in another instance different parameters might seem operative. What is significant is that the high point stands apart in some way from its environment, drawing the listener's attention to itself.

The notions of high point and dramatic curve provide another layer in describing the overarching emotional courses of music and text in Lieder. A Lied's expressive musical high point may well align (and often does) with the emotional peak of its poem, thus supporting and underlying the poem's emotional course. But again, the music's dramatic high point and the poem's emotional peak are not identical, as the latter stems from the text's semantic content, while the former is an outcome of musical factors alone.

Discussion of the music's dramatic curve is related to various intensities of basic emotions, such as sadness and happiness, and the examination of such intensities departs from Davies's ideas about music's capacity to express emotions. Even though I essentially agree with him that music can express only general emotions, unlike him, I feel that the quality and shade of these emotions may vary considerably, depending on such things as tempo, texture, dynamics, or figuration. Nicholas Cook has spoken about a somewhat similar issue, arguing that "music conveys not unnuanced emotion but emotionless nuance" (2001, 180). Instead of being able to express a variety of clearly individuated emotions, which require an object, Cook suggests that music can convey attributes (such as gentleness or storminess) normally associated with specific emotions, even though these specific emotions are not expressed in the music.

In this study, I combine aspects of Davies's and Cook's views. When discussing the work's expressive genre, I will refer only to the basic emotions of "tragic" and "joyful." This emotional juxtaposition is close to the one that Hatten (1994, 74–82) suggests when making a distinction between two primary affective categories, which he calls "tragic" and "nontragic." (The latter may be further subdivided into a category such as "buffa," "pastoral," or "high comic.") With more local expressions, by contrast, I will also discuss the individual qualities of these basic emotions. In other words, local factors such as texture may imply variations in expressive quality, suggesting, for example, a distinction between "inward" and "declamatory" qualities of either tragic or joyful. The inward quality may occur in situations in which the dynamic level is low and the music lacks gestures with strongly drawn profiles, while the declamatory quality may be suggested by clearly articulated, speechlike gestures (e.g., leaps), possibly combined with marked changes in dynamics (as in emotionally charged speaking). The harmonic structure in turn may suggest a distinction between an "uncertain" and a "confirming" quality. "Uncertain," for instance, may involve the avoidance of harmonic confirmation or a clear definition of key, while the "confirming" quality may arise from an unequivocal cadential progression. Such qualities and their changes may then form expressive processes in the music of a given Lied and find their counterpart in the Lied's text.[8]

So far, I have spoken about musico-poetic situations in which music and text express similar emotions and thus support each other. The opposite situation is also possible: music and text can express different, even conflicting emotions.[9] Such instances also occur in *Winterreise*. This coexistence of different emotions makes the interaction between the emotional qualities of music and text quite complex. I shall return to such situations in more detail below in connection with proposition 5.

3.4. Proposition 4: Music and Text in Lieder Can Have Similar Underlying Structural Features

Comparing the structures of different art forms—here, music and poetry—is necessarily a rather hazardous undertaking. The structure of a tonal musical work, for example, involves harmony, counterpoint, and voice leading, while much of the structure of a poem relies on words and their meaning.[10] So semantic meaning plays an important role in a poem's structure, while such meaning is not present in music or its structure. Owing to such different foundations, textual and musical structures cannot easily be compared. Yet we must be able to make comparisons if we believe that the two have similarities: without comparison such a statement would be unfounded.

Despite the differences in the foundations of musical and textual structures, there are points of contact. Both music and text can include tension and resolution, for instance. Or they both can exhibit binary oppositions, of which one is often normative, while the other is a source of contrast or tension. Such underlying tensions, resolutions, and oppositions can be described in an abstract sense at various structural levels. In music, this seems natural: music has no semantic content; hence, musical analysis examines, at least primarily, abstract relations. But the structure of a text can also be analyzed on an abstract level. The origins of such a structure are in the content of the text, but the structure can be described without making direct references to that content. In structuralist literary theory and semiotics, the structure of a text is often analyzed as a network of binary, functional oppositions occurring at various levels. These oppositions perform a certain role in the overall structure of the text.

In this study I will use Schenkerian theory to analyze the structure of music and Greimassian semiotics to analyze the poems.[11] Schenkerian and Greimassian theories provide somewhat similar means for analyzing the structures of music and text, respectively. Above all, both methods attempt to show underlying structural relations at various levels. (In chapter 4 I will further develop the topic of juxtaposing Schenkerian theory with ideas derived from Greimas. Here I will limit the discussion to general principles.) If we are able to analyze somewhat similar (but by no means identical) functional relations independently, both in music and in text—the postponement of the resolution of tension, for example, or the quest for primacy within the elements of a binary opposition—then we can argue that music and text are connected through abstract structural relations. Similarities like this may offer valuable insights into the interrelationships between music and text: they provide the means to describe associations without referring to semantic content.[12]

Such similarities also enable us to discuss the rapport between music and text at both the local and the global levels of the structure. At the global level, the overall structural tensions of text and music should be analyzed first, in my view, independently, without allowing the interpretation of one to influence the reading of the other. At this broad structural level, significant musical tensions can also occur in sections that would not seem to be connected to the text at local levels, for example, in moments when the singer is silent. Such a lack of local musico-poetic relationships does not necessarily mean that these musically significant elements have no part in the deeper-level musico-poetic connections. Important, deep-level text-music relations may arise in those parts of Lieder that have no imitation, emotional rapport, or local structural similarities between the music and the text. Moreover, Lieder may naturally include musical events that cannot be convincingly related to the text. Yet these may play a significant structural or rhetorical role in the course of the music; hence, a thorough analysis of a song should also take these events into consideration.

Even though a combination of Schenkerian and Greimassian methodologies primarily describes abstract, overarching relations, it may also form the basis for indirect and more local references to the content of the text by the music. If, for example, a certain significant musical motive includes aspects similar to those found in the structure of the text—textual features that grow out of the poetic content—we may suggest that the motive refers indirectly to the content of the poem. We can understand such a process of reference as being somewhat similar to Agawu's (1991) idea of "extroversive semiosis" described in his *Playing with Signs*. In order to understand this connection, we have to examine Agawu's ideas in some detail.

Agawu explored the interaction between two factors that he sees as essential for Classical music: inner, structural features, on the one hand, and the music's referential aspects, on the other. He calls the two layers "introversive semiosis" and "extroversive semiosis," respectively, using terms coined by the linguist Roman Jakobson. With the notion of extroversive semiosis (i.e., the music's referential aspects), Agawu means topics—characteristic features of the musical surface such as "singing style," Sturm und Drang, and "hunt style." These styles are defined historically and socioculturally. Agawu argues, however, that topics cannot provide a comprehensive picture of the course of a musical work; most importantly, they have no syntax and therefore cannot describe the logic of the music's temporal unfolding. By introversive semiosis, in turn, he refers mainly to Schenkerian voice-leading structure, the contrapuntal-harmonic framework. Schenkerian theory enables us to speak about the "beginning, middle, and end[,] . . . labels that denote not necessarily the temporal occurrence of particular passages, but their function. To recognize the signifying functions implicit in this paradigm is to recognize the possibility of playing with them" (Agawu 1991, 20). Schenkerian theory thus provides the kind of overall framework and functional logic that is lacking in extroversive semiosis.

A dialogue between extroversive and introversive semioses provides a tool for discussing the significance that motivic associations play in a Lied's musico-poetic network. Like topics, motives in a Lied can occasionally be understood as signs referring to some external aspects (in this instance, features of the text) and can thus be seen as examples of extroversive semiosis. In other words, a motive is presented through musical structure, yet it can be interpreted as a reference to the text. There is one significant difference between topics and motives, however; topics form general signs within a musical style, whereas motives operate within individual Lieder. But the principle of reference remains the same. In both, a certain musical configuration (a topic or a motive) refers to aspects outside of the musical structure (the general conventions of the Classical style or textual aspects of an individual Lied's poem). The introversive semiosis generally has a similar function in the Classical style as in an individual Lied: Schenkerian voice-leading structure provides the musical framework within which the topic or motive has its function. When a relationship between a motive and the content of the poem occurs, one can speak about a structural connection between a referential sign (the motive) and the object of reference (a certain factor in the poetic content).

I have outlined here two kinds of structural connections between music and text. First, there are the global connections, which can be described by using Schenkerian and Greimassian ideas. Such connections may be based on a quest for primacy between the elements of a binary opposition, for instance, or on postponement of the resolution of tensions. Second, there is the more local notion of motives as referential signs that are indirectly related to the content of the text. These two kinds of connections do not by any means exhaust the whole range of structural text-music relations. For example, I have left out the important similarities between the prosody in the poems and the meter and rhythm in the music.[13] I have restricted myself to the kinds of associations outlined above, since these will be examined in more detail in chapter 4 and then applied in the analytical chapters. Other, equally important kinds of connections are beyond the scope of this study.

3.5. Proposition 5: Relationships between Music and Text in Lieder Are Established through Ongoing and Interactive Interpretations

Examining the relationships between music and text in a Lied involves several stages, in all of which interpretation plays a significant role. If we say, for example, that a Lied's music imitates sounds described in its text, then this alleged association is based on interpretation. When the imitation is less specific, the significance of interpretation grows. Moreover, in musico-poetic analysis, interpretation is multilayered. To say that musical and textual structures exhibit similar features requires interpreting first the structures of the music and text and then the interaction between them.

The methodological choices that the analyst makes affect the ways in which interpretation operates in descriptions of word-music connections. Cook (2001) has examined the general significance of interpretive context in musical analysis in his study "Theorizing Musical Meaning," which provides a useful starting point for discussing the function played by interpretation in descriptions of musico-poetic associations. Cook argues that we should not speak about one fixed meaning of a given musical work. Rather, the meaning depends on the context and the interpreter. In Cook's view, both cultural and structural aspects affect the formation of musical meaning, and his purpose is "to outline a way in which we can understand at least some of the meanings ascribed to music as at the same time irreducibly cultural *and* intimately related to its structural properties" (173–74; emphasis in the original).

Cook seeks background for his ideas on musical meaning from studies of material culture. He quotes Daniel Miller, who argues that different societies emphasize different attributes of given objects. Miller suggests that "societies have an extraordinary capacity either to consider objects as having attributes which may not appear as evident to outsiders, or else to ignore attributes which would have appeared to those same outsiders as being inextricably part of that object" (quoted in Cook 2001, 178). Cook finds it significant that we can ascribe different meanings to the attributes of an object or choose altogether different attributes on which to base the object's meaning. So the meaning of the object is socially constructed, based on the choice and the interpretation of its attributes. Cook suggests that one can have a fundamentally similar standpoint to musical meaning. A given musical work has a bundle of attributes on which one can base the inference of its meaning, and these attributes can then be interpreted from various perspectives. In Cook's view, the meaning is not an inherent property of the work but rather an emergent quality defined in part by the interpreter and the interpretive context.

Similarly, I do not believe—nor, indeed, do I wish—that it were possible to say that there is one primary kind of text-music association in Lieder. We have seen above that, at the very least, there may be imitation, emotional relationships, and structural rapport, the last alone including a large range of possibilities. Hence, the choice of methodologies prescribes, at least in part, the nature of the musicopoetic associations to be described. Application of Schenkerian analysis and Greimassian semiotics, for instance, leads to word-music connections different from those arising when rhythm and prosody are emphasized. And even within a fixed theoretical context, the subjective analytical choices of the interpreter greatly affect the assessment of word-music relations. As a result, an analytical interpretation made within one theoretical context does not deny the existence or significance of other, different interpretations made in other theoretical contexts. Analysis of musico-poetic associations is therefore not a quest for the "true" assessment of text-music relationships but rather a process of seeking plausible interpretations of associations between music and text, interpretations that may well coexist with other equally plausible (but different) interpretations made in other analytical contexts.

As a hybrid art form, the Lied may also have an effect on the ways in which its individual components are read. Several scholars have suggested that the music of a Lied affects the manner in which its text is interpreted. Edward T. Cone (1974) was probably the first to address this topic in depth in his book *The Composer's Voice*. He examines Goethe's poem "Erlkönig" and Schubert's setting of it, suggesting that the poem may be read in various ways, of which Schubert's song is only one (5–11). Lawrence M. Zbikowski, in turn, has argued that "the music of the song does make a difference in how we understand the text of a song" (1999, 307). He then shows how three musical settings of Wilhelm Müller's poem "Trockne Blumen" led to three slightly different interpretations of the poem. Similarly, David Lewin contends that Schubert's setting of Müller's "Die Post" follows one of the possible interpretations of the text. Hence, Schubert's Lied involves "a mimetic reading of the text by the composer, a reading that is far from a simple musical translation. . . . So while it would be accurate enough to say that Schubert's reading 'represents' the text, one cannot go very far critically until one investigates how this particular representation, from among a number of plausible readings, interacts with musical structure to project an overall poetic conception of the poem that is the text" (Lewin 1986, 128–29). And Lawrence Kramer has suggested that "the relationship of the text to the music must always involve a critical interpretation of the poetry; merely to recount what the poem 'says' is not enough. The persona of a Romantic song is rarely content just to echo a text. On the contrary, it actively appropriates the text, which is to say that it both identifies and substantially revises the poetic persona's pattern of consciousness" (1986, 207).

The effect that the music of a Lied has on the interpretation of its poem is significant. The musical events may shade the interpretation of the poem or even justify the choice between different possible readings of the text. The need to acknowledge the effect of the music on the interpretation of the poem is especially acute when there is a conflict of some kind between the music and the most obvious reading of the poem. In such cases, the analyst may wish to abandon the straightforward interpretation of the text in order to reflect on the musical events. For example, in Jean Sibelius's song "Den första kyssen," the structural and emotional aspects of the music lead, in my view, to an interpretation of the poem that would be forced if the text were analyzed alone (Suurpää 2003).

Let us conclude by briefly summarizing the ideas presented in the five propositions. The music and the text of a Lied can be related, at least through imitation, emotional quality, or structural connections. (The last of these includes different kinds of structures, whose description depends on the analytical methods used.) But the music of a Lied cannot represent in the same manner as the visual and verbal arts. And finally, a description of a word-music relation is always an interpretation that reflects the viewpoint of the interpreter and the analytical tools that are used. Moreover, the music of the Lied may affect the interpretation of its text.

4 Musico-Poetic Associations: Principles of Analysis

4.1. Greimassian Theory

This chapter charts methodological issues of musico-poetic analysis, and I will begin by briefly explaining some basic ideas of Greimassian semiotics that I will use later in examining the poetic structure. A. J. Greimas (1917–92) was the leading figure of the so-called Paris School of semiotics. His work is characterized by an attempt to describe textual structure on a purely functional level. He shows such structures as sets of relations between binary oppositions, often applying quite complex formalizations partly derived from formal logic. In this manner, he is able to describe functional relations and tensions on a purely abstract level without directly referring to the semantic content of the text from which the structure has been abstracted.

The formal apparatus of Greimassian semiotics has clear advantages in musico-poetic analysis. Above all, it provides a means to describe textual structure without direct reference to the semantic content of the text. This may help to form a solid basis for describing text-music aspects; musico-poetic associations can thus be described on the level of abstract structures without suggesting that the music represents the content of the text in a straightforward manner. This is important, I believe, if one wants to avoid the impression that the music in some sense directly reflects the semantic content of the poem, an assertion whose problematic nature was discussed in proposition 1 in chapter 3. Once this kind of abstract relationship has been established, the text-music relations can then be extended to a more concrete level where the actual semantic content of the text is also taken into consideration. But this examination may be based on the underlying abstract structures as well.

This section provides a highly selective picture of Greimassian semiotics, concentrating only on a few basic concepts and leaving many fundamental ideas aside.[1] (I will not, for example, discuss the concept of "semiotic square," arguably the most significant notion from Greimas's later works.) Such a selective explanation of Greimas's theory is justified by at least two factors. First, when taken in its entirety, Greimassian theory is very complex and formal. As Therese Budniakiewicz has noted, the complex formalizations are both illuminating and problematic: "The strength of Greimassian narrative semiotics consists of its remarkable conceptual wealth and notional richness and its dramatic predicament is that of introducing idiosyncratic albeit powerful formalisms which prevent the interested outsider from navigating the simple conceptuality" (1992, 6–7). A thorough explication of Greimassian theory might therefore confuse rather than clarify my topic, so I will leave out much of the theory and simplify some of the ideas.[2] The second, and related, reason is that I will use Greimassian semiotics only to analyze the function of unattainable death and lost love, as well as the juxtaposition of reality and illusion more generally, in the short and relatively simple poems of *Winterreise*. This can be done without using the entire Greimassian theoretical apparatus.[3] Moreover, in the analyses I complement my interpretations with nonformal comments superimposed on the formally described underlying functional relations.

After explaining individual Greimassian technical concepts, I will clarify these by using them in an analysis of Wilhelm Müller's poem "Einsamkeit" (Loneliness), given below. This poem closes the first part of *Winterreise*, and the themes presented thus prepare us for the events of the cycle's second part.

Einsamkeit

Wie eine trübe Wolke
Durch heitre Lüfte geht,
Wenn in der Tanne Wipfel
Ein mattes Lüftchen weht:

So zieh' ich meine Straße
Dahin mit trägem Fuß,
Durch helles, frohes Leben,
Einsam und ohne Gruß.

Ach, daß die Luft so ruhig!
Ach, daß die Welt so licht!
Als noch die Stürme tobten,
War ich so elend nicht.

Loneliness

As a dark cloud moves through clear skies when a faint breeze blows through the tops of the firs,

so I go on my way with dragging feet, through a bright, joyful life, alone and greeted by no one.

Alas, that the air should be so calm! Alas, that the world should be so bright! While the storms were still raging, I was not so miserable.

Throughout his work Greimas makes references to Vladimir Propp's *Morphology of the Folktale* (originally published in 1928), a book that clearly functioned as a kind of starting point for Greimas. Propp had analyzed Russian folktales, and his aim was to show that they follow a limited number of underlying structural schemata. Propp started out to clarify this by giving four events:

What methods can achieve an accurate description of the tale? Let us compare the following events:

1. A tsar gives an eagle to a hero. The eagle carries the hero away to another kingdom.
2. An old man gives Súčenko a horse. The horse carries Súčenko away to another kingdom.
3. A sorcerer gives Iván a little boat. The boat takes Iván to another kingdom.
4. The princess gives Iván a ring. Young men appearing from out of the ring carry Iván away into another kingdom, and so forth.

Both constants and variables are present in the preceding instances. The names of the dramatis personae change (as well as the attributes of each), but neither their actions nor functions change. From this we can draw the inference that a tale often attributes identical actions to various personages. This makes possible the study of the tale *according to the functions of its dramatis personae*. (Propp 1968, 19–20; emphasis in the original)

Propp describes seven "spheres of action" and thirty-one "functions." Spheres of action are characters or dramatis personae in a tale, such as "the hero," "the villain," and "the princess (a sought-for person) and her father." The functions, in turn, describe significant structural events in a tale, such as "one of the members of the family is absent from home," "the hero leaves home," "the hero and the villain join in direct combat," "the villain is defeated," and "the hero is married and ascends the throne." The structure of the tale consists of a sequence of functions; the functions given above, for example, could underlie numerous tales. Hence, the actual content is not crucial for a tale's structure; rather, the role of the different characters and the function their actions play in the underlying plot are the crucial factors.

Greimas went further in abstracting the underlying structure of a narrative. Fundamental to his ideas is a distinction among three pairs of "actants" that correspond, in his theory, to Propp's dramatis personae: subject versus object, sender versus receiver, and helper versus opponent. The first two pairs are primary, while the third functions as a kind of auxiliary pair. Actants operate at the level of narrative syntax; hence, their relations are functional and can be described without direct reference to the content of the stories. In practical analysis, actants are abstractions made of the story that is being examined, and Greimas used the term *actor* when referring to the actual characters of an individual discourse. One actant may consist of several actors and vice versa. Here I will confine myself to explicating the two primary pairs of actants: subject versus object and sender versus receiver.[4]

Subject (hereafter S) can be described as the protagonist of a narrative. Greimas (1983, 202–203) said that his subject corresponds, in some ways, to the hero in Propp's theory. The object (O) can be defined through its relation to the subject; the object is something that the subject desires, wants, or contemplates and attaches value to it. Greimas showed the syntactic relation between the subject and the object by connecting them with an arrow: S → O. The arrow signifies a mutual interdependence between subject and object. It can thus be understood in the same way as in formal logic, as a reference to the connective "if-then."[5] Such an utterance can be either a "doing utterance" or an "utterance describing a state" (Greimas 1987, 89). In other words, the relation between subject and object can either include an action (the subject can act, for example, in order to attain the object) or describe a state (the subject can own the object, for instance).

The subject and the object can be either conjoined or disjoined. Greimas showed conjunction as S ∩ O and disjunction as S ∪ O. Both define a state, and a narrative can be described as a sequence of such states. The motion from one state to another can be indicated with a double-line arrow (⇒). If, for example, we want to show the underlying structure of a story in which the subject (say, a prince) seeks the object (say, a princess) and finally finds it (or her in our tale), we can describe this structure as (S ∪ O) ⇒ (S ∩ O). Subject and object are initially disjoined (the prince is separated from the princess), and, after a transformation or action (the search for the princess, indicated by the double-line arrow), the pair are conjoined (the prince has found the princess).[6]

The discussion of conjunction and disjunction does not, of course, presuppose narrative activity. Greimas (1983, 139) made a distinction between factors that are "dynamic" (such as narrative) and those that are "static" (such as a state or an impression) (see also Greimas 1987, 89). Often poems consist of only one state and hence can be called static. A poem's underlying idea may consist, for example, of longing for something, in which case the formalization might be S ∪ O; or the idea might be delight in having attained something, in which case the formalization would be S ∩ O. The juxtaposition of S ∪ O and S ∩ O can also be shown as static. For example, the underlying idea of a text may be a situation in which the protagonist does not know whether or not he will reach the object of his desire and is contemplating this uncertainty (say, whether a girl loves him or not). In such a case the formalization might be (S ∪ O) versus (S ∩ O).

To clarify the concepts of subject and object, let us analyze their role in Müller's "Einsamkeit," whose text was given above. The protagonist wanders alone, observing in the first two stanzas the calm weather. At the same time, he refers to his dragging feet, to his weariness. These lines have a deeply melancholy air, an atmosphere made all the more desolate because this emotion is prompted by images that ordinarily have positive associations. The poem's last two lines introduce an important change. The protagonist recalls past storms, saying that when the weather raged, he was not so miserable. He deems this condition positive (again contrary to the usual associations) and would like to regain a not-so-miserable state. But this positive situation is ultimately an illusion; his present is unavoidably tied to misery, which is represented by the gentle weather.

In the poem the protagonist functions as the subject (S); it is he who is making the observations, and it is his inner feelings that are described. The text's emotional world consists of an opposition between the miserable present and the not-so-miserable past, which the narrator would like to recapture. The state when he did not feel so miserable (and which he hopes to regain) is considered positive; it

Table 4.1. "Einsamkeit," underlying structure of the poem

a. Underlying static state
reality
$(S \cup O)$

b. Narrative layer

state 1		state 2
reality,		illusion,
contemplation		contemplation
of the present		of the past (and an indirect hope for a future)
$(S \cup O)$	$\Rightarrow$	$(S \cap O)$

c. Two forms of sender

state 1		state 2
present, reality, negative		past, illusion, not-so-negative
primary		secondary
$([Sr_1 \rightarrow R] \rightarrow [S \cup O])$	vs.	$([Sr_2 \rightarrow R] \rightarrow [S \cap O])$

Actant	Reference
S	the protagonist
O	a not-so-miserable state
Sr_1	the calm weather
Sr_2	the storm
R	the protagonist

is therefore the poem's object (O). The relationship between the protagonist and the positive state he contemplates can thus be formalized as $S \rightarrow O$. In the poem, however, the object is ultimately an illusion; it cannot be obtained. So the subject and the object are fundamentally disjoined $(S \cup O)$ (table 4.1a).

Superimposed on this static state is a narrative layer in which the protagonist first contemplates the unhappy present reality (the first two stanzas and the first two lines of the final stanza), while in the poem's last two lines, he speaks about the more positive illusion. This narrative activity can be formalized as $(S \cup O)$ $\Rightarrow (S \cap O)$ (table 4.1b). In effect, the poem moves from describing the negative present (in which S and O are disjoined) to describing a more positive illusion in which misery is not so strongly felt (so that S and O are conjoined). The poem implies that the speaker would like to attain such a state in the future, a state that occurs in a temporal location ahead of the poem's present (in addition to being a recollection), hence, the notion of narrative activity. In the poetic analyses in this book, I will complement such transformations by superimposed references to the content of the poems. When reference to the content is added, this narrative layer of "Einsamkeit" can be described as shown in table 4.1b. In the poem, this narrative action is fundamentally secondary, however; the underlying first state ($S \cup O$) is primary, and, therefore, the more positive second state ($S \cap O$) is and remains an illusion.

The opposition of subject and object gives us preliminary tools for discussing death, or, more generally, illusion, in *Winterreise*. The wanderer, the protagonist, is interpreted as the subject. In the poems to be discussed, illusion (the object) assumes two guises: lost love and death. When the global unfolding of *Winterreise* is addressed, these two will be referred to as O_1 and O_2, respectively. The subject is situated in the real world, whereas the object (the lost beloved and death) occurs only in the subject's mind and hence does not exist in present reality. Yet the protagonist contemplates and longs for the unreal, for the objects he cannot have. The subject is therefore disjoined from the object ($S \cup O$). Since the subject and the object are abstract functional concepts, the object can assume various guises in the poems themselves without losing its structural relation to the subject. In other words, the function of the object (as well as the distinction between O_1 and O_2) remains effective, even in those poems that do not refer directly to the beloved or to death.

Let us now move to the second pair of primary actants in Greimas's theory, namely, the relationship between the sender (Sr) and the receiver (R), formally described as $Sr \rightarrow R$.[7] The relationship between sender and receiver describes communication; the sender is the source of information, which the receiver then obtains. In addition, the information concerns the object, so the relation between Sr and R is also related to O. We can clarify these relationships with a tale in which a hero seeks a hidden treasure and a fairy tells him where it is buried. The hero is the subject, while the treasure, or finding the treasure, is the object. The fairy is the sender who tells the hero the location of the treasure and hence causes him to look in the right place. Thus, in addition to being the subject, the hero is also the receiver. (The same character often represents, as here, both the subject and the receiver.)

We can clarify the sender and receiver by continuing the analysis of Müller's "Einsamkeit." In the poem, the weather functions as the sender and the protagonist as the receiver. The protagonist observes that the weather makes him feel either miserable or not so miserable, so the quality of the weather is the source of his emotions. The sender assumes two forms, Sr_1 and Sr_2. The first, Sr_1, refers to calm weather, so it is connected to the disjunction of S and O, the reality. Formally, this can be indicated as in the first state of table 4.1c: the gentle weather observed by the protagonist makes him realize that he cannot reach a state in which he does not feel miserable. By contrast, the second, Sr_2, refers to the storm and is associated with the conjunction of S and O, the illusion. Formally, this can be shown as in the second state of table 4.1c. The two forms of the sender are therefore directly related to the poem's two states.

The $Sr \rightarrow R$ relation will be important in several poems of *Winterreise* and will feature prominently in the discussion of death and lost love, as well as in the juxtaposition of reality and illusion. As suggested above, the protagonist can be understood as the subject and the illusion as the object. In several poems, something makes the protagonist contemplate the illusion. So we may say that this something is the sender, the protagonist is the receiver (in addition to being the subject), and the illusion and its contemplation are the object.

The analytical observations of the underlying structural relations of Müller's poem suggested above could have been made, in principle, without the formalizations. We could have spoken only about the content of the poem: the protagonist, the different kinds of weather, and their associations with the protagonist's different emotions. The use of the rudimentary formalizations used above, however, has three advantages. First, and most evidently, such formalizations clarify poetic tensions and relations that may be intuitively grasped but conceptually hidden. Thus, they can elucidate poetic connections that are not immediately evident. Second, using these formalizations, we can speak about the tensions and structural relations within the poems without directly referring to the content. This is important for interpreting the text-music relation; it is then possible to speak about abstract structural relations between music and text and hence avoid basing the musico-poetic reading on the notion that certain musical events directly represent the semantic content of the poems. Third, in an analysis of the texts of *Winterreise*, formalizations can show how those outwardly very different referents—serving as various actors in the poems—nevertheless fulfill the same underlying functions in the poetic structures, that is, they function as invariable actants. The significance of this is most apparent when *Winterreise* is examined as a cycle in chapter 13.

4.2. Motivic Connections and Freer Associations

In discussing structural text-music relationships in section 3.4, I referred to the notion of "extroversive semiosis," a term used by Kofi Agawu and meaning the referential layer in Classical music. I argued that we can understand motives in Lieder as instances of extroversive semiosis (i.e., as references to something outside of the music), but now the music is not referring to the general characteristics of a musical style (as in the case of topics) but rather to the text of an individual Lied. In order to understand how such extroversive semiosis functions, it is important to define what I mean by the term *motive,* as well as by the related notion of *freer associations.* Because analysis of voice-leading structure will figure significantly in the following analytical chapters, here as elsewhere I will be using the term "motive" in a Schenkerian context.

In *Free Composition,* his last and most significant theoretical work, Heinrich Schenker did not use the term *motive* except in a pejorative sense. Yet the kinds of relations that more recent Schenkerian literature normally calls motivic do appear in his monograph, although Schenker calls such connections "concealed repetitions," examining them under the heading of "the achievement of organic relationship through repetition" (1979, 98–100, and fig. 119).[8] Such repetitions do not, however, play a significant role in most of his examples.[9] Schenker argued that these "concealed repetitions," occurring at deeper levels, can be revealed by studying the voice leading, since "all diminution must be secured firmly to the total work by means which are precisely demonstrable and organically verified by the inner necessities of the voice-leading" (98).[10]

Since the motivic connections appearing at deep levels are an outcome of voice leading, they tend to be quite simple, often appearing as linear progressions, arpeggiations, neighbor notes, or combinations of these. Allen Cadwallader (1988, 5) has coined the term *first-order motive* to describe the prolongations that can appear at the first level of the middleground and may then be repeated at more immediate structural levels.[11] Such motives are no longer aspects of specific pieces only, Cadwallader argues, but stem directly from the features of the tonal system. By contrast, Charles Burkhart (1978) emphasizes that motives are primarily aspects of individual pieces. Unlike Cadwallader, he suggests that mere local repetitions of some patterns occurring at the deepest levels do not suffice to form motivic parallelisms. If the *Ursatz* of the entire work, for example, is repeated at more local levels—a procedure Burkhart calls "*Ursatz* parallelism"— this still does not make a motivic association. Yet even *Ursatz* parallelisms, in Burkhart's view, may form significant motivic associations if the parallelisms are similarly elaborated in their individual appearances. In other words, the common elaboration makes the parallelism an aspect of a given musical work, not just a repetition of a fundamentally abstract phenomenon.

In this study I adopt a view of motivic relations resembling Burkhart's. I will consider simple deep-levels elements—the *Urlinie*, for example—as motivic factors only in situations in which these are treated in some specific manner that underlines their motivic quality. More generally, I will try to explain how the motivic design helps to shape the unique character of each individual song rather than to make note of repetitions per se. Such piece-specific motivic connections can form (and often do form in *Winterreise*) dramatic traits that permeate entire compositions. Edward Laufer (1988) has discussed this possibility in suggesting that a characteristic feature of several fantasies is an underlying dramatic idea in which the music first loses its way, so to speak, and finds it again in the end. In his analyses, this kind of dramatic arch is seen to a great extent as an outcome of motivic aspects of the fantasies.

Motivic connections as discussed by Cadwallader, Burkhart, and Laufer appear at various structural levels and can be revealed through analysis of voice-leading structure. In addition to such motivic connections, I will also examine freer associations, other kinds of relations that have specific significance within the context of a given song. The most frequent of these associations is the "pitch-class motive," wherein the same pitch class (often exhibiting two distinct enharmonic functions) figures prominently in a work.[12] I will also discuss other kinds of freer associations that can be directly related to the voice-leading structure yet do not form motivic connections in the sense discussed above. A cover tone, for example, may conceal the structural top-voice line in a way that affects the dramatic quality of the music considerably. There may also be instances in which such associations do not arise directly from the voice-leading structure. Register or rhetorical emphasis, for example, may associate pitches that are not connected with each other through voice leading. Or an association may be related to meter; deviations from a steady hypermeter, for instance, may appear in a similar way in various parts of a piece. Furthermore, changes in texture may draw clear associations. A unison texture, for example, may alternate with a fuller texture, creating a dramatic trait. In these and numerous other instances, these kinds of aspects may be used with such consistency that it could be argued that they shape significantly the work in which they occur.

To take an example of freer associations that are nevertheless elucidated in a Schenkerian context like the ones I will discuss, let us consider Carl Schachter's analysis of the Prelude from Bach's Suite No. 4 for Violoncello Solo. Schachter discusses such associations, arguing that they form a dramatic arch extending through the entire work, creating motion from a state of incompleteness to fulfillment: "The contrast between the opening and closing pedal points is a contrast between disruption of a musical process and its completion, between musical frustration and fulfillment. And the tonal events between the two pedal points are what makes the music achieve completion and fulfillment in so overpoweringly convincing a way" (1994, 71). Perhaps the three primary elements of Schachter's discussion of the piece are (1) the disposition of the upper voices of the underlying four-part texture so that the *Urlinie* occurs in the "tenor" voice; (2) the introduction of the pitch class D♭ as a destabilizing factor at the outset and its rhetorically underlined correction into a D♯ only at the end; (3) the manner in which the chromatic pitches are introduced (all five rising pitches that do not belong to the tonic scale are heard in the first part of the piece, with their falling enharmonic equivalents in the latter part). Only the first of these is directly related to the voice-leading structure, whereas the other two are based on freer associations.

4.3. Music and Text: An Analytical Model

So far, this chapter has provided a theoretical foundation on which the kinds of structural text-music relations outlined in section 3.4 can be based. It is now time to draw the different lines together and introduce an analytical model that will be applied in the analyses in chapters 5–11. The model consists of three consecutive stages: analysis of the music, analysis of the text, and analysis of the musico-poetic aspects. The main novel feature here is the initial separation of music and text; each is first studied without any recourse to the other, and their relationships are addressed only in the final, third stage. (The relationship of this principle to ideas presented in earlier literature on text-music connections will be discussed in section 4.5.) At each of the three stages one should avoid too strict a prescription of how to carry out the analysis; because individual songs differ from each other in manifold ways, an analytical model should be able to cope with the idiosyncrasies of a given Lied. Furthermore, the nature of individual analyses also depends on the analytical approaches used in musical and textual interpretations. As a result, the outcome is different in a study such as this one, which applies Schenkerian and Greimassian methodologies, as opposed to a study that examines rhythm and prosody, for example. Despite such different methodological approaches, the actual analytical stages may be similar.

1. Analysis of the Music

The analysis of the music of a Lied provides the basis for interpreting its text-music relationships; as suggested in proposition 5 in chapter 3, the music of a Lied may influence the interpretation of its text. This first stage may analyze both structural factors and aspects related to the emotional and dramatic quality of the music. Ideally, the text should not affect the analysis of the music. In practical analysis, there are two kinds of instances where I find it justifiable to depart from this principle. First, in some subtle analytical details (where it is difficult to decide between two analytical alternatives, for example), the text may help achieve the most plausible interpretation. I do not believe, however, that textual factors should generally guide the analytical decisions. Second, in presenting the analysis, the choice of musical features to be examined in detail may be based on text-music relations to be discussed only later. The analyst should not, however, leave aside musical aspects that are important for the overall organization of the music, even though these may not play a direct role in the subsequent text-music analysis. In other words, one should not leave out of the analytical discussion elements that are of great significance for the musical unfolding. If this were done, then the musical aspects to be examined would be extracted from the large-scale structure, so their overall function would remain unspecific. This would diminish the explanatory power they have in illuminating the text-music associations; such associations would then be based on musical details only, without taking into consideration the function of these details in the large-scale organization of the music.[13]

In the analytical chapters to follow, I provide voice-leading graphs for entire songs, even when the verbal commentary concentrates only on certain passages and motives (or other kinds of associations). In this manner, I provide a larger musical context for those musical aspects that will be examined more thoroughly, aspects that function prominently in the examination of the text-music relations. Hence, the musico-poetic associations affect the choice of musical features to be discussed in detail, but I will try to avoid allowing them to affect the music-analytical interpretations. In addition to the structure, I will comment on the form and emotional aspects of the music at both the local and the global levels. At the global level, I will concentrate on two basic emotions, the tragic and the joyful. As proposition 3 in chapter 3 argues, following the ideas of Stephen Davies, music cannot express higher emotions requiring an object. The emotional features extending through entire works will be indicated by Robert Hatten's term *expressive genre*, introduced in section 3.3. More locally, I will take account of various qualities and intensities of the basic emotions of the tragic and joyful. These local shades thus constitute a more nuanced expressive narrative of the music. The differences in the emotional intensities of the expressive genre will also be discussed by referring to a "dramatic curve," indicating significant high points (as explained in section 3.3). I distinguish between global high points of entire songs, on the one hand, and more local dramatic peaks of individual musical sections, on the other.

2. Analysis of the Text

Once we reach the text analysis (or, at least, once this analysis is presented), the musical features will already have been examined. Therefore, the results of the musical analysis might have influenced the analysis of the text had the poems been read solely from the standpoint of the musico-poetic aspects. At this second analytical stage, however, the poems are to be read and analyzed only as text. If the poems are first interpreted in this way, without recourse to the music, then the actual manner in which the music shapes their reading can be explained more clearly. (Section 4.5 will discuss difficulties that may emerge when one chooses, as I do here, to first study the poem of a Lied without considering the music.) In the analyses of the poems, I will concentrate on describing the themes of the lost beloved and death, as contemplated by the protagonist, and then relate these topics to the more general theme of juxtaposing reality and illusion.

3. Analysis of Musico-Poetic Aspects

While the music and the text will be analyzed independently in the first two stages, they will be related to each other in the third stage, which includes discussion of structural associations, emotional aspects, and imitation.

No single formula can be given for comparing musical and textual structures. The musical factors to be taken into consideration are manifold: in this study, they stem primarily from the voice-leading structure, form, meter, motivic design, or the kinds of freer associations discussed in the previous section. Hence, the description of structural musico-poetic relations should show sensitivity to the nature of musical and textual features in the individual songs.

The structural aspects of music and text that form abstract musico-poetic relations in a Lied need not be aligned, so to speak; that is, they need not be heard at the same time. Consider, for example, a situation in which both the musical and textual structures form a similar dramatic arch, moving from tension—such as a juxtaposition of two conflicting elements—to release. This underlying relation remains effective, even if there is no direct contact between the factors creating this tension in the musical structure, on the one hand, and those creating the textual tension, on the other—if these two do not, in other words, appear together on the surface. The similar tensions in the musical and textual structures suffice, in my view, to draw a link between the two.[14]

Yet such underlying abstract associations between the structures of music and text are enhanced if the musical and textual aspects forming these relationships meet in the foreground. We can think of a situation, for example, in which a certain motivic configuration in the music can be associated with a certain element in the textual structure. If lines or individual words of a poem significant for the text's underlying structure are set by a foreground occurrence of a recurring musical motive, then we may say that this coexistence supports the deep-level relation. Motivic factors that participate in such connections can be called instances of extroversive semiosis, as discussed in proposition 4 in chapter 3.

Imitation and the expressive qualities of the music and text can often be related to these abstract, structural musico-poetic connections. In that way, they can considerably strengthen structural text-music relations; the kind of foreground encounter between musical and textual aspects discussed above, for example, can be underlined by imitation or similarities between the emotional qualities of music and text. One should be careful, however, not to connect structural relations to imitation and emotions too closely; these may be clearly associated in some Lieder, while in others there may be no such connections.

Imitation always occurs on the surface. Since there must be some sort of resemblance between the music and the sounds or gestures of the external world imitated, how the musical surface sounds cannot be changed if the connection is to be drawn. Indirectly, however, such imitations can be related to deeper levels. There may be, for instance, motivic elements that appear on the surface in the sections that include imitation. These same motives may also be enlarged in the music and form abstract connections with the structure of the text. By contrast, emotional rapport between the music and text can be analyzed at both the local and the global levels. In both layers, the text and music may exhibit similar (or conflicting) emotions.

If there are conflicts between certain aspects of the music and those of the text, then these can be discussed in stage 3. Since the music and the text have been analyzed independently in the first two stages, any disagreements between them may now lead the analyst to revise the interpretation of the poem. (As discussed in proposition 5 in chapter 3, the music may at this time affect the interpretation of the text in the Lied.) If the revisions are made here instead of in stage 2, when the poem is first analyzed, the extent and actual manner in which the music affects the reading of the poem can be assessed more clearly.

4.4. Some Previous Studies on the Text-Music Relationship in Nineteenth-Century Lieder

The model and analytical methodology presented above do not, of course, introduce a totally new way of understanding musico-poetic connections in Lieder, so a discussion of how my approach is related to ideas presented in earlier literature is in order. In this section, I introduce some pertinent literature from among the studies with a Schenkerian orientation. I have two reasons for my selection. First, as suggested above in proposition 5 (section 3.5), the choice of analytical perspective defines the nature of the analytical outcome (but not its actual content). Hence, those studies that share my method of musical analysis are more likely to illuminate my topic than studies with a different point of departure. Second, the amount of literature on the nineteenth-century Lied is simply so vast that choices must be made, and I believe that a selection based on methodology is the most fruitful. Furthermore, I will concentrate on studies that examine the structural connections between music and text (proposition 4). This is because I believe that the imitation and rapport between the emotional qualities of music and text—the other two sources for musico-poetic relations outlined above—are easier to grasp.

Owing to this selection of literature, I must leave aside many texts that would be highly significant for studies on *Winterreise* whose methodological orientation differs from mine. To take but two examples: in a study examining *Winterreise* in the context of Schubert's late song output, Susan Youens's *Schubert's Late Lieder: Beyond the Song Cycles* (2006) provides valuable material, in particular on the Lieder whose poems feature the notion of death, the topic of my study as well, while Yonatan Malin's analytically oriented study, *Songs in Motion: Rhythm and Meter in the German Lied* (2010), which concentrates on the interaction of poetic and musical meters, provides comprehensive theoretical and analytical background for a study emphasizing prosody and rhythm.

In his valuable article "Theory and Practice in the Analysis of the Nineteenth-Century *Lied*" (1992), Kofi Agawu sought to lay a theoretical foundation for a "Schenkerian poetics of song," a secure basis for describing text-music relations. Throughout his article, Agawu stresses the need to go beyond musico-poetic foreground correspondences (and noncorrespondences, as he argues). Lieder often include, he suggests, sections that would not seem to show direct connections between words and music. Yet these sections may play a significant function in the overall unfolding of the Lieder: "An enduring problem for the song analyst is deciding what to do with those aspects of [musical] structure that appear not to participate directly in the signifying process of the text" (24).

Agawu's solution to this dilemma is to distinguish three general layers in a Lied, which form the basis for analysis: the music, the words, and the song, the last of which describes the musico-poetic network. A song analysis can then be carried out in three stages that reflect these layers. The first stage concentrates on musical structure and includes the development of "metaphors for 'purely musical' devices" (Agawu 1992, 11). Hence, the musical structure should be dealt with as such before references to the text are made. The second stage consists of the analysis of the text as well as a preliminary comparison of musical and textual aspects. At this stage, the analyst does not interpret the poem alone but rather attempts to read it as the composer did, so that, in Agawu's view, the music affects the interpretation of the poem. Finally, the third stage is an explicit interpretation that proposes a reading of the musico-poetic network. As in my analytical model (discussed in section 4.3), Agawu's schema provides a way to elucidate the independence of music and text as well as their interaction.

In his essay "The Blossoms of 'Trockne Blumen': Music and Text in the Early Nineteenth Century" (1999), Lawrence M. Zbikowski also examines the interaction between music and text, the methodological standpoint for describing this relation, and the significance of interpretation for this relationship. I will confine myself to those aspects of Zbikowski's complex argument that are pertinent to my approach. Zbikowski draws his methodological perspective from research on cognitive linguistics and rhetoric and specifically from the notion of "conceptual integration networks" (CINs), which consist of at least four "mental spaces." Central to a network constituting a CIN are two "input spaces," that is, two contrasting levels, or aspects, of the object under analysis. In a Romantic poem that juxtaposes the protagonist and nature, for example, these input spaces might be "nature space" and "human space." The input spaces operate within the boundaries defined by the "generic space." And finally, there is the fourth space, the "blended space," which is a combination, or fusion, of aspects of the input spaces. To oversimplify: the generic space provides the general boundaries for the quality of the object's aspects to be analyzed; input spaces show two contrasting features of the object; and the blended space is the outcome of the juxtaposition of the input spaces.[15]

In analyzing Lieder, Zbikowski suggests that one of the input spaces can be devoted to music, while the other can be reserved for text. This provides a theoretical framework for the discussion of the text-music relationship, namely, an examination of the structural similarities between the two: "This leads to the possibility of a CIN in which one of the input spaces is built up from language, and the other from music. This CIN could then be used to explain how concepts associated with a given text combine with concepts associated with specific music to give rise to the phenomenon of song" (Zbikowski 1999, 314).

Zbikowski stresses the dynamic and nonfinal quality of CINs: "Mental spaces are dynamic structures, as are the CINs that are built from them. . . . [A given CIN is] a sort of 'snapshot' of this particular network, framed with the intent of capturing its essential features but making no claim to exhausting the possibilities for description" (1999, 311–12). So interpretation again plays a central role, and different methods could lead to different analytical readings. Yet the interpretation must be based on structural similarities, Zbikowski argues; otherwise, it would be unfounded.

Zbikowski's theory functions as a kind of metatheory. The general requirement in discussing structural musico-poetic relationships is very similar to the one advocated in this study: if we want to discuss structural text-music connections, then there must be a layer in which the two structures can be compared, in which they are in dialogue with each other. Such a layer is provided by the two input spaces that are devoted to musical and textual structures, respectively. The musico-poetic interpretation then occurs in the blended space. Zbikowski makes it clear that the structural elements discussed in the input spaces can include information arrived at via several analytical methods. Thus, they might also consist of readings that employ Schenkerian and Greimassian theories, the two approaches I use here. Indeed, one of Zbikowski's examples, Schubert's "Trockne Blumen," comes close to this possibility; here the aspects of the text space consist of a binary opposition underlying the text, while the music space includes features described with a voice-leading graph (1999, 333).

The Schenkerian analytical literature on Lieder includes several studies in which the structural relations between text and music are described in a highly illuminating manner. This literature often addresses issues similar to those I raise here: primarily, the global courses of the music and text (and their interactions), as well as the function of motives as references to the poems. Even though this literature does not usually make use of formalization to describe the poems the way I do, the writers often seem to share my view that the music does not directly represent the poetic content. They, too, prefer to examine the musico-poetic associations at an abstract level, speaking, for example, about motion from uncertainty to clarity in both the music and the text, or about a central image of a poem and its relations to the music. To illustrate this literature, I will briefly discuss studies by Edward Laufer, Charles Burkhart, Carl Schachter, David Lewin, and Walter Everett.

In their writings, Laufer and Burkhart have referred to an overarching narrative underlying a poem and its relations to musical structure. Laufer shows how several aspects of the music of Brahms's "Wie Melodien zieht es mir," op. 105, no. 1, interact with certain features of the text. He speaks about the structural nature of such relations: "The words are not merely set: the poem, its structure, and the thought behind the discourse as well become organically part of the composition" (Laufer 1977, 255). Laufer reads the poem as a motion from the ineffable and indefinable idea of beauty in the mind of a poet at the beginning of the poem to its expression through art at the end. He then shows how such a motion from an indefinite state to a definite one is reflected in several aspects of the music: its melodic material, harmonic structure, and motivic features. Burkhart, in turn, discusses a somewhat similar "progression from vagueness to relative clarity" (1990, 157) in Schumann's "Schöne Fremde" from *Liederkreis*, op. 39. The principal harmonic-contrapuntal means by which this progression appears in the music are, on the one hand, the underlying harmonic structure—an auxiliary cadence extending through the entire song—and, on the other hand, a large-scale arpeggiation leading to the *Kopfton* only in the third and final phrase of the song. In addition to voice-leading structure, this idea of progression from vagueness to clarity is reflected in the metrical structure of the music. The first two phrases contain expansions—hence suggesting metrical vagueness—whereas the last is a stable eight-measure phrase.

Schachter's examination of Schubert's "Nacht und Träume," which appears in his essay "Motive and Text in Four Schubert Songs" (1999b, 209–20), is particularly pertinent here: as in my study, Schachter discusses the juxtaposition of reality and illusion. Whereas the underlying structures of the poems in the songs examined by Laufer and Burkhart consist of a motion or progression, the structure of Matthäus von Collin's poem "Nacht und Träume" consists of a state—dreams that are, at least implicitly, juxtaposed with reality. Schachter argues that the image of a dream is reflected in the motivic and tonal structure of the work. In the B-major song, a recurring melodic motion in the foreground is the progression F♯–F𝄪–G♯ and its reverse, G♯–G♮–F♯. This motive also permeates the deeper levels. Mm. 15–19 center around an unprepared G-major triad whose bass note, G, proceeds unconventionally, in m. 20, to A♯, thus forming an augmented second. Schachter argues that the structural origin of the G-major passage is a chromatic passing-tone F$\times$ (an outcome of motivic enlargement), the chord's stability in the foreground notwithstanding.

> By combining in a single sonority two different and contrasting orders of musical reality, Schubert gives this song a great central image; the song embodies a musical symbol of dreams. The G-major section crystallizes around a most transitory musical event—a chromatic passing tone. Yet, while we are immersed in it, it assumes the guise of that most solid tonal structure, the major triad. Only at "wenn der Tag erwacht" [when day awakens] does its insubstantiality become manifest; it vanishes, never to return except as an indistinct memory in the G♯s of the coda. (1999b, 217–18)

In his discussion of Schubert's "Ihr Bild" (in *Schwanengesang*), David Lewin examines, among other things, the relationships between two issues: the temporal organization of Heine's poem set by Schubert and the various musical locations where the underlying *Urlinie* might be seen to close (2006, 135–47). Lewin's starting point is that Schubert's music affects the way in which Heine's poem is understood. Whereas if read alone, the poem ends in an outcry of grief, the poem as set by Schubert closes with the narrator's refusal to accept the loss of his beloved (136–38). Lewin then discusses how different Schenkerian interpretations, particularly the location of the arrival of the concluding background $\hat{1}$, affect the way in which we understand the poem's end in the musico-poetic network. One Schenkerian option would be to interpret the closure of the *Urlinie* as taking place in m. 34, in the B♭-major cadence. If the background were interpreted this way, then the poem would end in the "'present of denial' or 'the delusive present'"—the main poetic idea of this end then being "to make the picture come to life" (139, 143). If, on the other hand, the arrival at the $\hat{1}$ is seen to occur only in the song's final bar, in B♭ minor, then the poem would end in "the present of 'reality,'" where the narrator has to accept that he has indeed lost his beloved, thus reflecting the "real reality" (139, 145).

In Lewin's *Urlinie* interpretation, the way in which an element of the background structure is understood affects the way we read the poem and consequently the entire text-music network. He distinguishes between two layers of present at the poem's end, and the one we deem to be primary reflects our interpretation of the background structure. Background is not, therefore, an abstract framework but an active player in the song's musico-poetic web.

Walter Everett has published extended and detailed Schenkerian analyses of several songs in *Winterreise* (1988, 1990); his topic and approach are close to those presented here. He discusses various poetic themes found throughout the cycle (in particular, delusions and illusions, memories and dreams, and the traveler's grief) and examines how they are reflected in the music of various songs. Thus, he addresses cyclical aspects along with the musico-poetic associations in individual Lieder. Particularly valuable is his association of the $\hat{6}$–$\hat{5}$ progression in the minor mode with grief in the poems, an association he sees in several songs. He argues that "various textual references to grief are given a consistent motivic treatment in the music. A Schenkerian approach is well suited to such a study because of the rigorous way in which it allows musical motives, along with their hidden repetitions at different structural levels, to be defined, thus facilitating a meaningful correlation of musical and literary motives" (Everett 1990, 157). Everett's aim is therefore to show that "the decoration of the fifth scale degree with its semitone upper neighbour note . . . is Schubert's principal means of portraying the wanderer's grief, thus unifying the individual songs in a cohesive cycle" (157).

4.5. The Point of View of the Present Study and Earlier Approaches to Musico-Poetic Associations

All of the theorists mentioned in the preceding section have points of contact with the methodology introduced in this study: the analytically oriented studies by Laufer, Burkhart, Schachter, Lewin, and Everett approach musico-poetic associations in a way that is very close to my viewpoint in several respects, while the more methodological essays by Agawu and Zbikowski share significant general points of view with my approach. Most importantly, all of these writers argue that the music's voice-leading structure (which is often seen to interact with its motivic material) is related to the underlying structure of the poem.

Yet there are significant differences. Most important, my methodology begins with a strict distinction between music and text; that is, I suggest that each be first studied independently of the other. The musico-poetic associations are then examined only after the music and text have been analyzed separately. At a general level, Agawu's three-part scheme comes closest to this view in the literature referred to above. (Some indirect similarities can also be found in Lewin's view that there are different ways of understanding Heine's "Ihr Bild.") Yet Agawu's analytical framework differs from mine; he suggests that the influence of the music should be immediately considered while the text is being addressed, whereas I argue that this influence is better discussed only after musical and textual structures have first been examined separately.

To be sure, there are studies that emphasize the significance of examining the poem as such before considering musico-poetic associations, so I am not suggesting that my approach is unique in this respect. To take an example, in discussing two lyric poems by Goethe set by Schubert, Robert Hatten (2008) suggests that we should also consider the musical quality of the poems themselves in order to understand how the music makes the texts correspond to the musical features that Schubert adds. In his view, the poems might lose some of their distinctive features in the musical setting, so we should avoid "a tendency to approach text settings of the masters as though everything were calculated for the best of all possible reasons, and to hear poetic texts primarily through the filter of their compositional setting" (Hatten 2008, 11).

Despite my insistence that music and text first be studied independently, the analyst can hardly approach the two in a complete void, as my model implies. Unavoidably, there is at least a tentative idea of the relationship between the music and the text when we begin to analyze any Lied. While conceding this provisional knowledge, I have attempted to put aside the text as much as possible in analyzing the music, and I have done the same with the music in analyzing the text. This strategy has great advantages. At a general level, it provides a concrete and clearly articulated foundation (the independent views of the music and the text) on which to base a musico-poetic interpretation. In other words, if the music and the poem have been studied without recourse to each other, then we can at least maintain that both have been approached first on their own, as it were, and not through those features that arise in the study of musico-poetic associations.

There is an additional advantage in songs whose music seems to affect how the poem is understood (and there are several instances of this in part 2 of *Winterreise*). If we are able to see how the interpretations of a poem differ when the text is read on its own, rather than as part of a Lied, then we can present a justified hypothesis of how Schubert's music affects our understanding of a poem. This not only increases our understanding of music's function in a given Lied but also deepens our view of the musico-poetic network. Unless we at least attempt to understand the poem first as an independent entity, we cannot clarify such added nuances—or indeed occasional new meanings—that music creates in the poetic signification. Although I concede that the analyst often already knows both music and text when allegedly approaching them independently, I believe that it is possible to bracket out that knowledge when analyzing poem and music separately, and the benefits described above are well worth the effort.

Because in this book we are dealing with a song cycle, the differences between the interpretations of a single poem either as an independent entity or as part of a musico-poetic network may also indicate how Schubert's poetic interpretations mold the overall narrative of *Winterreise*. The view of the cyclical organization therefore brings up another advantage of my methodology. Although the content of the individual poems may vary greatly, the poems might nevertheless be elaborating the same underlying themes, and in such instances, the Greimassian formalizations enable us to describe such interconnectedness. If we used only the imagery derived from the content of individual poems (as is usually done in studies of Lieder), then these associations would easily remain hidden. The actantial formalizations, by contrast, make it possible to trace the evolution of the underlying themes of the poetic cycle, even in instances where the concrete images in the poems do not necessarily seem to address the same overarching topics.

For example, in the analysis of Müller's "Einsamkeit" presented in section 4.1, it is significant that the "not-so-miserable state" can be referred to as the "object." This is the first poem in the cycle in which the longed-for object is not the beloved but a state in which misery is not felt. Later, in part 2 of *Winterreise,* such a state is unequivocally termed death. (Sections 1.2 and 1.3 discussed the cycle's underlying narrative, which moves from longing for a past love to longing for the coming death.) "Einsamkeit" is thus the first song in the cycle in which the initial longed-for object (the beloved or O_1 in Greimassian symbols) is replaced by the idea of a state in which the poor wanderer has managed to escape his misery (death, a not-so-miserable state, or O_2). Thus, this song signifies a turning point in *Winterreise,* or at least it anticipates one. Using Greimassian symbols, we can follow the course of such invariant poetic themes in individual poems (such as O_1 and O_2 in the overarching cycle), even where the actual concepts that Müller uses in individual poems differ from each other. (Here, for example, Müller is not referring to death, yet the not-so-miserable state of "Einsamkeit" can be associated with the O_2 of the cycle's overall narrative.) If the poetic analysis only used concepts derived from individual poems, such connections would be more difficult to decipher.

The formalizations are also valuable in that they provide the means for discussing both the structures of individual poems and the cycle's overall narrative with the same symbols. This is important when the functions of individual Lieder and their musico-poetic associations are interpreted from the global perspective of the entire cycle: the role that each Lied plays in the whole can be clarified by referring to the poems' function in the overall narrative. In other words, this view also provides an important layer in the musico-poetic network, which clarifies how any given Lied participates in the larger context. This view of textual structure thus provides a starting point for discussing both local and global musico-poetic associations, as well as the connections between the two.

Part 2. Songs

5 The Emergence of Death as a Positive Option: "Der greise Kopf"

5.1. Music

"Der greise Kopf" is the second song of part 2 in *Winterreise*. It is slow, contemplative, and in a minor key, thus contrasting sharply with part 2's opening song, "Die Post," which is fast and in major. "Der greise Kopf" is in a ternary form, framed by an introduction (mm. 1–4) and a brief coda (mm. 43–44). The A¹ section (mm. 5–16) closes on a tonicized major-mode dominant, while the B section (mm. 17–29) ends on the dividing dominant of the underlying interrupted structure (example 5.1). The relationship between these two dominants is complex; in spite of their shared sonority, I do not read them as structurally connected, as would be expected in this kind of ternary organization. The concluding A² section (mm. 30–42) includes two cadential progressions, the first ending on a major-mode tonic in m. 39, the second on a minor-mode chord in m. 42. I read only the latter of these as structurally conclusive.

The song's expressive genre is governed by the tragic, the only deviations from this primary expression occurring around the G-major chord of mm. 14–16, the Ab-major chord of m. 20, and the C-major chord of m. 39 (example 5.1). There are thus three passages in which the music escapes the prevailing gloom. The song is mostly dominated by quiet music, but there are two climaxes that depart from this low dynamic level: one, in mm. 19–22, where a registral expansion and crescendo lead to the song's high point in m. 22, signaled by the arrival at an Eb-major chord; the second, in mm. 40–41, when a dramatic peak underlines the second of the A² section's cadences, the one in the tonic minor. (As explained in section 4.3, I use the term *high point* when discussing the global dramatic culmination of an entire song and the term *peak* when referring to more local climaxes.)

The song's local events occur within this global structural and expressive framework. Example 5.2 shows my analysis of mm. 1–29: introduction, A¹, and B sections. The opening tonic governs the music up to m. 10, and the tonic pedal in the bass underlines the stability of this chord. As the staff above the graph in example 5.2b and the asterisks indicate, a neighbor note above G (Ab) is a significant motivic element, and we will see that it plays an important function in the expressive drama of the song as well. At the outset, this pitch is rhetorically underlined, specifically in mm. 3 and 9, where it is stressed by declamatory ges-

Example 5.1. "Der greise Kopf," an overview.

tures that interrupt the rather inward quality of the tragic mood prevailing at the song's beginning (example 5.2b). The occurrence of A♭ in m. 9 has gestural and metrical significance. Gesturally, it is part of a rhetorically intensified repetition of the harmonic motion toward the tonic in mm. 7–8, while metrically, m. 9 is understood as the repetition of the penultimate bar of the steady four-bar hyper-measure of mm. 5–8 (see the metrical analysis in example 5.2b).

A♭ also features prominently in the modulation to G major (mm. 11 ff.), which follows the opening tonic. In m. 11, A♭ is transformed into its enharmonic equivalent, G♯, so it now functions as a chromatic passing tone. Mm. 11–14 also feature a neighboring motion above G, hence drawing further motivic associations with the preceding music. Now, however, the neighbor note is A♮, not A♭; the enharmonic transformation of A♭ into G♯ has thus affected the motivic configuration. The pairing of the enharmonic A♭ and G♯ receives further clarification through gestural and metrical means. As in mm. 9–10, mm. 15–16 repeat the harmonic arrival at the tonic (this time in G major), gesturally intensifying the harmonic

64 Songs

= broken chord; = A♭ / A♮ –G; * = A♭ / G♯

Expression: tragic · joyful · tragic implied · joyful · tragic

Quality: inward declamatory (rep.) searching · confirming hesitant declamatory · hollow · resigned

Example 5.2. "Der greise Kopf," mm. 1–29, voice-leading sketch.

closure (with the significant G♯ repeated as an upbeat to m. 15) and metrically repeating the last two bars of the preceding hypermeasure.

The musical expression reflects these motivic events. The G-major environment changes the opening tragic emotion into the joyful. Yet this new expression has a somewhat searching local quality at first (example 5.2b). In the same way that the diminished-seventh chord at the end of m. 11 could still be resolved to a C-minor triad (in which case there would be an A♭, not a G♯), the newly joyful expression is not firmly established immediately. It is only the arrival on an A♮ (an element indicating that the preceding pitch was a G♯, not an A♭) that announces the approach of a joyful expression, which is then confirmed by attaining a tonicized G-major sonority in m. 14. The arrival at the joyful is thus a gradual process.

It is unusual to modulate into a major-mode dominant in a minor-mode piece—that is, to use modal mixture in this manner.[1] Here this uncommon mixture is underlined by the stress on the two-line E♮ in m. 13 (and its repetition in m. 15). The *Kopfton*, E♭, is weakly expressed at the beginning of the song, and m. 13 is the first rhetorically underlined statement of 3̂. This chromatically inflected *Kopfton* and the tonicized G major together result in an unusual juxtaposition of major and minor: through its tonicized dominant, the C-major diatony attempts to displace C-minor diatony, as it were, yet without bringing the key of C major into the foreground.[2] The tension related to 3̂ also has its effect on the musical expression: the opening C-minor area (with an undermined ♭3̂) has an inward emotional quality, while the G-major section (with the explicit ♮3̂) has a more con-

Emergence of Death as a Positive Option 65

firming expression (example 5.2b). The music seems more willing to stress the major than the minor, as it were.

But the function of the tonicized G-major chord as a significant middleground goal is challenged in the B section. As example 5.2a indicates, the G-major chord is transformed in m. 19 into a $^6_4$ harmony, which acts locally as a dominant of A♭ major, a key tonicized by a strong gesture in mm. 19–20. Owing to the rhetorically stressed arrival at an A♭-major harmony and the unusual major mode of the previously tonicized G chord, I consider this G harmony to be a transitory element, part of an extended unfolding in the lowest voice (example 5.1) rather than a middleground *Stufe*.

Once tonicized in m. 20, A♭ major governs as a key area up to m. 25. Mm. 20–23 lead the music from the tonic of A♭ major into its dominant, an E♭-major triad, whose arrival in m. 22 is underlined by a wedgelike motion in the outer voices, a harmonic preparation with an augmented sixth chord, and a crescendo. In addition, this harmony is stressed by metrical factors: for the first time in the song, four-bar hypermeasures, occasionally extended by repetitions, are abandoned (see the metrical analysis in example 5.2b).[3] Owing to this emphasis, I take the E♭-major chord of m. 22, rather than the preceding A♭-major harmony, as the structurally primary middleground element (example 5.1). The E♭-major harmony ultimately functions as part of a I–III–V arpeggiation, an enlargement of the opening thematic gesture of the song.[4]

The musical material of mm. 17–22 features a kind of commentary on the events that earlier tonicized G major, and this dialogue retrospectively affects the function of the G-major passage. First, the mixture encountered in the G-major tonicization is canceled, as it were, by a fleeting tonicization of a C-minor chord in mm. 17–18. Second, the G-major chord turns out to be a contrapuntal element rather than a middleground *Stufe*. Third, in m. 20 A♭, as a pitch class, brings back the motivically significant A♭ after the A♮ of mm. 12–13. Fourth, E♭ is heard emphatically in the two-line octave in m. 22, that is, the *Kopfton* is underlined in its diatonic form, hence displacing the E♮ stressed in m. 13 in the high register. Thus, all of the main elements of mixture encountered in the A¹ section, borrowed from C major, are replaced in 17–22 by elements belonging to C minor. The major diatony and its joyful expression were therefore, as it now turns out, just a passing glimpse of something more positive. Once these major-mode implications have vanished, the music, in the unison passage of mm. 24–29, completes its motion to the dominant of the underlying interrupted structure (example 5.2). The unison creates a somewhat hollow expressive quality in the measures that bring to an end the deep-level motion to the dividing dominant.

The structural elements of the B section are again in dialogue with the musical expression (example 5.2b). The joyful established at the end of the A¹ section is interrupted in m. 18 when the fleetingly tonicized C minor cancels the preceding C-major diatony. The joyful immediately reappears with the A♭ major, however, and the arrival at the dominant of this key in m. 22 forms the dramatic high point of the song (example 5.1). Even though this chord locally has a joyful air (as the dominant of A♭ major), it also includes a seed of the tragic expression.

= broken chord; = Ab / A♮ –G; * = Ab / G♯

a)

30   ^3 33   38 39 40   ^2 41   ^1 42

I   II 6/5   V   I

b)

30 *   *   ^3 *   36 *   39 ♮^3   *   ^2   42 ^1   *

I   V⁷ I♮ II 6/5   V   I

1   2   3 4, (3 4,) 1   2   3   4,   1   2 3,   1   2,

Expression: tragic   joyful   tragic

Quality: inward   declamatory   searching   tentatively   solidly   declamatory
                                                      confirming   confirming

Example 5.3. "Der greise Kopf," mm. 30–44, voice-leading sketch.

In the deep middleground, it functions as a III, a third dividing the I–V progression into two units. In addition, it is embellished by a neighboring minor-mode $^6_4$ chord. The chord's tragic possibility immediately materializes in the ensuing unison bars, whose music exhibits a hollow expressive quality. This unison prolongs a predominant chord, thus announcing the approaching dividing dominant. When this chord finally arrives in m. 29, the expressive quality is somewhat resigned: the unavoidable tragic goal has been attained, and the joyful turned out to be only a fleeting emotion.

The A² section, whose voice leading is shown in example 5.3, returns to many of these dramatic and structural factors. It repeats the thematic material of the A¹ section, with the material heard earlier in G major now in the tonic major, a mode that cadences in mm. 38–39. The minor is immediately brought back after this harmonic closure, however, and a new cadence (mm. 41–42) closes the song's background structure in the tonic minor. Also, the A² section includes mixture, but this is much more conventional than in the opening section: now the music simply moves in the parallel major. The staff above the graph in example 5.3b and the asterisks show that mm. 36–39, the C-major passage, also return to the motivic material associated with G major in the A¹ section. The motivically significant Ab is now enharmonically reevaluated as G♯, a reevaluation that leads again

Emergence of Death as a Positive Option 67

to a G–A♮ motion. (A♮ now functions as a passing tone rather than as a neighbor note; see example 5.3b. This does not, however, remove the motivic association.)

The broken-chord motive, encountered on the surface at the outset of the two A sections and in the middleground as the bass progression underlying the A¹ and B sections, returns in the A² section, albeit in a somewhat distorted form (see the staff below the graph in example 5.3b). A succession of notes forms an arpeggiation from tonic to dominant, with the arpeggiating third being E♮, which results from mixture. These notes do not constitute a structural entity, however; the low D in m. 38 is so strongly marked by the register that I take it as the principal bass note filling the space between tonic and dominant.[5] This distorted, broken-chord motive can be interpreted in a dramatic way: just as the major-mode dominant chord that ends the A¹ section (a result of mixture) is not given significance in the voice leading at the deepest levels, so the E♮ underlined here (also resulting from mixture) is not part of the middleground progression. It could be argued that the C–E♭–G motion underlying the A¹ and B sections represents, so to speak, the reality of the music (arpeggiating the minor-mode tonic chord), while the distorted motivic C–E♮–G motion represents illusion (mixture).

The top voice of the A² section takes part in juxtaposing major and minor and in securing the primacy of the latter (example 5.3b). The C-major cadence ends in m. 39 on a tonic chord with Î in the uppermost voice. However, there is no linear connection between this Î and the preceding *Kopfton*. Rather, the Î is, at deep levels, an inner-voice note: it closes a fourth-progression ascending from g¹. As a result, the major-mode cadence of mm. 38–39 provides no final closure. Similarly, as a musical expression, the cadence signifies only a tentatively confirming quality (example 5.3b). In m. 39 the structural top-voice line is transferred to an inner voice from where it descends, in the minor-mode cadence of mm. 41–42, into the concluding background Î.[6] In this closing cadence, the vocal part has lost its melodic independence: it simply executes a G–C motion, which follows the course of the bass. (Example 5.3a shows a registral simplification of the top voice.) It is as if the vocal part attempted to close the structure in C major, but when this attempt does not succeed, it loses its power to take part in the course of the primary musical material. Accordingly, the piano alone is active in the cadence that closes the song's structure.

In the musical expression, the minor mode provides a strongly confirming expressive quality, at the same time functioning as the expressive peak of the A² section. The expressive culmination enhances the significance of the structural closure; thus, together, the two emphasize the C-minor closure that displaces the previously attempted major ending. The staff above the graph in example 5.3b indicates that the final cadence and the brief postlude bring the motivically important A♭–G neighboring motion back, hence displacing the preceding G–A♮ neighboring motion, as was also done after the A¹ section.

From a gestural perspective, the structural cadence recalls a common pattern in the song whereby arrival at the tonic is followed by repetition of that arrival. In the earlier occurrences, the repetitions have metrically consisted of reiterating the last two bars of a hypermeasure (see mm. 9–10, 15–16, and 34–35 and their metrical analyses in examples 5.2b and 5.3b). Now this pattern is only partly repeated (example 5.3b). Unlike the earlier versions, this time the mode (and consequently the expression) of the two harmonic arrivals is not the same; the first harmonic arrival (m. 39) takes place in the joyful major, whereas the latter (m. 42) occurs in the tragic minor. Likewise, the metrical situation is different from the earlier versions (example 5.3b). As the second, minor-mode cadential progression has a significant structural and expressive function of its own, it is not simply a repetition of the conclusion of the preceding hypermeasure as before. Rather, mm. 40–42 form an independent metrical unit. At its conclusion, the song therefore recalls an element that has ended all tonal trajectories in its A sections (repetition of the cadential closure) but now revises it so as to juxtapose directly the two primary modes and expressions. In this way, the struggle of the minor and sorrow with the major and joy is foregrounded at the song's end, and the primacy of the first two is conclusively settled.

5.2. Text

Der greise Kopf

Der Reif hat einen weißen Schein
Mir über's Haar gestreuet.
Da glaubt' ich schon ein Greis zu sein,
Und hab' mich sehr gefreuet.

Doch bald ist er hinweggetaut,
Hab' wieder schwarze Haare,
Daß mir's vor meiner Jugend graut—
Wie weit noch bis zur Bahre!

Vom Abendrot zum Morgenlicht
Ward mancher Kopf zum Greise.
Wer glaubt's? Und meiner ward es nicht
Auf dieser ganzen Reise!

The Gray Head

The frost has sprinkled a white sheen upon my hair. I thought I had already become an old man, and I rejoiced.

But soon it melted away; I have black hair again, so that I shudder at my youth— how far it is still to the grave!

Between dusk and dawn, many a head has turned gray. Who would believe it? And on this whole journey mine has not!

As so often in *Winterreise,* the main tension in the poem grows out of the juxtaposition of reality and illusion. In the first stanza, the protagonist observes that his hair is sprinkled with frost, implying that he has turned gray and become old. He is overjoyed, since old age will bring death closer. The significant theme of death as a positive option thus occurs for the first time.[7] In the second stanza, the frost melts away, and the wanderer again has black hair. This frightens him: death is still far away. The third stanza is an aside or comment on the preceding.[8] The protagonist observes that many a head has turned gray in only one night (that is, death has come near), something for which he too longs. But death does not come for him, all the misery of his journey notwithstanding.

Table 5.1 shows the underlying structure of "Der greise Kopf." Table 5.1a describes a narrative level, while 5.1b shows a static underlying state. In 5.1a the structure consists of two states and a motion from one to the other. The first state represents illusion and has positive associations. Of its two binary statements, the first shows a relationship between sender and receiver. I interpret the hair in the poem as the sender and have made a distinction between the gray hair, Sr_1, and the black hair, Sr_2. The protagonist functions as the receiver. The gray hair, Sr_1, is positive for the receiver, so a conjunction between subject and object occurs in state 1. (I interpret the speaker as the subject and the closeness of death as the object.) This first state of the poem's underlying structure is only an illusion, however, and hence unobtainable. A transformation, indicated by the double-lined arrow, leads to the second state, which, like the first, consists of two binary statements. This time, the first statement has Sr_2, representing black hair. This image has negative implications, so that subject and object are disjoined. The second state, standing for reality, is unavoidable. The transformation between the two states represents the melting of the frost—the turning of the gray hair to black—or motion from Sr_1, representing illusion, to Sr_2, representing reality.

This underlying narrative structure appears in the poem's first two stanzas. From a structural perspective, the third stanza does not add anything new to the poem. When taken alone, however, it presents a structure similar to that in the first two stanzas together: the first two lines represent the first state shown in table 5.1a; the last two, the second. So it sums up the preceding structure. Moreover, it provides the larger context for the poem (the entire journey of the wanderer), stressing the inability of the speaker to influence his own fate: the wanderer would like to attain the first state in the underlying structure, but as this is unobtainable, he must remain in the unavoidable second state.

At a still more fundamental level, shown in table 5.1b, the second state dominates the poem: the first two lines, which mention frost, refer to the past, so the protagonist knows all along that he has not actually turned gray. Hence, the transformation described in table 5.1a is something the protagonist only imagines, well knowing that the first state is an illusion. Ultimately, this transformation occurs within the framework of the static state shown in table 5.1b, which represents present reality.

5.3. Musico-Poetic Aspects

Both the poem and the music of "Der greise Kopf" feature the juxtaposition of two factors: something that is stable and unavoidable versus something

Table 5.1. "Der greise Kopf," underlying structure of the poem

a. Narrative level of the poem

state 1		state 2
illusion		reality
positive		negative
unobtainable		unavoidable
$[(Sr_1 \to R) \to (S \cap O)]$	$\Rightarrow$	$[(Sr_2 \to R) \to (S \cup O)]$

b. Underlying static state
reality
negative
unavoidable
$(Sr_2 \to R) \to (S \cup O)$

Actant	Reference
S	the protagonist
O	the closeness of death, a state in which misery is no longer felt
Sr_1	the gray hair, a symbol of the closeness of death
Sr_2	the black hair, a symbol of the great distance from death
R	the protagonist

that does not last or is not attained in a conclusive manner. As table 5.1a shows, the narrative level of the poem consists of an opposition of two states: the second is primary and real yet creates negative associations, while the first is unobtainable and illusory but creates positive associations. The music of song, in turn, juxtaposes minor and major through mixture, the minor mode being structurally primary and the major mode being ultimately unobtainable, or at least not firmly established in the music. In the song's expressive genre, as in its text, the primary element of the underlying juxtaposition (the minor) is associated with negative emotions, and the secondary element (the major) is associated with positive ones.

These abstract text-music associations provide a framework for the more local musico-poetic factors. The opening C-minor phrases set the poem's first two lines, which present the situation in a neutral manner: there is frost on the speaker's hair. The protagonist thus contemplates his situation, a quality well matched by the music's inward expression (with brief declamations; see example 5.2b, lowest line). The next two lines mention the illusion of old age, represented in the underlying structure by the first state (table 5.1a). Similarly, the music for these lines includes the tonicization of a G-major chord—a factor resulting from mixture—and the G–A♮–G motive, elements that are subordinate to the underlying C-minor diatony and the G–A♭–G motion associated with it (example 5.2b). The arrival at a motivically significant A♮ is prepared by an enharmonic reinterpretation of A♭ as G♯. In other words, the minor is displaced by actively reinterpreting one of its elements, just as the poem interprets the frost as gray hair. The poem's third line suggests uncertainty ("Da glaubt' ich"), and this is reflected in the searching quality of the musical expression.

In the B section, the C-minor key returns immediately (mm. 17–18), albeit only in passing, setting the passage in which the frost has melted. The mixture vanishes in the music, just as the illusion disappears in the poem, and the tragic expression reappears fleetingly. The mention of black hair, represented in the underlying structure by the second state, coincides with the completion of the extended 5–6 progression above the opening tonic and the return of the G–A♭ motive. (The G of m. 19 supports a ⁶₃ harmony, which still prolongs the preceding G-major chord, transforming it into an active element.) These factors indicate, retrospectively, that the structural stability of the G-major chord was ultimately an illusion. The reference to youth, the reality, is accompanied by the arrival of the E♭-major chord in m. 22, an element that occurs at the first level of the middleground and is part of the C–E♭–G broken-chord motive: the music returns to the underlying deep-middleground structure, the "reality" of the composed-out tonic triad, just as the poem returns to the real state of affairs. The significance of the arrival at the musical and textual reality is underlined by the simultaneous occurrence of the song's expressive high point.

The speaker feels dismay when he realizes that he is still young, and this emotion can be seen to have its counterpart in the musical structure. The middleground function of the E♭-major chord, a III in C minor (a minor-mode context), is disguised in the foreground by its local function as the dominant of A♭ major (a major-mode context). The musical tensions are thus similar to those in the text where the speaker shudders at reality and would like to avoid it. He cannot, however, and accepts it in the final line of the second stanza. This line is set within a phrase that completes the motion to the dominant of the first branch of the underlying interrupted structure (example 5.2). The hollow expressive quality of the low unison matches the text very well: the protagonist observes that the grave is still far away, the hoped-for goal still unattainable. In sum, the acceptance of reality in the poem coincides with the completion of the first structural background entity, as well as with the extended broken-chord motive in the bass (see the staff below the graph in example 5.1); both the music and the text have left the illusion of mixture and gray hair behind. When the dominant arrives, the musical expression has a resigned quality: reality cannot be avoided. The singer is silent when the dominant is achieved in m. 29; the wanderer does not take part in the ultimate attainment of the inevitable goal.

As has been observed, the third stanza does not bring anything new to the poem's narrative organization. Rather, it sums up the underlying structure of the first two stanzas, thereby emphasizing the inability of the protagonist to influence his fate, to affect the unavoidable reality. This aspect of the poem can be seen to be reflected in the music's thematic design: the A² section introduces no new material. The inability of the speaker to affect his fate, in turn, can be seen to have its musical counterpart in the application of mixture and in the two cadential progressions. The C-minor phrases set the final stanza's first two lines, which describe something positive that has happened to others (death) but not to the speaker. He hopes this will happen to him too but observes that it does not, the misery of his journey notwithstanding. This vain hope can be seen as being related to the mixture occurring in mm. 36–39, the C major and G–A♮ motion momentarily replacing C minor and G–A♭ (with the A♮ again prepared by an enharmonic reinterpretation of A♭ as G♯). Yet in the music, a stable major mode is not possible, a situation underlined by the distorted version of the broken-chord motive, the structurally inconclusive cadential progression in mm. 38–39, and only a tentatively confirming musical expression. Similarly, in the poem, the speaker does not turn gray. Final closure arrives only in C minor when the final words, "auf dieser ganzen Reise," referring to the long journey, are repeated in the musical setting. This word repetition may be seen to reflect the idea that this journey does not end as soon as the speaker would like—it does not end with the C-major cadence—but rather goes on. The wanderer cannot affect the course of his journey; likewise, he has only a passive role in the final cadence, where the *Urlinie* descends in the piano part and in an inner voice, a closure underlined by a strongly confirming musical expression.

The finality of the outcome is enhanced by the commentary made by the repeated cadences (first in major and then in minor) on an earlier pattern. So far in the song, repetitions of harmonic arrivals have been nonindependent reiterations of earlier material (see mm. 9–10, 14–15, and 34–35 and their analyses in examples 5.2 and 5.3). In these earlier repetitions, the singer was silent, so the reiterations underline the contemplation of the preceding words, as it were, but avoid drawing final conclusions. By contrast, in mm. 39–41, the mode changes, the singer joins the music, and there is an independent metrical unit. Instead of mere contemplation, the singer now must accept the unavoidable conclusion that he has not become old, and his journey therefore continues.

To close this analysis, we can turn from these descriptions of the direct musico-poetic aspects back to the similarities between the underlying tensions discussed earlier. I suggested that the juxtaposition of reality and illusion constitutes the main tension of the poem and that a significant factor in the music is the juxtaposition of minor and major, a result of mixture. Now that we have analyzed the foreground and interpreted several musical factors as referential signs related to the poetic content, we may suggest that the contrast between minor and major mode can also be understood as such a sign. The primary element, the minor mode, refers to the unavoidable reality that table 5.1b shows underlying the entire poem. The secondary factor, the major mode, refers to the unobtainable illusion, the first state in table 5.1a, which is absent from the deeper-level table 5.1b. The unobtainable quality of the illusion is emphasized by the return of the song's opening material in the coda. This return can be seen to reflect the idea that the transformation shown in table 5.1a is framed, at still deeper levels, by the static table 5.1b. In other words, the protagonist knows all along that he has not turned gray. Similarly, in the music, the tension between minor and major is framed by the same material in minor.

The thought of death as a positive option—an idea that will prevail throughout the second part of *Winterreise*—first emerges in "Der greise Kopf." In the song, however, death remains an illusion, a situation the wanderer laments. In the next Lied in the cycle, "Die Krähe," the protagonist continues to reflect on death as a positive option. This song can be understood as forming a pair with "Der greise Kopf": in addition to their contemplation of death, the two songs are connected by various musical factors.

6   Death Contemplated: "Die Krähe"

6.1. Music

"Die Krähe" is in C minor, the key of the immediately preceding song, "Der greise Kopf," which creates a direct association between the two. Indeed, I will argue that the songs form a pair, connected by common motivic material, voice-leading procedures, and textual associations, in addition to the shared key. "Die Krähe" is in ternary form, preceded by an introduction (mm. 1–5) and followed by a coda (mm. 38–43). In m. 13, at the end of the A^1 section, E♭ major is tonicized, and at the same time the expressive genre arrives at the contrasting emotion of the joyful (example 6.1). In the B section (mm. 16–24), an unfolding in the bass leads to a dividing dominant (m. 24), which completes the first branch of the interrupted structure. The A^2 section (mm. 25–38) includes the second branch of the background structure and arrives at the structural dominant in m. 32. Instead of immediately resolving the dominant, the music returns to what was heard in mm. 29 ff., thus bringing a repetition of what led to the dominant. The V is regained in m. 37, and this time it is resolved, in the ensuing bar, in the tonic. The repetition has a powerful dramatic effect: with the postponement of the closing tonic, the sense of dramatic resolution is deferred as well.[1] The song's dramatic curve underlines this deferral: the high point in mm. 32–33 combines the arrival at the structural dominant with the initial avoidance of its resolution.

As in "Der greise Kopf," the introduction (mm. 1–5) establishes motives that will turn out to be significant. Most importantly, A♭ is also heard in this song as an emphatic neighbor note above G, both in the top-voice figuration and in the 5–6 unfolding of the bass (example 6.2b).[2] This unfolding (mm. 3–4) creates associations with later events in the song: as a gesture, the deceptive cadence postponing the arrival of the tonic anticipates the events of the A^2 section in which the parenthetical repetition (shown in example 6.1) postpones the arrival of the concluding tonic. In addition, the use of A♭ as an underlined motivic element draws direct connections to "Der greise Kopf." As a result, the motivic material along with the shared key suggests that "Die Krähe" continues from where "Der greise Kopf" left off.

The thematic material of the A^1 section (mm. 6–15) is based on the introduction's top voice, now sounded in a lower register. Despite the thematic similarity, the texture is very different in the two sections. Whereas the introduction has independent top-voice and bass lines, in the A^1 section the two lines merge to create

Example 6.1. "Die Krähe," an overview.

unison. But the relationship between the vocal part and the piano's left hand does not remain constant through the unison bars, mm. 6–13. In mm. 6–11, where the tonic chord is prolonged, the piano doubles the top voice. In other words, if we consider the underlying four-part harmonic framework (indicated in example 6.2b), the piano's left hand does not represent the structural bass line but rather follows the top voice.[3] (The actual pitches of the bass part do, however, appear in the piano's left hand. But rhythmically and gesturally, many of the pitches, such as the G in m. 8, the root of the dominant, appear as embellishing elements rather than primary ones.) In mm. 12–13, when E♭ major is tonicized, the roles of the vocal line and the piano's left hand are reversed. Here, the piano part assumes the function of a bass line (see in particular the cadential E♭: I⁶–V–I in example 6.2b). As a result, the vocal line now doubles the bass. The right hand of the piano part, in turn, adopts the function of the structural top voice, leading the *Urlinie* from the opening $\hat{5}$ to the $\hat{3}$ in m. 13.

This reversal of functions subtly affects the way the tonal framework is understood. In mm. 6–11 the primacy of the top voice, doubled by the piano's left hand, suggests that the uppermost voice (the high register) is being emphasized. Mm. 12–13, by contrast, suggest the primacy of the bass line: now the vocal line

Example 6.2. "Die Krähe," mm. 1–15, voice-leading sketch.

doubles the bass part, and the latter (the low register) assumes textural emphasis. Accordingly, mm. 6–11 stress the top voice and mm. 12–13 the bass, even though the actual register remains the same.

The Eb-major cadence in mm. 12–13 (repeated in mm. 14–15) shifts from the initial expression of the tragic to the joyful while at the same time leading the music into the B section (mm. 16–24). As example 6.3b indicates, mm. 13–23, the first phase of the B section, consist of a sequential progression moving from the tonicized Eb-major chord via an F-major triad (mm. 20–21) to a G-major sonority (m. 23) that assumes the function of V in the tonic key, a chord one expects to be resolved to the tonic in m. 24. Owing to the preceding tonicized F major, the music prepares a major chord, not a minor one, so the tonic is assumed to reappear in the joyful expression that has governed the B section, not in the song's initial tragic expression. Instead of this tonic, a deceptive cadence evades the expected tonic resolution by moving to VI (thus exhibiting the G–Ab motive in the bass), and the G-major chord turns out to have a contrapuntal rather than a cadential function; the bass-note G is part of an unfolding that provides consonant support for a passing-tone D in the top voice (example 6.3a). With the arrival of Ab in the bass, the allusions to C major (rather than minor) also vanish. The structural dominant ending the first branch of the interrupted structure is reached in m. 24, the arrival emphasized by the recurrence of the motivic G–Ab–G in the uppermost voice.

The B section plays a significant role in the song's expressive course. The song opens with an inward expressive quality that changes in mm. 12–13 from the ini-

Example 6.3. "Die Krähe," mm. 13–24, voice-leading sketch.

tial tragic to joyful expression (example 6.2b). The B section begins with short thematic gestures that suggest a more declamatory expressive quality (example 6.3b); the musical gestures address an outside listener, as it were. The declamation continues until m. 24, where the singer ends his part and the initial inward quality returns. At the same time the deceptive cadence and the return to C minor (after the preparation of C major) bring the opening tragic emotion back. The declamation is therefore associated with the outwardly joyful sections, while the tragic sections are governed by inward expression. It is as if the music

Example 6.4. "Die Krähe," mm. 25–43, voice-leading sketch.

accepted the tragic (inward) but at the same time tried to overcome it (by joyful declamation).

The material of the B section is related in several ways to the preceding song, thus further stressing the association between "Der greise Kopf" and "Die Krähe." First, in both songs the motivically important A♭ is enharmonically reinterpreted as G♯, a pitch that prepares a tonicization of a major chord, resulting from mixture (cf. mm. 11–14 and 36–37 in "Der greise Kopf" and mm. 19–22 in "Die Krähe"). Second, after an A♮ sounded in a major-mode tonicization, A♭ returns powerfully in the bass in both songs, both times as part of an extended unfolding (cf. m. 20 in example 5.2 and m. 24 in example 6.3). Third, the structural dominant that closes the first branch of the interrupted structure arrives in the piano part alone. All this suggests that the B section is a kind of commentary on certain elements of "Der greise Kopf," thus continuing the argument initiated in the earlier song.

The A² section repeats the music of the opening formal unit up to m. 28, when the tonic is transformed into a ♮⁴₂ chord, which is resolved in m. 29 to a IV⁶, a chord functioning as a predominant supporting the top-voice $\hat{4}$ (example 6.4). From here on, the Urlinie descends in the piano part only, the $\hat{3}$ and $\hat{2}$ appearing moreover in an inner voice. (This again establishes associations with the closure of "Der greise Kopf," in which the Urlinie descends in the piano's inner voice.) The predominant IV⁶ of mm. 29–31 is also important from the motivic point of view: it introduces the significant A♭ into the bass, resolving it to G when the structural dominant arrives in m. 32. The progression toward the dominant is underlined by a crescendo, creating the impression that the music is on the threshold of a conclusive closure. But the resolution to which the dominant aspires is frustrated, as we have seen; instead of arriving at the tonic, the music of mm. 29–32 is repeated, with minor changes, in mm. 34–37.

The repetition underlines the significance of the A♭–G motion by repeating it in the bass. The repetition is also related to two other significant issues in the song. First, on a general dramatic level, the repetition continues to avoid the resolution of a chord that initially sounds like a cadential dominant, a procedure encountered earlier in the two bass unfoldings (mm. 3–4 and 23–24). Second, the repetition in the piano's right hand occurs at a lower octave, exhibiting a registral descent similar to what happens gradually from the introduction to the B section. All of these features—motivic A♭–G motion, postponement of the resolution of the dominant, and registral descent—occur again in the coda, emphasizing their significance in the song (example 6.4b).

The A² section's structural factors discussed above interact with the song's expression (example 6.4). The arrival at the predominant IV⁶, with the motivically significant A♭ in the bass, coincides with the increased declamation. The song's high point, indicated in example 6.1, arrives when the predominant moves to what initially sounds like a cadential dominant (m. 32). But this V is not immediately resolved, lending the expression a rather frustrated quality. When the cadential preparation is repeated in mm. 34–37, the dynamic level drops to piano, and the music returns to the initial inward quality of expression. This decrease in intensity is reflected in the structure. Now that it is clear that the declamation and high point of mm. 27–32 were not able to lead to a structural resolution, the singer gives up his active role in the music's unfolding. In mm. 37–40, the singer merely observes the closure without actively participating in it.

6.2. Text

Die Krähe

Eine Krähe war mit mir
Aus der Stadt gezogen,
Ist bis heute für und für
Um mein Haupt geflogen.

Krähe, wunderliches Tier,
Willst mich nicht verlassen?
Meinst wohl bald als Beute hier
Meinen Leib zu fassen?

Nun, es wird nicht weit mehr gehn
An dem Wanderstabe.
Krähe, laß mich endlich sehn
Treue bis zum Grabe!

The Crow

A crow has accompanied me from town; up to now it has been flying incessantly around my head.

Crow, you strange creature, will you not leave me? Do you plan soon to seize my body here as prey?

Now, there is not much further to go with my walking staff. Crow, let me at last see faithfulness unto the grave!

In "Die Krähe," the protagonist continues to contemplate death. The first stanza describes the reality in a neutral manner: a crow has been flying above the wanderer's head ever since he left the town where his beloved lives. The second stanza becomes more personal. The speaker begins to ask if the crow is an omen of death, an idea he states clearly in the third stanza, where he utters the hope that he is close to the end of his journey, close to death.

The poem again juxtaposes reality and illusion (table 6.1a): the present wretched journey is juxtaposed with death as a wished-for state. The poem includes no narrative action; rather, it reflects this static opposition. Yet there are various stages during which the protagonist becomes aware of this opposition. In the first stanza, the situation, the flying crow, is described in a neutral manner. In the second stanza, the protagonist becomes aware of the possibility of the crow as an omen of death; from the Greimassian perspective, the crow here assumes the function of the sender (table 6.1b). In other words, the wanderer asks, in a quite macabre manner, whether the crow intends to grasp his body as prey. At the same time, the protagonist's questions introduce the juxtaposition of illusion (the hoped-for state 2 in table 6.1a) and reality (state 1). In the final stanza, the illusion

Table 6.1. "Die Krähe," underlying structure of the poem

a. Underlying opposition in the poem

state 1		state 2
reality		illusion
present		future
$(S \cup O)$	vs.	$(S \cap O)$

b. The crow as sender

$Sr \rightarrow O \rightarrow R$

Actant	Reference
S	the protagonist
O	the closeness of death
Sr	the crow
R	the protagonist

is further contemplated when the protagonist utters his wish to be close to death. But there are no signs of death; the association of the crow with death has no concrete foundation, so uncertainty continues to the end of the poem, since no trustworthy signs of approaching death challenge the miserable reality.

In the poem's final stanza, there is a bitter and indirect reference to the lost beloved. Susan Youens has remarked that the last words of the poem ("laß mich endlich sehn / Treue bis zum Grabe!") "are taken from the marriage service and the traditional vow to be faithful 'until death do us part'" (1991, 241).[4] In other words, the wanderer says that although the beloved was not faithful, let death be true. But death is not true, at least not at this stage of the wanderer's journey. The end of the poem thus clearly juxtaposes the two forms of desired objects that the protagonist contemplates in *Winterreise*, objects that are doomed to remain illusions: the beloved (with the reference to the marriage vow) and death (of which the crow is an omen).

6.3. Musico-Poetic Aspects

The music juxtaposes two registers, high and low, in a meaningful way. I will argue that the registers are related to the poem's two characters (or actors in Greimassian terminology), the crow and the protagonist, respectively. Ultimately, this association stems from an imitation of the crow flying high in the sky (a high register) and the protagonist wandering on the earth (a low register). Indirectly, the two registers, if examined together with the music's motivic material and voice-leading structure, can be associated with the poem's two underlying states, as shown in table 6.1a.

The introduction and its high register can be understood as imitating the flight of the crow high above the protagonist's head. The speaker reflects on the bird in mm. 6–13 during the poem's first stanza, set to the thematic material of the introduction. But the use of the lower register indicates that the wanderer's perspective is the prevailing one. In these measures, the musical structure interprets the poem, adding additional poetic layers: the course of the music suggests that, in the poem's first stanza, the protagonist gradually becomes aware of the crow's possible function as an omen, an issue addressed directly in the second stanza. In mm. 6–13 the vocal part and the left hand of the piano move in unison, but their relationship is not consistent. First, in mm. 6–11 the piano part doubles the top voice; that is, the "higher" part (the top voice) is emphasized (example 6.2b). Poetically, the protagonist (in the vocal part) observes the bird (the high register) flying above his head while he repeats the introduction's thematic material. In mm. 11–12 the situation is reversed; now the vocal part doubles the bass (although the thematic material associated with the crow continues), so the "lower" part (the bass) is underlined. At the same time, E♭ major is tonicized, and the expressive genre moves from tragic to joyful. The interpretation of the crow as an omen arises in the protagonist's mind, so his register (low) is stressed at the end of the crow's (high) thematic material. And because the idea of death is positive, the expression moves from tragic to joyful. In this sense, the music goes farther than the poem; if the end of the poem's first stanza is read without the music, there is no corresponding idea of interpreting the crow from the protagonist's perspective.

The commentary on the textual structure in example 6.1 clarifies this interpretation. The music that precedes m. 12 introduces the sender, the crow. The tonicization of E♭ major and the emphasis on the "bass" part then interpret the sender, thus anticipating the object and, indirectly, the opposition of the two states shown in table 6.1a. This opposition is then explicitly stated in the music's B section, where death is contemplated. The shared key, E♭ major, associates the beginning of the B section with mm. 12–13, where the protagonist begins to interpret the crow. The change of the expressive genre to the joyful suggests that the protagonist wants to believe in the illusion, that is, in the interpretation of the crow as an omen; thus, state 2 in table 6.1a (S ∩ O) is emphasized. The speaker's questions in the poem's second stanza are reflected in the declamatory quality of expression (example 6.3b): the declamation mimics the questions, as it were. This musico-poetic interpretation is supported by motivic material. As in the preceding song, the motivically significant A♭ can be associated with reality, while its chromatic variant, A♮, prepared by G♯, stands for the illusion. In "Die Krähe" this pitch appears prominently in mm. 20–22 (example 6.3b). This motivic connection underlines the wanderer's willingness to believe in what will ultimately be shown to be an illusion.

In the poem the questions asked in the second stanza do not receive a direct answer; the larger context only implies that the closeness of death is ultimately an illusion. The music, by contrast, provides a clear answer, so again the music goes farther than the poem. In m. 23 the text of the second stanza ends in a question. In this measure, the joyful expression and declamatory quality support this stage of the expressive genre, A♮ has displaced A♭, and the local context suggests a cadential progression that will end in a major-mode tonic chord in m. 24. All of these features imply that it would indeed be justified to see the crow as an omen and hence believe in the closeness of death (S ∩ O). But none of these musical factors is firmly established: in m. 24 the tragic expression and inward quality return, A♭ corrects the preceding A♮, and the deceptive cadence eliminates the option of a C-major tonic. That these unavoidable events appear in the piano part only suggests that the protagonist has no power over them. The futility of desiring death here is enhanced by the associations drawn to the previous song, in particular, to the manner in which the illusion of death's nearness was denied there. The two songs both return to the tragic expression and A♭, which function as signs of reality, after the feelings of joy and A♮, referring to illusion. Moreover, both songs feature an extended unfolding in the bass, which reintroduces the significant A♭. Briefly, the songs, both together and on their own, suggest that the time of death is not yet nigh.

The A² section foregrounds, as it were, the tension between reality and illusion, as well as the futility of the attempt to trust in illusion. The description of the textual structure in example 6.1 outlines the musico-poetic process. The music tries to close the structure when the text of the final stanza ends in m. 33.

The power of the attempt is emphasized by the music's high point occurring here. The piano plays in a high register, thereby referring to the crow, the sender that initially suggests the possibility of death to the protagonist. This attempt to confirm the illusion is represented in example 6.1 by the designation "(S ∩ O)?" The tonal closure does not arrive in m. 33, however, so the high register's claim of primacy turns out to be false, a factor underlined by the frustrated quality of the musical expression. In order to attain tonal closure, the poem's final words have to be repeated, and they only bring closure this second time. The low register of the cadence in mm. 37–38 suggests that the protagonist and his journey (representing reality) are primary, while the high register and the crow (referring to illusion) are secondary, shown in example 6.1 by "(S ∪ O)!" This interpretation is confirmed by the coda, in which the material of the introduction (which brought in the idea of death in the first place) is repeated an octave lower than at the start. In the local expression, the song ends in the initial inward quality; just as the declamation led only to frustration, so the protagonist has to accept that he cannot reach the unobtainable.

The A² section also makes clear structural and musico-poetic references to "Der greise Kopf." First, the repetition of the poem's final words leads in both cases to a situation in which the music's structural closure is postponed from the desired first attempt, representing illusion (C major in "Der greise Kopf" and a high register in "Die Krähe"), to the successful closure in the second attempt, representing reality (C minor in the former song and a low register in the latter). Second, the *Urlinie* closes in an inner voice in both songs. This suggests that the protagonist cannot alter the course of reality (the organization of the background tonal structure), so he has no choice but to remain passive when the events he has been trying to avoid inevitably take place.

Although there are associations elsewhere in *Winterreise* between consecutive songs (the triplet figuration that begins "Der Lindenbaum" can be seen as growing out of the accompanimental figuration of the preceding "Erstarrung," for example), "Der greise Kopf" and "Die Krähe" form the clearest pair in the entire cycle. Their pairing emphasizes the essential turning point in *Winterreise*. If the focus has been on the lost love up to this point, from here on the emphasis is on the possibility of approaching death. The close connections between the two songs underline the protagonist's new perspective by describing its emergence in a unified dramatic form. Yet it is not easy for the protagonist to accept death as a positive option, even though he expresses it so clearly in "Der greise Kopf" and "Die Krähe." He needs more time to become fully convinced of the choice between abandoning the search for love and seeking death instead. In other words, he must define a context for the idea of death that has begun to emerge here, something he does not do in "Der greise Kopf" or "Die Krähe." The following song, "Letzte Hoffnung," presents the next step taken by the protagonist toward accepting death as the new, primarily desired object.

7 From Hope for the Past to Hope for the Future: "Letzte Hoffnung"

7.1. Music

"Letzte Hoffnung" is one of the most complex and perplexing songs in all of *Winterreise*. Its emotional range is enormous: it includes unsettled and restless features, stemming from harmony, key areas, and meter, for instance, as well as calm serenity.[1] Example 7.1 is an overview of this through-composed work: an introduction (mm. 1–4), followed by the main body of the song (which I have divided into four sections, shown by the boxed numbers), and a coda (mm. 43–47). An interruption divides the voice-leading structure into two phases. The first (mm. 8–25) consists of a I–III$^{\sharp}$–V arpeggiation in the bass and prolongation, in the top voice, of $\hat{5}$ throughout, raised when the III$^{\sharp}$ arrives. Even though the underlying structure of mm. 8–25 prolongs an E♭-major chord (which both initiates the background structure in m. 8 and is arpeggiated, in the bass, in mm. 8–22), the musical surface strongly features the key of E♭ minor: the dominant that opens the song (mm. 1–6) suggests a resolution to a minor-mode tonic, and the dominant that closes the first structural phase (mm. 22–25) again refers to the key of E♭ minor.

E♭ minor is established even more firmly in m. 26, when the structure's second phase begins. Now we also have a minor-mode tonic chord, not only its dominant. The significance of the minor tonic is emphasized by the extended top-voice arpeggiation, which arrives in m. 32 for the first time at the *Kopfton* $\hat{3}$. Owing to the minor mode, this scale degree is first heard in a lowered form (G♭). But the major mode is ultimately primary, and in m. 35 a voice exchange transforms the E♭-minor triad of m. 32 into an E♭-major sixth chord. At the same time, the character of the music changes drastically: whereas thus far the song has had a restless and rhythmically complex quality, it now assumes a calm chorale-like texture. In m. 39 the lowered *Kopfton* is replaced by ♮$\hat{3}$, after which the structure closes in E♭ major.

The juxtaposition of minor and major substantially affects the song's expressive genre (example 7.1). E♭ minor, which features significantly in the key-area design until m. 35, initially establishes the tragic as the dominating expression, with only fleeting moments of the joyful in mm. 7–8 and 17–18. The dramatic curve suggests an unsettled quality at the song's beginning, as the music is initially unable to establish the tonic key (or any other key) firmly. Attainment of an

8 13 22 26 32 35 39 40 41   43

♭$\hat{3}$ — ♮$\hat{3}$ — $\hat{2}$ $\hat{1}$

(arpeg.)

IN

(=3   2 II)

(V) I III♮ V II I♭ ——— ♮   IV V$^{6-5}_{4-3}$ I

| Form: | intro. | 1 | 2 | | 3 | | 4 | | + coda |

Expressive genre: tragic (mingled with fleeting joyful)   joyful, serene

Dramatic curve: unsettled   settled, peak   high point, quiet

Textual structure: (S ∪ O₁)   ⇒   (S ∩ O₂)

Example 7.1. "Letzte Hoffnung," an overview.

unequivocal E♭ minor in mm. 26 ff. clarifies the tonal uncertainties, so the dramatic curve moves from an unsettled situation to a settled one. The ambiguities appear to have been resolved. At the same time, the forte dynamic level and the clarified tonal situation suggest a peak in the music's dramatic unfolding. But this peak is not the end of the song's drama. From m. 35 on, a serene and joyful expression reigns, with only a passing reference to the tragic and the minor mode in mm. 41–42. The remarkable and unexpected affective and textural change suggests that the dramatic peak of m. 26 was a local climax; the song's global high point arrives only in m. 35, when the dynamic level descends to piano, major mode replaces minor, and serene joyful is established as a new expression. This is an unusual high point in that it is marked by a drop in the dynamic level, not an increase. As the joyful reigns until the end, the song's expressive genre exhibits a situation in which the initial expression (the tragic) differs from the concluding one (the joyful). This is rare in *Winterreise;* along with "Letzte Hoffnung," such a change of state can be found only in "Frühlingstraum," which begins with a joyful expression but ends in the tragic.

α = G♭ / F♯ ; β = B♮ / C♭

a)

V I III♮

b)

β α β α β β α β

V I III♮

intro.

1

Expression: tragic   joyful   tragic

Quality: searching,   confirming,   searching,
               unstable   stable   unstable

Example 7.2. "Letzte Hoffnung," mm. 1–14, voice-leading sketch.

If the global course is unusual in "Letzte Hoffnung," so are the events at more local levels. The song begins with a diminished-seventh chord whose function is uncertain at first. The underlying V is sounded only in m. 2 as the appoggiatura C♭ descends to B♭, and it is only here that the role of the diminished-seventh chord as a VII^7 of E♭ becomes clear (example 7.2b). At the start, however, the listener does not assume E♭ to be the tonic. The preceding two songs have been in C minor, and when "Letzte Hoffnung" begins, the opening diminished-seventh chord is at first associated with the previous tonal context; in other words, one assumes that the pitch is B♮ rather than C♭, so that the harmony sounds as if it were a VII^7 of C minor rather than of E♭ minor. The enharmonic ambiguity of the diminished-seventh chord thus creates a link between "Die Krähe" and "Letzte Hoffnung."[2]

The rather ambiguous harmonic opening introduces a searching, unstable quality of expression (example 7.2b); neither the key nor the meter is initially established clearly. At deeper levels, the introduction is governed by the dominant of E♭, whose primary top-voice pitch is F. In the top voice there are two chromatically altered pitches of great significance, C♭ and G♭, so that E♭ minor, rather than major, is suggested (example 7.2b; G♭ and C♭, as well as their enharmonic equivalents, F♯ and B♮, will be indicated in the examples by α and β, respectively). The dominant is still being prolonged in m. 5 when the song's first main formal section begins, and the vocal line opens with an extended utterance of the important C♭–B♭ motion (see the staff above the graph in example 7.2b). The structural tonic finally arrives in m. 8, but in an unexpected way: it is a major chord rather than a minor one. Moreover, the sonority is fleeting, lasting only one measure, so the structural tonic is not strongly established in the foreground. It is like a vision of something not quite clearly perceived. The fleeting quality of the tonic has an effect on expression. In mm. 7–8, when the tonic arrives, a joyful expression briefly replaces the tragic, and the perfect authentic cadence in these measures temporarily switches the searching and unstable expressive quality to a confirming and stable one. But as the tonic is relinquished almost immediately, the joyful, confirming, and stable expression also slips away.

After the tonic of m. 8, the dominant reappears in m. 9; likewise, the searching and unstable expressive quality returns. This time the dominant is not resolved to the tonic but proceeds instead, in m. 13, to a III⁵. Within this harmonic progression, the important pitch classes C♭ and G♭ are enharmonically reevaluated as B♮ and F♯ (see the staff above the graph in example 7.2b). At the same time, their tendency of resolution changes. Whereas C♭ and G♭ suggest downward resolution, B♮ and F♯ have upward-resolving tendencies.[3] Both B♮ and F♯ are underlined in the foreground rhetoric: B♮ is the top voice of the deep-level III⁵, whereas F♯ (m. 12) is a chromatic passing tone whose significance is stressed by the sudden unison texture and a metric expansion (shown below the graph of example 7.2b), in which an entire measure is given to this pitch.

The III⁵ arrived at in m. 13 adds a new element to the song's harmonic uncertainty. It first implies a function of a V of C minor, particularly after a seventh (F) is added to the chord in m. 14. The tonic of C minor never arrives, however, nor is the seventh (F) resolved downward. Instead, in m. 18 the G-major chord (III⁵) is tonicized, so its function is transformed from an illusory dominant into a local center. At the same time, a joyful expression fleetingly peeps through the primary tragic (example 7.3b) yet without displacing the searching and unstable quality. As example 7.3b indicates, in my view the unresolved seventh (F) of m. 14 is related to the important pitch F♯ (m. 17), which, as a leading tone, is the agent tonicizing G major: F ultimately has the very unusual function of a chromatically altered anticipation of F♯. It might be argued that the upward tendency of F♯ (contrasting, as mentioned above, with the downward tendency of its enharmonic G♭) is here so strong that it assimilates, so to speak, the initially descending tendency of the F of mm. 14–16 into its ascending aspirations, a process leading to the F–F♯–G motion.

As shown in example 7.1, the III⁵ functions in the deep middleground as a third divider and continues into a V in m. 22. At the local levels, the enharmonic pairs B♮/C♭ and F♯/G♭ feature prominently in this III⁵–V progression. The third between the bass notes G and B♭ is filled in with a passing tone, A♭ (example 7.3a). (On the surface this bass note is only implied, since the unison texture in m. 21 momentarily leaves out the structural bass part.) The A♭ supports a minor chord (IV⁵), and its top-voice note is C♭, a neighbor note ♭6̂. It is remarkable that the ♭6̂ is enharmonically equivalent to the preceding ♮5̂, the top-voice note of the III⁵; that is, α = G♭ / F♯ ;   β = B♮ / C♭

Example 7.3. "Letzte Hoffnung," mm. 13–26, voice-leading sketch.

Expression: tragic   joyful   tragic

Quality: searching,   declamatory,
             unstable   stable

Example 7.4. "Letzte Hoffnung," mm. 26–47, voice-leading sketch.

the two enharmonic versions of one pitch class have different functions, ♮5̂ being a chromatically altered stable scale degree, ♭6̂ a neighbor note. Here the enharmonicism of the song is highlighted in an extraordinary manner.[4] Example 7.3a indicates that before the C♭ arrives, the ♮5̂ is transformed into its diatonic form in m. 20, so the B♮, a note that at least initially had an ascending tendency, descends instead. At the same time, the bass note G is lowered to G♭. Thus, both the B♮ and F♯ of mm. 13–18 are replaced in mm. 20–21 by their enharmonic equivalents C♭ and G♭, thereby highlighting the tension between the two enharmonic pairs.

Mm. 21–25 prepare E♭ minor, rather than major, as a tonal center. When the tonic chord returns in m. 26, it is indeed a minor harmony, which temporarily confirms the preceding minor implications. This is the song's first tonic sonority that is also clearly established in the foreground, so the expressive quality changes from an unstable to a stable tragic expression, which can be further described as declamatory, owing to the speech-like vocal gestures of mm. 26–27 (example 7.4b). Moreover, the confirmed E♭ minor forms a peak in the song's dramatic curve (example 7.1). The music thus implies that minor will outweigh the previous, fleeting, major-mode associations. The sense of arrival is underlined by the top voice, which now has reached an E♭, the second note of the extended top-voice arpeggiation shown in example 7.1. The lowered *Kopfton* (the motivically important G♭) is finally attained in m. 32. The significance of E♭ minor is further enhanced by a cadence in mm. 29–30, a harmonic progression whose expression suggests a pleading quality (example 7.4b). Yet the stability of E♭ minor is

Example 7.5. "Letzte Hoffnung," the end of the song recomposed in minor.

not quite complete; in mm. 26–34 the meter consists of three-bar hypermeasures, whose asymmetry lends the harmonically secure music an air of instability. The meter thus reminds us that the drama is not yet over.

M. 35 brings the song's greatest surprise: the restless third section in E♭ minor is followed by a calm, stable, and serene chorale-like fourth section in E♭ major (with symmetrical four-bar hypermeasures). The major-mode chorale functions as the song's global dramatic high point, thus retrospectively annulling the significance of the peak of m. 26 (example 7.1). The impression of the primacy of the minor mode implied by mm. 26 ff. turns out to have been premature. Here the serene chorale, somewhat paradoxically, takes on greater dramatic significance than the declamatory outburst of mm. 26 ff.

Although the expressive contrast between the third and fourth sections creates a sense of discontinuity, there is a significant motivic parallelism that closely associates the two sections; in both, there is a top-voice skip of a third from E♭ to the *Kopfton* (see the brackets in example 7.4a). But although the $\hat{3}$ is lowered in m. 32, it appears in the major-mode form in m. 39. We have here still another juxtaposition of minor and major, now emphasized by the motivic parallelism and the deep-level function of the *Kopfton*.

The fourth section structurally resolves the tension between major and minor that has prevailed so far in the song. Although an E♭-major chord underlies the first phase of the structure at deep levels, locally, minor implications have been stronger, and the second phase indeed opens with a Iᵇ. One would expect E♭ minor to continue. It would have been perfectly possible to end the song in minor: Schubert occasionally closes works that start in major in the parallel minor.[5] Example 7.5 shows a recomposition of the song's fourth section in minor. The serenity and calmness remain, but the strangely transfigured and nontragic quality has disappeared.

Once the ♮3̂ has arrived in the fourth section, the structure closes in major, thus sealing its primacy over the minor mode. Yet the important descending, minor-mode versions of the enharmonic pairs (C♭ and G♭) return as decorative elements within the cadential progression (see the staff above the graph in example 7.4b). Earlier, these pitches created associations with the minor mode, and they featured prominently in the song's third, minor-mode section. Here they sound like recollections: they no longer suggest primacy for the minor but refer to the conflict between minor and major that has now been left behind. The coda enhances the impression of recollection. The texture returns to the searching quality that began the song. But now the harmonic environment is clear, so the instability of the earlier occurrence of this material is replaced by stability (example 7.4).

7.2. Text

Letzte Hoffnung

Hie und da ist an den Bäumen
Manches bunte Blatt zu sehn,
Und ich bleibe vor den Bäumen
Oftmals in Gedanken stehn.

Schaue nach dem einen Blatte,
Hänge meine Hoffnung dran;
Spielt der Wind mit meinem Blatte,
Zittr' ich, was ich zittern kann.

Ach, und fällt das Blatt zu Boden,
Fällt mit ihm die Hoffnung ab,
Fall' ich selber mit zu Boden,
Wein' auf meiner Hoffnung Grab.

Last Hope

Here and there on the trees, many colored leaves can still be seen, and I often stand before those trees, lost in thought.

I watch one leaf, hanging my hopes on it; if the wind plays with my leaf, I tremble from head to toe.

Ah, and if the leaf were to fall to the ground, hope would fall with it; I too fall to the ground and weep on the grave of my hopes.

"Letzte Hoffnung" has been considered one of the most intensely emotional and desperate poems in the cycle. Susan Youens, for example, has said that "an extraordinary range of emotions is compressed into these twelve lines. . . . Müller travels from somber reflection through anxiety and terror to profound grief at the end. There are other psychologically rich poems in the cycle, but none with this emotional range" (1991, 246).

The poem consists of three stanzas and is about loss of hope. The wanderer is standing in front of a tree that still has its autumn-colored leaves. He looks at one leaf and makes it a symbol of his hopes: if the leaf falls, his hopes will be lost; if it stays on the tree, his hopes will remain high. The wind plays with the leaf, and the speaker trembles with nervous anxiety. Finally, the leaf falls, and the poem ends in deep despair. The protagonist too falls to the ground, weeping and lamenting his lost hopes.[6]

Fundamentally, the poem moves from uncertainty to certainty, from the juxtaposition of two options to the dominance of one. Table 7.1a shows the underlying narrative structure. The first state includes the two options. Option 1 is preferred: the leaf will stay on the tree (represented by Sr_1), leading to a fulfillment of the protagonist's hopes, a conjunction between subject and object. Option 2 is

Table **7.1.** "Letzte Hoffnung," underlying structure of the poem

a. Narrative level of the poem

state 1 (illusion)			state 2 (reality)
option 1 (unobtainable)	option 2 (unavoidable)		reality
preferred	not preferred		not preferred
$[(Sr_1 \rightarrow R) \rightarrow (S \cap O)]$	or $[(Sr_2 \rightarrow R) \rightarrow (S \cup O)]$	$\Rightarrow$	$(Sr_2 \rightarrow R) \rightarrow (S \cup O)$

b. Underlying static state
reality
not preferred
$(Sr_2 \rightarrow R) \rightarrow (S \cup O)$

Actant	Reference
S	the protagonist
O	the fulfillment of hope
Sr_1	the leaf staying on the tree
Sr_2	the leaf falling from the tree
R	the protagonist

From Hope for the Past to Hope for the Future 93

not the desired one: here the leaf will fall (Sr₂) and hope will be lost; subject and object are disjoined. The main tension grows out of the opposition between Sr₁ and Sr₂; the disjunction or conjunction between subject and object depends on which option turns out to be primary. Option 2 ultimately becomes reality, as the second state in table 7.1a indicates, so option 1 is fundamentally an illusion. Subject and object are in the end disjoined, an outcome not preferred by the subject.

It might be argued that in the poem, the leaf staying on the tree (Sr₁) does not ultimately represent a realistic option, and the protagonist knows this, at least subconsciously. At this moment in *Winterreise,* it would be unthinkable for his hopes suddenly to be fulfilled and misery left behind. Nevertheless, the wanderer wants to consider the unobtainable, even though he knows it cannot be attained. So the entire first state, with its two options, is basically an illusion, as is shown by the underlying static state shown in table 7.1b.

7.3. Musico-Poetic Aspects

The musical complexity of "Letzte Hoffnung" is reflected in the subtlety and intricacy of its musico-poetic relationships. At the most fundamental level, both the music and the text juxtapose two kinds of factors. As table 7.1 shows, the underlying structure of the poem consists of two states: the first juxtaposes two options, while the second shows that the second option—the one not preferred— becomes reality. The two options result from the juxtaposition of two senders (Sr₁ and Sr₂). In the music, in turn, major and minor are again juxtaposed. On the musical surface, the hierarchy between the two is uncertain throughout much of the song. In addition, two other kinds of oppositions feature prominently: the two enharmonic pairs (G♭/F♯ and C♭/B♮) and the juxtaposition of the rhetorically undermined structural tonic chord in mm. 1–25 with the stable tonic in mm. 26– 47. Moreover, the G♭/F♯ pair and the juxtaposition of minor and major are related to the pairing of ♭3̂ and ♮3̂ in mm. 32 and 39.

These musical and textual issues show similarities. Both feature two different aspects of one factor: in the poem, there are two versions of the sender (representing the one leaf either staying on the tree or falling to the ground), while the music exhibits the major and minor forms of the tonic and the *Kopfton,* as well as the two enharmonic pairs in which one pitch class has two different functions. In the poem, the first state in table 7.1a (the one with the two options) extends through the first two stanzas, set in the song's first two sections (mm. 5–25). The uncertainty encountered in the text of these two stanzas finds its counterpart in the unsettled character of their musical settings: the first structural tonic chord (m. 8) has only meager emphasis (it opens the background structure but hardly stands out in the surface rhetoric), and the status of the major-mode tonic key remains vague. Uncertainty concerning the key areas extends beyond doubt about the mode of the tonic key. At the beginning of the song's second section (and the poem's second stanza), C minor is suggested as a center by its dominant (mm. 13–16), yet the tonic of C minor never arrives. Instead, the G-major chord is tonicized (m. 18), but the music also abandons this chord immediately. So the first two sections (mm. 5–25) have no rhetorically underlined tonic in any key, a factor that creates an impression of indecision, resembling that of the poem's first two stanzas. This tonal uncertainty is reflected in the music's local expression, where the emotional quality of the tragic is searching and unstable throughout (apart from the fleeting sense of confirming and stable joyful in mm. 7–8, which sound the structural tonic) (examples 7.2b and 7.3b).

In spite of this local uncertainty, the deep levels in mm. 8–22 exhibit a stable progression, an arpeggiation of an E♭-major chord in the bass, which provides the music with a solid harmonic foundation (example 7.1). Likewise, in the poem, the protagonist knows, deep down, that only the second option is possible (table 7.1b). So both the music's first two sections and the poem's first two stanzas contrast the uncertainty of the surface with an underlying stability. The unconscious layer of the narrator's mind thus maps the deep-middleground structure of the music.

The song's third and fourth sections (mm. 26–43) set the poem's third stanza, the one representing the not-preferred state 2 of table 7.1a. The minor key prevailing in the third section and the song's first firmly stated tonic chord in m. 26 seem to underline the attainment of the poem's tragic conclusion; in other words, the music's arrival at the first definitely established tonic chord appears to coincide with the poem's arrival at the resolution of its initial tension. In the local expression, this apparent certainty of resolution is reflected in the declamatory and stable emotional quality that replaces the preceding searching and unstable expression (example 7.4b). Accordingly, one assumes that the drama of the song has now reached its conclusion. But the fourth section, with its major mode and solemn chorale-like texture, removes the impression of having arrived at the conclusion, thus apparently contradicting the poem's tragic ending. The declamatory and stable tragic expressive quality now gives way to a serene and stable joyful emotion (example 7.4b). In the underlying dramatic curve, in turn, the rhetorical and tragic outburst of mm. 26 ff. retrospectively turns out to be a local peak, while the serene and joyful chorale of mm. 35 ff. provides the global high point. I will address this emotional conflict later.

The musico-poetic aspects of "Letzte Hoffnung" discussed so far have appeared on a global level. I now turn to how the text and music interact at more immediate layers, especially how the two enharmonic pairs function. In mm. 1–10 the protagonist states the poem's opening situation: there are colorful leaves on the trees, and he stands before them. In these measures, G♭ and C♭ feature prominently. M. 11 brings a significant change: the speaker stands lost in thought, reflecting on the one leaf and whether it will stay on the branch or fall. So the standpoint changes from a description of the outer world to a depiction of the narrator's innermost thoughts. When these thoughts are mentioned in mm. 11–18, the other enharmonic versions, F♯ and B♮, appear in the music. In m. 18 the poem returns to the outside world (the wind), and at the same time G♭ and C♭ return. So it might be argued that G♭ and C♭ are associated here with the outside world, whereas F♯ and B♮ appear when the speaker's inner thoughts are explored. Indeed, such a poetic interpretation of the enharmonic pairs extends throughout the song.

There are two instances of imitation of the text in the song's first two sections. The first appears in m. 12: the expansion (shown in the metric analysis below example 7.2b) and the consequent retardation of motion clearly depict the protagonist lost in thought and hence not moving. The second instance of imitation takes place in mm. 22–24: the neighboring motions prolonging the dominant, and the sixteenth-note figuration of m. 23, quiver, much as the protagonist says he trembles when looking at the wind playing with his leaf. The first instance of imitation refers to the protagonist's inner world (with an underlined F♯), while the second reflects the outer reality (with a stressed C♭). Imitation is now combined with the enharmonic pairs to juxtapose the inner and outer worlds.

In the song's third section, the music clearly establishes E♭ minor as a center. The firmness of the key area suggests that the vagueness of the music's first two sections has been replaced by a stable key area, the underscored I♭, a stability further emphasized by reaching the *Kopfton*. Likewise, in the poem, uncertainty has been left behind, and the second of the underlying states has been reached (table 7.1a). The pitches G♭ and C♭ of the two enharmonic pairs feature prominently, so these can still be associated with the outer reality, the falling leaf.

So far, there have been clear correspondences between music and text, yet the musico-poetic interpretation of the song's fourth section is highly problematic. In the poem, the protagonist weeps over the loss of hope. One would expect his intense despair to be accompanied by tragic music, perhaps something along the lines shown in the hypothetical recomposition of example 7.5. But Schubert does something very different: he introduces new, chorale-like music in the major mode, a passage whose emotion is far removed from the deep despair expressed in the poem.

What is the musico-poetic function of the apparent incompatibility between the emotion of the music and that of the poem? Commentators have attempted to explain this situation in various ways. Eytan Agmon, who examined the use of the enharmonic C♭/B♮ pair in the song, suggests that "Schubert may have felt the need, from a purely musical point of view, to bring back B towards the song's ending [mm. 35 and 39–40] in a kind of synoptic statement of the C♭/B♮ issue." Moreover, Agmon associates B♮ with hope and says that since "the grave is in any case the grave *of hope*," B♮ is an appropriate pitch at the end (1987, 54; emphasis in the original). Susan Youens, on the other hand, suggests that, for the protagonist, any solution is better than uncertainty: "Müller's poem epitomizes *Angst* at its most acute, barely this side of a psychotic break and so intense that even catastrophe is better because certain" (1991, 248).[7] In my view, neither the need to reintroduce B♮ nor the eventual solution suffices to justify the music's emotional character, which appears to contrast so strongly with that of the poem. We therefore need to seek a different interpretation.

It would be possible to explain the emotional contrast between the text and the music at the end of the song as an ironic or bitter reaction, for instance, as the protagonist ironically recalling the hopes he once had for love, hopes that he should have known to be vain from the beginning (as suggested by the second stanza of the cycle's second song, "Die Wetterfahne"). But in my view the music's solemn quality precludes such an interpretation. I believe that a viable explanation of the emotional contrast should include some kind of hope or positive associations.

In order to explain this emotional conflict, I believe we should examine "Letzte Hoffnung" as part of *Winterreise* as a cycle rather than as an individual song. As I have suggested throughout this study, *Winterreise* features basically two forms of illusion: one associated with the past, the lost love (songs 1–13), and one associated with the future, the hoped-for death (songs 14–24). In chapters 5 and 6 we saw that in "Der greise Kopf" and "Die Krähe" the desire for death is clear, and this desire has not been altered when "Letzte Hoffnung" is heard.

These two forms of illusion can explain the emotional contrast at the song's end. The hope that is lost in the poem is related to the first form of illusion, the lost love from the past. In the present state of the wanderer's journey, love has been permanently lost. This is probably how the poem would be interpreted without taking the music into consideration (and how its structure is shown in table 7.1), namely, as an expression of frustration resulting from the impossibility of regaining love. But the musical setting leads me to revise the interpretation of the poem. As the end of the song has a solemn, strangely positive, and almost religious air, I cannot take it as a description of deep despair.

In my interpretation, the hope that is lost in the poem is the first form of illusion, the hope of having the beloved back. But this loss, the present reality, opens the possibility for the second form of illusion—death—which would free the protagonist from his misery. This form of illusion also has positive associations and is thus desired. But this second form of illusion cannot be gained before the first has been firmly left behind; the protagonist cannot at the same time wish to return to his beloved and also wish to die. Now that death has been contemplated as a positive option in two preceding songs ("Der greise Kopf" and "Die Krähe"), the protagonist is about to abandon for good his hope of attaining the first form of illusion (love) and concentrate instead on the second form of illusion (death). In other words, the death contemplated in the two previous songs in isolation, as it were, is now contextualized and considered alongside the lost love, the theme governing songs 1–13. Death in "Der greise Kopf" and "Die Krähe" is now tied to the wanderer's journey and juxtaposed with its initial impulse, lost love.

Table 7.2 shows a revised Greimassian interpretation of the poem that reflects the song's end and the need to reconsider the poetic structure it suggests. State 1 summarizes the reading presented in table 7.1; the leaf falls from the tree, and consequently, the subject and object are disjoined. The addition of state 2 and the transformation from state 1 to state 2 reflect the solemn fourth section of the song. Instead of the one form of object in table 7.1, we now have two. O_1 in the first state represents the poem's initial hopes, associated with the past, and here subject and object are disjoined. In the second state, by contrast, the subject is conjoined with the object, this time with O_2 referring to the hope for death, as-

Table 7.2. "Letzte Hoffnung," a revised interpretation
of the underlying structure of the poem

state 1	state 2	
negative	positive	
reality	illusion	
$(S \cup O_1)$	$\Rightarrow$	$(S \cap O_2)$

Actant	Reference
S	the protagonist
O_1	initial hopes (associated with the past and love)
O_2	concluding hopes (associated with the future and death)

sociated with events in the future. The second state has positive implications. It is this conjunction with the object occurring in state 2 (the hope for death but not its arrival) that, in my interpretation, explains the music's strangely positive emotion at the end of the song: the loss of the initial hope opens the way for a new hope. But since the wanderer finds neither death nor peace, this second state too is ultimately only an illusion.

It is thus the musical features of the song's fourth section that justify the poem's revised interpretation.[8] Example 7.1 aligns the middleground voice leading with the poetic structure indicated in table 7.2, thus clarifying the function of the song's fourth section in this textual reinterpretation. The protagonist has known all along how the tension associated with the one leaf will be resolved: the leaf will fall, and his hopes will be lost. But when he admits the unavoidable loss of love $(S \cup O_1)$, he becomes aware of its positive consequences $(S \cap O_2)$. The idea of becoming retrospectively aware of something previously only implied also governs the musical structure. The positive major, which brings forth the newly positively conceived O_2, becomes clearly manifest in the foreground only in the fourth section. Yet the major-mode tonic underlies the deep middleground throughout the first two sections of the song (the E♭–G–B♭ arpeggiation in the bass), hence forestalling, as it were, the major-mode conclusion without emphasizing the major in the foreground. It is as if the music knew subconsciously the primacy of the major mode throughout in the same way as the narrator is subconsciously aware of the possibility of death, the positive consequence of abandoning the hope for love. The rather religious-sounding chorale texture of the fourth section enhances this reading by strengthening the music's associations with death.

In the fourth section, the major mode is reinforced in two phases, so to speak. The section consists of two subphrases, mm. 35–38 and 39–43 (example 7.4). The first concludes with a deceptive cadence, and E♭ governs its top voice, whereas the second establishes ♮3 and then closes the background in the structural cadence. So the second subphrase is a closing, whereas the first has a somewhat searching air. One might suggest that the subject only gradually becomes aware of the positive O_2 in the same way as the music reaches a cadence only in the second subphrase of the fourth section.

The two enharmonic pairs play an interesting role in this section. Above, I suggested that C♭ and G♭ can be understood as signs referring to the outer reality, whereas B♮ and F♯ refer to the protagonist's inner thoughts. Both of these pairs are present in the fourth section (see the staff above the graph in example 7.4b); for the first time in the song, the pairs together set the same words. (F♯ is not heard, however, so G♭ alone represents the enharmonic pair G♭/F♯.) This coexistence is justified by the coexistence of outer reality and inner thoughts at the song's end. In the outside world, the leaf has fallen. In the narrator's inner thoughts, past hopes are gone, but, at the same time, new hope emerges.

"Letzte Hoffnung" is one of the key songs in *Winterreise*. Chapters 5 and 6 indicated that at the outset of the cycle's part 2, the protagonist begins to consider death as a positive option, showing frustration that the signs he interprets as indicating its nearness (his graying hair and the crow) turn out to be false. Yet he has not considered how this positive view of death is related to the lost love, the theme contemplated in the first part of the cycle. This contemplation takes place in "Letzte Hoffnung." By the end of the song, the wanderer understands that relinquishing the beloved leads to the possibility of death and to peace; indeed, this is the prerequisite for peace, since he cannot hark back to the past and simultaneously anticipate the future. The next three songs ("Im Dorfe," "Der stürmische Morgen," and "Täuschung") show three different views of the situation the protagonist now faces—whether truly to seek death, an endeavor that would mean abandoning the beloved for good.

8 Reflecting Lost Hope: "Im Dorfe," "Der stürmische Morgen," and "Täuschung"

In the next three songs, "Im Dorfe," "Der stürmische Morgen," and "Täuschung," the protagonist reflects on the situation he faced at the end of "Letzte Hoffnung." As he considers abandoning the hope for happiness and embracing the possibility of death, the wanderer goes through a range of emotions, from nostalgia to rage. This chapter treats the three songs as a unit whose coherence is suggested by textual rather than musical factors.

8.1. "Im Dorfe"

"Im Dorfe," composed in ternary form, is mostly governed by the joyful emotion, with occasional passing shades of the tragic in the A sections and the introduction (example 8.1). The fleeting tragic emotion primarily results from the occurrence of two chromatically altered pitches borrowed from the parallel minor: B♭ and F♯. The present analysis will largely concentrate on the function of these pitches and the different contexts in which they appear. B♭ is introduced as part of a modally inflected predominant harmony in the introduction (m. 3) and heard again in the A^1 section when the same material is repeated (mm. 9–10). The entire A^1 section consists of one extended cadential progression (I–II♭$^6_5$–V$^{6-5}_{4-3}$–I), and the predominant of mm. 9–10 (with the tragic B♭) continues in m. 12 to the cadential six-four chord. The resolution of this V is considerably delayed, and the tonic finally arrives in m. 18.[1] Within this prolonged dominant, the tragic B♭ is heard again in m. 17 as a local neighbor note in the accompaniment's sixteenth-note figuration.[2] The tragic expression of m. 17 is emphasized by the F♯ of the preceding measure, which transforms the cadential six-four chord prolonged from m. 12 onward into a minor sonority. When the tonic finally arrives in m. 18, it is a major chord.

The B section is in G major (example 8.1).[3] This section opens with a prolongation of a home-key IV that has a contrapuntal voice-leading function: its top-voice G provides consonant preparation for the seventh of the ensuing V^7 (mm. 29–30), a chord that is then resolved to the tonic. There are no traces of the

Example 8.1. "Im Dorfe," middleground voice leading.

tragic expression in the main body of the B section, and its thoroughly joyful pastoral quality clearly contrasts with the A¹ section's somewhat declamatory air, which is colored with tragic undertones. In m. 29 the retransitional dominant brings the pitch B♭ back, thus reintroducing the tragic shades that again occur when the ensuing A² section begins.

The two A sections begin similarly but end differently (example 8.1). Instead of the one overarching harmonic motion as in A¹, A² consists of two phrases, both ending in a cadence (mm. 39–40 and 45–46). The structural role of these cadences differs. In the first, both the vocal part and the uppermost voice of the piano end on an F♯, so tonal closure is avoided, and the background still prolongs the $\hat{3}$. In the second cadence, the piano has D in the top voice, so the $\hat{2}$ and $\hat{1}$ of the *Urlinie* occur in mm. 45–46. Yet even here the sense of closure is considerably weakened by the singer's F♯, which covers the piano's $\hat{1}$ in m. 46. The musical situation is thus left partly open, even though the background arrives at structural closure.[4]

The two cadential progressions are motivically related to the significant B♭, which so far in the song has been associated with the tragic shades. When first heard in the A² section (m. 33–34), B♭ conveys a tragic quality (example 8.1): it is part of a predominant chord that seems to prepare a cadence in D minor (instead of major), an assumption enhanced by the apparent cadential six-four chord in m. 36 (a chord including F♯, the other important chromatically altered pitch in the song). But the chord of m. 36 does not ultimately function as a cadential six-four chord. Rather, it is transformed into a V_5^6 of B♭ major, a key briefly tonicized in m. 37. During this tonicization, the chromatic pitches so far associated with the tragic expression (B♭ and F♮) change their expressive significance, so that now they appear together in a joyful, major-mode environment.

The remote ♭VI creates a rather dreamy emotional quality in the local expression. The flat-side softness of the chord (a "purple patch," to use Donald Francis Tovey's evocative term) distances the chord from the primary D-major environment. In the voice-leading structure, the bass note B♭ functions as an incomplete neighbor above the dominant of the first cadential progression (example 8.1). B♭ major is also tonicized in the second, structurally primary cadential progression (in mm. 41–42), with expressive implications similar to its first occurrence. This is the last sounding of the important chromatic pitch B♭; its final occurrence is thus heard as part of the joyful expression, rather than the tragic sense it initially signaled. The other important chromatic pitch, F♮, is still heard in m. 44 as a chromatic passing tone in the song's final brief recollection of the tragic, the expression that has loomed behind the joyful throughout the work.

The two tonicizations of ♭VI feature significantly in the song's dramatic curve (example 8.1). Dynamically, "Im Dorfe" is soft throughout, so the song's high point is not signaled by a change in intensity. Instead, I argue that the sonic remoteness of the significant ♭VI, together with the texturally differentiated, chorale-like cadential progressions that follow this chord, form the dramatic climaxes. Because there is a hierarchical difference between the two cadential progressions, the two ♭VI chords also signify climaxes at different levels. The first progression does not lead to a structurally conclusive cadence and therefore functions as a local peak, while the second precedes the background closure and thus also functions as a global high point.

The A^2 section's two cadential progressions are texturally associated with the end of the previous song. In mm. 38–40 and 43–45 chorale-like chords interrupt the textural activity, a procedure resembling the end of "Letzte Hoffnung." Moreover, in both songs, a chorale-like texture appears at the moment a cadential progression begins; in other words, the chorale-like passage functions in both works as an indicator that closure, arrival at the goal, is at hand. And as in "Letzte Hoffnung," the chorale creates a somewhat pious or religious local expressive quality in "Im Dorfe" (example 8.1).

Im Dorfe

Es bellen die Hunde, es rasseln die Ketten.
Es schlafen die Menschen in ihren Betten,
Träumen sich manches, was sie nicht haben,
Tun sich im Guten und Argen erlaben:
Und morgen früh ist alles zerflossen.—
Je nun, sie haben ihr Teil genossen,
Und hoffen, was sie noch übrig ließen,
Doch wieder zu finden auf ihren Kissen.

Bellt mich nur fort, ihr wachen Hunde,
Laßt mich nicht ruhn in der Schlummerstunde!
Ich bin zu Ende mit allen Träumen—
Was will ich unter den Schläfern säumen?

In the Village

The dogs bark, their chains rattle. People are sleeping in their beds, dreaming of much they do not have, refreshing themselves in good and bad, and early in the morning all will have vanished. Well, they have enjoyed their share and hope to find again on their pillows what they still have left to enjoy.

Drive me away with your barking, you watchful dogs; let me not rest in this hour of slumber! I am finished with all dreams—why should I linger among the sleepers?

"Im Dorfe" is one of the few poems in *Winterreise* that is not divided into stanzas of equal length, usually four lines each. Instead, it is asymmetrically divided into two units of eight and four lines, respectively. The poem's reigning emotion is the tragic, or, more specifically, bitterness. The wanderer contrasts his position with that of the people in the village, who are asleep and dreaming beautiful dreams that symbolize their hopes. In addition, the protagonist contrasts his present state with his own past, when he too still had hopes. These juxtapositions are shown in table 8.1a. State 1 represents reality, where any hope for happiness is futile, a state accepted by the protagonist at this stage of *Winterreise;* state 2 shows illusion and dreams, which represent the sleeping people and the speaker's earlier hope for happiness. Coming as it does after "Letzte Hoffnung," "Im Dorfe" emphasizes the conclusion of the preceding poem, namely, that all hope of regaining the former joyousness is gone.

The poem also has indirect narrative activity. On a general level, its first unit (lines 1–8) refers to the people sleeping in the village and their dreams. But the dreams are not real; the people are dreaming of things they do not have, and when the morning comes, all will have vanished. Thus, the poem's first unit juxtaposes the two states indicated in table 8.1a. The poem's second unit (lines 9–12) becomes more personal. Now the protagonist speaks in the first person, saying that he has dreamed all his dreams, so he must leave the village where people still have hopes. This personal statement makes the poem's conclusion all the more bitter and final. The second unit represents only the first state of the underlying opposition shown in table 8.1a, the reality accepted by the protagonist, so the poem has shifted from the juxtaposition of the two states to the first state alone (table 8.1b).

As in "Letzte Hoffnung," the emotions of the poem and those in the music conflict in "Im Dorfe." Although the poem of "Im Dorfe" is tragic and bitter, the music is predominantly joyful, albeit with frequent, passing tragic undertones. In my view, this conflict is related to the one examined in the preceding song. In other words, in these two songs Schubert consistently departs from the most ob-

Table 8.1. "Im Dorfe," underlying structure of the poem

a. Underlying opposition

state 1		state 2
reality		illusion
accepted		contemplated
$(S_1 \cup O)$	vs.	$(S_2 \cap O)$

b. Narrative level of the poem

state 1		state 2		state 1
reality		illusion		reality
accepted		contemplated		accepted
$(S_1 \cup O)$	vs.	$(S_2 \cap O)$	$\Rightarrow$	$(S_1 \cup O)$

Actant	Reference
S_1	the protagonist in the present
S_2	the people sleeping in the village and the protagonist in the past
O	the hope of happiness

vious interpretations of Müller's poems, giving the text new and subtle significance. As we saw in the previous chapter, the lost hope in "Letzte Hoffnung" leads to the awakening of new hope, signaled by the solemn expression at the song's end. I argue that "Im Dorfe" continues to deal with this new hopeful state, although without remaining solemn in its expression.

Like "Letzte Hoffnung," "Im Dorfe" includes a reinterpretation of an initially tragic element as positive. In its music the loss of hope, the fact that the time for dreaming is over, ultimately creates positive associations, hence, the primacy of joyful expression in the music. But the wanderer is merely contemplating this new idea; therefore, the tragic expression still has a significant role in the song. In the A^1 section, the tragic associations result from the pitches B♭ and F♮, which can be understood to represent the futility of the dreams of those in the village (and the past dreams of the protagonist). These pitches are thus associated with state 1 in table 8.1a. The pastoral expressive quality of the B section, in turn, refers to the dream world of the sleepers. In Schubert's time, the pastoral was understood to refer to a lost, ideal, and better world.[5] This pastoral expression is connected to state 2 in table 8.1a.

In the A^2 section, the musico-poetic significance of B♭ and F♮ as well as the emotional references become quite complex. B♭ is first heard (mm. 33–34) with tragic associations when the protagonist remarks that he does not want to rest in the hour of sleep ("laßt mich nicht ruhn in der Schlummerstunde!"). Here the music and the text-music associations are similar to those in the A^1 section. The tragic expression is enhanced by the F♮ in m. 36. When the protagonist observes that he has already dreamed all of his dreams ("Ich bin zu Ende mit allen Träumen"), he recognizes the same positive implications of this idea that he remarked on at the end of the previous song: giving up hope for the past opens up new hopes, so the associations are positive. In other words, the arrival at the second unit of the narrative structure indicated in figure 8.1b clearly unveils the positive associations of the loss of dreams. This is reflected in the music by the avoidance of the D-minor cadence, which the pitches B♭ and F♮ suggest in mm. 33–36, and by the tonicization of B♭ major in m. 37, an event that introduces both B♭ and F♮ in a joyful expression. The narrator thus reinterprets the signs referring to the tragic expression (the futility of dreaming) as positive (the former dreams were about the beloved, but giving her up altogether brings new hope for peace and death). The significance of this poetic reinterpretation is enhanced by the dramatic peak and high point that underline the important ♭VI chord. But this change in the poem is justified only in Schubert's Lied; Müller's poem, if read only as text, does not provide a foundation for such a reading.

The reinterpretation of an initially negative factor as positive is reinforced by the chorale texture of the A² section's two cadences as well as by the association this texture creates at the end of "Letzte Hoffnung." As in the preceding song, the chorale too now signals the emergence of the positive consequences of giving up optimistic dreams. The chorale, in fact, sets the words with which the narrator asks himself why he should remain in the company of those who still believe in dreams. The connection to the previous song is further enhanced by the passing ♮3 of the cadential six-four chord in m. 44, a pitch that clearly recalls the ♭3 in m. 41 of "Letzte Hoffnung." The narrator is thus still considering the option that emerged in that song.

Yet at this stage of his journey, the protagonist is merely contemplating the novel idea of drawing positive conclusions from lost hope and giving up dreaming; he has not yet declared his decision to abandon hope. This uncertainty is reflected in the song's end. The first cadential progression (which introduces the positive associations of pitches B♭ and F♮ as well as the chorale texture) brings no tonal closure. The poem's last two lines have to be repeated (the narrator must consider his conclusions further, as it were), and the background is closed only in the second cadential progression. But the protagonist still leaves the situation somewhat open by singing F♯ (3̂) in m. 46. The time for the final declaration that death is a new hope has not yet come.

8.2. "Der stürmische Morgen"

The next song, the brief "Der stürmische Morgen," is a violent outburst. By far the shortest of the songs in *Winterreise*, it features a juxtaposition of two different characters: on the one hand, the tragic and raging music in mm. 1–9 and 14–19 in the D-minor tonic; on the other hand, the joyful (and somewhat pompous) B♭-major music in mm. 10–13. In spite of its harmonic and expressive stability, the contrasting B♭-major section has the air of insubstantiality, for even though there are two clear V–I harmonic progressions that establish this key (in mm. 11 and 13), B♭ major does not stand out as a fully confirmed key center.

Example 8.2. "Der stürmische Morgen," chordal reduction (*a*) and middleground voice leading (*b*).

The rather unstable impression of mm. 10–13 is an outcome of both structural and formal factors. As example 8.2b indicates, the top voice of mm. 10–13 prolongs an inner-voice neighbor note B♭. As a result, the structural top-voice line is temporarily given up in mm. 10–13, a factor that suggests a kind of parenthetical quality for the entire section. Also, the bass note B♭ is unstable when studied in the large context. One might assume that it would function as an upper incomplete neighbor (6̂) above the dominant. However, instead of being resolved downward to A, in the middleground B♭ ascends in m. 14, an augmented second rising to C♯. Example 8.2a shows in schematic form the function of the B♭-major chord. It results from a 5–6 progression above the tonic. Thus, the bass note B♭, which is sounded in the foreground, ultimately functions as an inner-voice note located below the structural bass line. As a result, the ensuing C♯ is a neighbor note prolonging the tonic.[6] In other words, the B♭-major chord and its bass have a purely contrapuntal and decorative function, their emphasis in the foreground notwithstanding. In the schematic form shown in example 8.2a, the B♭ of the B♭-major sonority provides a consonant preparation for the seventh of the ensuing ♯VII⁷, a function that is quite evident on the musical surface when the lowest register is abandoned in m. 14.

The formal organization also contributes to the relative insubstantiality of mm. 10–13. Measures 10–18 (up to the third beat) can be understood as a modified sentence structure in which the B♭-major section constitutes the presentation (the basic idea in mm. 10–11 and its repetition in mm. 12–13). Thus, mm. 10–13 have an initiating function, leading in m. 14 to the continuation with a medial function and ultimately in m. 18 to the cadence with a concluding function. In other words, the B♭-major section does not form an independent and closed phrase-structural unit despite its V–I harmonic progressions.[7] In sum, the harmonically and expressively contrasting B♭-major section creates an impression of being almost a parenthetical event in the middle of the stormy D-minor music.

The B♭-major section's local expression interacts subtly with its embellishing structural function (example 8.2b). The quality of the expression is quite pompous; it is as if the music attempted to convince itself of the significance of the contrasting joyful emotion. The pomposity is futile, however, as the tragic unavoidably returns. The song's dramatic high point arrives in mm. 16–17, the measures that precede the return of the tonic chord. This climax is the conclusive indicator that the tragic and D minor are primary.

The distribution of the *Urlinie*'s pitches is unusual (example 8.2b). In m. 5 the top voice ascends from D to E, and one assumes F (3̂) to be the next step of the initial ascent. This is indeed what happens at deep levels. In the foreground, however, a reaching-over brings a 1̂ to the top voice before the arrival of the *Kopfton*, a 3̂ locally sounded as the top voice of a ♯IV in m. 8.[8] Near the song's end, the *Kopfton* is regained in the latter part of m. 18, and the *Urlinie* descends quickly in the next bar, the song's last. What is significant here is that all of the pitches of the *Urlinie* occur in the piano part only and, furthermore, in passages during which the singer is silent. Thus, the vocal part has no role to play in the course of the deep-level top voice; the singer passively observes, as it were, the song's deepest-level events.

Der stürmische Morgen

Wie hat der Sturm zerrissen
Des Himmels graues Kleid!
Die Wolkenfetzen flattern
Umher in mattem Streit.

Und rote Feuerflammen
Ziehn zwischen ihnen hin.
Das nenn' ich einen Morgen
So recht nach meinem Sinn!

Mein Herz sieht an dem Himmel
Gemalt sein eignes Bild—
Es ist nichts als der Winter,
Der Winter kalt und wild!

The Stormy Morning

How the storm has torn apart heaven's gray gown! The tattered clouds flutter around in weary strife.

And red flames of fire flash between them. This is what I call a morning that really suits my mood!

My heart sees its own image painted in the sky—it is nothing but winter, cold and savage winter!

The poem is divided into three stanzas. The first describes the raging storm in a neutral manner, while the second ends with a more personal tone as the protagonist remarks that he enjoys such weather.[9] The final stanza is the most personal. In it, the wanderer likens his inner emotions and heart to the storm; both are cold and wild. Table 8.2a shows the poem's underlying structure. The storm is interpreted as the sender (Sr), the element that initiates the contemplative process of the poem. The object of contemplation (O) is the similarity between the storm and the wanderer's sentiments. Table 8.2b shows that the object appears in two guises. The secondary positive refers to the similarity between the wild storm and the protagonist's inner thoughts (the second stanza); in such a wild atmosphere, the wanderer does not feel anxiety over his lost love, the starting point of his journey. The primary negative quality of the object, on the other hand, refers to coldness, the idea that giving up love also signals the inability to feel human emotions (the third stanza).[10] Now that the protagonist has reached a state in his journey in which he considers renouncing love and accepting death as a positive option, he has to cope with the negative consequences of this possibility.

The restless music of the D-minor sections reflects the storm in an imitative manner; the music's brief gestures, its frequent and unexpected accents, and its emphatic dissonances can all be heard as imitating the storm, the sound of thunder, and the unpredictable intervals between the flashes of lightning. Furthermore, the similarity between the storm and the protagonist's sentiments is reflected in the largely unison texture. In other words, much as the wanderer's sentiments are connected to the storm, the vocal line is tied to the piano part,

Table 8.2. "Der stürmische Morgen," underlying structure of the poem

a. Textual structure
Sr → O → R

b. Two qualities of the object

secondary		primary
O (positive)	vs.	O (negative)

Actant	Reference
Sr	the storm
O	the unity of the storm and the protagonist's emotions
R	the protagonist

which introduces the unison already in mm. 1–3. This creates the impression that the protagonist is almost a passive observer; unable to affect the course of events, he must follow his destiny, just as his vocal line follows the piano part. The idea of the wanderer being without power over his own fate is mirrored in the background voice leading. All pitches of the *Urlinie* occur in passages in which the singer is silent. Thus, the protagonist does not take part in the most basic top-voice events of the song.

The text in the opening D-minor section (mm. 1–9) describes the storm, thereby introducing the sender of the underlying textual structure (example 8.2b). In m. 10 the musical expression changes from the tragic to the joyful. Together with the tonicization of B♭ major, this change reflects the part of the text in which the protagonist expresses more personal sentiments, including his pleasure in experiencing the storm. The rather pompous expressive quality of the music attempts to confirm the joyful emotion. But these positive associations are only secondary in the poem. The likeness between the storm and the wanderer's heart primarily refers to coldness and wildness; a cold heart cannot love and suggests the loss of the speaker's ability to experience positive emotions.

This duality of the poetic object is conveyed by the structural function of the music's positive factor, the B♭-major chord. Even though it is strongly established on the surface, structurally, the chord has a purely contrapuntal, decorative role (example 8.2a); formally, it has no concluding function, and its uppermost voice does not represent the structural top-voice line (example 8.2b). When the primary bass line returns with the C♯ in m. 14, the tragic, negative expression again holds sway. At the same time, the poem refers to coldness of heart, the primary aspect of the object shown in table 8.2b. The primacy of the tragic is enhanced by the music's dramatic high point, which underlines the return of the tonic D minor, displacing the more positive B♭ major. The storm enjoyed by the narrator inevitably signals coldness of heart and the loss of a capacity for warm emotions, particularly love.

"Der stürmische Morgen" shows another reaction to the loss announced by "Letzte Hoffnung." If "Im Dorfe" portrayed a fundamentally positive reaction, with bitter undertones, "Der stürmische Morgen" is certainly negative; the wanderer laments his cold heart and the loss of his ability to experience positive emotions and love. Yet he cannot change the course of his journey but must accept the inevitable. This is conveyed musically by the unison texture (the singer follows the piano, much as the wanderer follows his fate) and by the descent of the *Urlinie* in the piano part (the singer does not take part in the principal top-voice events, much as the speaker cannot affect the course of his journey). But the negative reactions of the brief "Der stürmische Morgen" are expressed only as a fleeting outburst, and the next song returns to a more positive expression. The protagonist is on his way to making the unequivocal choice of death, the option he has contemplated since "Der greise Kopf" and that he sees as ultimately positive. The brief outburst of "Der stürmische Morgen" does not suffice to turn the wanderer's course.

8.3. "Täuschung"

"Täuschung" makes a strong contrast with "Der stürmische Morgen," whose tragic rage is now replaced by mostly joyful nostalgia. The song is in ternary form, preceded by an introduction (mm. 1–5) and followed by a coda (mm. 40–43) (example 8.3). The introduction and the A sections include almost literal repetitions of material: they are made solely of phrases that, in the bass, consist of a descending fourth A–E followed by the return of A (I–V–I) and, in an inner voice (or the top voice in the introduction), an ascending fourth E–A (5̂–1̂). The structural top voice of each of the A section phrases, in turn, consists of 3̂–2̂–1̂ progressions, the last of which constitutes the *Urlinie*. Even though the bass keeps repeating the descending A–E motion, it is subdivided differently (see the separate staff in example 8.3). In mm. 6–12, the repetition in mm. 14–20 (not shown in the example), and in mm. 31–37, the fourth is subdivided into a second and a third. In other words, the G♯ supports the dominant in the first inversion, thus functioning as the upper third of the forthcoming V. The F♯, in turn, is a passing tone within the prolonged dominant. In mm. 1–5 and 37–40, on the other hand, the G♯ supports a V⁴₃ of VI, so G♯ functions as a passing tone. As a result, the descending fourth is subdivided into a third and a second, and the F♯ is an

Form:	intro.	A¹		B	A²		+ coda
Expressive genre:	joyful			tragic	joyful		
Expressive quality:	playful			lamenting	playful		
Dramatic curve:				high point			
Textual structure:		(S ∩ O)		(S ∪ O)	(S ∩ O)	(S ∪ O)	

Example 8.3. "Täuschung," middleground voice leading and motivic fourth.

incomplete neighbor. The juxtaposition of the two subdivisions creates a subtle difference between the two versions of the same contrapuntal framework. The emphasis on F♯ and VI has darker undertones not heard in the phrases stressing G♯ and V$^6_5$.

The two forms of the descending fourth are most directly juxtaposed in the A² section. An exact repetition of mm. 6–13 would lead to a definitive closure in m. 37, an end that would be followed by a two-bar repetition of the singer's cadential gesture in the piano. However, after m. 37, the repetition of the cadential figuration is evaded.[11] Instead, the cadential arrival in m. 37 overlaps the beginning of a new phrase whose bass emphasizes the F♯ in the descending fourth, rather than G♯, as in the preceding phrase, mm. 31–37 (example 8.3). Owing to the background closure in mm. 39–40, the structural dominant is achieved via the version of the descending bass emphasizing VI and F♯, rather than the one stressing V$^6_5$ and G♯. The background closure thus follows the descending fourth that suggests those darker undertones.

The expression opening the B section differs from the rest of the song. Now a tragic and lamenting emotion fleetingly replaces the joyful and playful expression that dominates elsewhere. The section begins with an A-minor triad whose role is far from clear. Initially, it suggests a function of I$^\natural$, a chord that would transform the major-mode tonic ending the A¹ section into a minor harmony. However, when the entire B section is taken into consideration, the situation seems different. The A-minor triad begins a harmonic progression leading to a dominant harmony tonicized in m. 27, so within the context of the B section, it functions as a IV$^\natural$ in E major. Example 8.3 clarifies this view by showing an auxiliary cadence directed toward the V in m. 27.[12]

The uncertainty of the A-minor triad's function has subtle dramatic consequences. The initial assumption that the chord is a minor-mode tonic transforms the expressive genre from the joyful, which has reigned so far, to the tragic (example 8.3). Moreover, the expressive contrast makes mm. 22–23 the dramatic high point of the song; the lamenting expressive quality clearly distances these measures from the earlier playfulness. But the retrospective reinterpretation of the chord as the initial harmony of the auxiliary cadence removes the tragic in the same way that the larger context denies the function of the sonority as a modally inflected tonic. In other words, the later events cancel the durability of both the structural and expressive functions that the A-minor chord initially suggests. This process of reevaluating the A-minor sonority is paralleled by the reinterpretation of the C♮ in m. 22 as B♯ in m. 30; the pitch class that first signaled the onset of the tragic expression later occurs when the joyful music that started the song is about to be heard anew (see the asterisks in example 8.3).[13]

Täuschung

Ein Licht tanzt freundlich vor mir her;
Ich folg' ihm nach die Kreuz und Quer;
Ich folg' ihm gern und seh's ihm an,
Daß es verlockt den Wandersmann.

Ach, wer wie ich so elend ist,
Gibt gern sich hin der bunten List,
Die hinter Eis und Nacht und Graus,
Ihm weist ein helles, warmes Haus,
Und eine liebe Seele drin—
Nur Täuschung ist für mich Gewinn!

Delusion

A light dances, friendly, before me. I follow it here and there; I follow it gladly, seeing that it lures the wanderer. Ah! Anyone as wretched as I gladly falls for the beguiling trick that shows him, beyond ice and night and horror, a bright, warm house and a beloved soul within—even delusion is a prize to me!

The poem is not divided into stanzas but rather consists of a single entity. As the title "Täuschung" (Delusion) suggests, this poem deals directly with the theme of illusion. The protagonist follows a light, assuming that it will lead him through the cold and dark to the warm house of his beloved. But he acknowledges that these assumptions are only delusions, and yet he defends his willingness to follow them by his wretched state of mind. This poem has larger significance in *Winterreise.* This is the last time the wanderer refers directly to his beloved and now concedes without any protest that all positive associations with her are illusions. When this assertion arrives at this point in *Winterreise,* it confirms beyond any doubt that the hope of regaining the beloved must be well and truly abandoned, an idea the wanderer has contemplated since "Letzte Hoffnung."

Table 8.3a shows the opposition underlying the poem. On the one hand, there is the illusion that the subject (the protagonist) and the object (happiness and love) are conjoined; on the other hand, there is the reality—subject and object are disjoined. Table 8.3b indicates that the light, mentioned at the poem's beginning, functions as the sender; the protagonist follows the light, believing it will lead to the beloved yet at the same time admitting that this is only a delusion.

The two forms of descending fourth can be associated with the opposition shown in table 8.3a. I interpret the subdivision emphasizing G♯ as a reference to illusion and associate the one highlighting F♯ (the one with darker expressive undertones) with reality (example 8.3). As in the poem, here too there are contrasting views of one and the same element (in the poem, light either leads to the beloved or deludes the wanderer; in the music, a descending fourth emphasizes either G♯ or F♯). The introduction includes the version emphasizing F♯; the singer is still silent, and the reality is shown as it is. In the A¹ section, the protagonist follows the light and the delusion, so the version of the fourth emphasizing G♯ is heard. In mm. 17–21, at the very end of the A¹ section, the narrator concedes, for the first time in the poem, that the positive associations are only delusions. As a result, the B section begins in the tragic expression; the speaker remarks on how wretched he is. This brief admission of the miserable reality coincides with the song's dramatic high point and the only moment of directly tragic expression. But in the poem, the protagonist mentions his unhappy state only to explain why

Table 8.3. "Täuschung," underlying structure of the poem

a. Underlying opposition

illusion		reality
chosen		rejected
(S ∩ O)	vs.	(S ∪ O)

b. Sender as the source of illusion

Sr → O → R

Actant	Reference
S	the protagonist
O	happiness and love
Sr	the light
R	the protagonist

he follows the light, the delusion. Similarly, in the music the tragic A-minor triad is interpreted as the initial element of an auxiliary cadence tonicizing E major (rather than as a modally inflected tonic), and the pitch C♮ is reinterpreted as B♯. Accordingly, the tragic is given no chance to establish itself securely either in the poem or in the music.

At the song's end, both the music and the protagonist have to acknowledge reality. In the poem's final line, the wanderer concedes that all he ultimately gets from the light is delusion. These words appear in mm. 37–40, which stress F♯ in the bass line, the sign of reality. Furthermore, the somewhat intrusive beginning of the phrase in m. 37 evades a firm closure of the preceding phrase, whose text speaks about the beloved and stresses G♯ in the descending bass. In other words, the closure of the musical phrase referring to delusion (S ∩ O) is avoided, while the closure of the phrase referring to reality (S ∪ O) is emphasized by the completion of the *Ursatz*. Delusion is unreal and will remain so.

"Täuschung" completes the three-song unit in which the protagonist reflects on the circumstances suggested at the end of "Letzte Hoffnung." The three Lieder show very different responses to those circumstances. In "Im Dorfe," the loss of hope of regaining the beloved is recognized as inevitable, and there is a somewhat bitter undertone, even though the sense of relief introduced at the end of "Letzte Hoffnung" prevails. But the protagonist is still uncertain how to react, and thus his vocal line ends on 3̂, avoiding closure and leaving it to the piano to end the *Urlinie*. "Der stürmische Morgen" is a violent outburst, lamenting the loss of any chance of experiencing warm emotions, which will be an inevitable outcome of accepting the loss of love. But the song is so brief that it does not eradicate the protagonist's fundamentally positive attitude to giving up the hope of love. The third song, "Täuschung," is nostalgic. The wanderer concedes that there is a delusion (the idea of returning to the beloved), yet he still likes to think of her. He has accepted his fate, and the song, unlike "Im Dorfe," closes with the singer's clear î. The end thus affirms that the thought of recapturing love can only be a delusion.

After contemplating the loss of love in these three songs, the protagonist is now ready to draw the inevitable conclusions about his circumstances. It is time to seek death consciously, to move toward the second form of hope, which emerged in the concluding chorale texture of "Letzte Hoffnung." This choice is made in the next song, "Der Wegweiser."

9 Choosing Death: "Der Wegweiser"

9.1. Music

"Der Wegweiser" is one of the most important songs in the dramatic trajectory of *Winterreise*. Its deep intensity culminates in highly chromatic music toward the end of the song, a more extreme departure from a firm tonal framework than anything else in the cycle. "Der Wegweiser" is in ternary form, preceded by an introduction and followed by the chromatic coda (example 9.1). Most of the song is dominated by a tragic expression from which the music escapes only briefly at the beginning of the B section, in which the minor-mode tonic of the A^1 section is transformed into a major sonority. The B section then proceeds from its opening I^6 via ♮III^6 (m. 29) to the dominant (m. 39), which ends the first branch of the interrupted deep-level structure. During this harmonic progression, the primary tragic expression returns. The G-minor tonic reappears in m. 37 without any harmonic preparation, and this unexpected and somewhat horrifying event forms a peak in the song's dramatic curve. The A^2 section repeats the music of the opening section almost note for note (thus, example 9.1 shows the events only in schematic form). The concluding coda differs in two significant respects from all other codas in *Winterreise*: first, it is larger than any other coda in the cycle, taking up about one-third of the song; and second, aside from "Der Leiermann," it is the only coda in which the singer is not silent. The coda also includes the song's dramatic high point, another factor that distinguishes it from all other songs in *Winterreise*.[1]

The introduction and the A^1 section launch a motivic element that will permeate the song: E♭ ($\hat{6}$), which usually, but not always, functions as an upper neighbor to D ($\hat{5}$). This pitch first occurs in m. 3 in the bass, where its descending tendency is made clear by the augmented-sixth chord (example 9.2b). It also features significantly in the two phrases that constitute the A^1 section (mm. 6–10 and 11–21, respectively). In the first phrase, E♭ functions in mm. 7–9 as in the introduction, that is, as the bass of the predominant leading to the dominant (example 9.2b). In the second phrase, however, its function is far from clear.

The second phrase begins in m. 11 with the motivically significant E♭ sounded immediately in the bass. The lowermost voice then descends in the next bar to D, thus providing another instance of the descending E♭–D motive. The chord of m. 12, however, does not fulfill its immediate tonal implications and function as a V^7. Instead, the progression of mm. 11–12 is sequentially repeated, and the four-bar sequential unit ends in m. 14 on the dominant of F minor, a key that is to-

$\hat{3}$ $\flat\hat{3}$ $\flat\hat{3}$ $\hat{2}\| \; \hat{3} \; \hat{2} \; \hat{1}$ (unfolding)   (unfolding)

(musical score)

-6

I   (♮VII♭ V I)   I♮   ♮III♯   V ‖ I V I   V I   V I

Form: intro. A¹   B   A²   coda

Expressive genre: tragic   joyful   tragic

Dramatic curve: peak   high point   peak

Textual structure: $(S \cup O_1)$ $\Rightarrow$ $(S \cap O_2)$

Example 9.1. "Der Wegweiser," an overview.

nicized in mm. 14–15. Example 9.2a clarifies the middleground voice leading: a $^6_3$ sonority over E♭ (m. 11) is transformed into a $^6_5$ chord on E♮ (m. 14; in the foreground, the root C is added below the E♮). In other words, in the middleground the IV of the main key becomes the V of F minor. Therefore, at deeper levels, the E♭ of m. 11 does not descend, as the bass note E♭s have done so far, but rather ascends to E♮. This creates tension between the immediate and deeper levels of structure. On the surface, and more apparently, the E♭ descends to D, while in the middleground, and in a more covert manner, it ascends to E♮. The tension between the two directions from the pitch E♭ (descent to D or ascent to E♮) will feature significantly in the rest of the song.[2]

The remote F-minor chord tonicized in m. 15 creates great harmonic contrast. In the middleground, it functions as the upper third of the V arrived at in m. 17 (example 9.2). The motion from this embellishing ♭VII♭ (m. 15) to the primary V (m. 17) brings back the tension between E♭ and E♮. At the end of m. 16, a C-major chord (V of F minor) is transformed into a C-minor triad (IV of the tonic key), which proceeds in the next measure to the home-key dominant. Now m. 16 reverses the E♭–E♮ progression of mm. 11–14: E♮ descends to E♭ (rather than ascending to F, as would be expected of a leading tone). Ultimately, the line continues to D, yet another instance of the E♭–D motive. Right before the cadence closing the A¹ section, m. 16 thus corrects the middleground ascent from E♭ (encountered in mm. 11–14) back to the primary descent to D.[3]

This play with descent or ascent from E♭ interacts with the local expression (example 9.2b). After the inward quality of the tragic that prevails at the song's beginning, the sequential unit of mm. 11–14 intensifies the affective quality; the

Example 9.2. "Der Wegweiser," mm. 1–19, voice-leading sketch.

middleground ascent from E♭ thus intertwines with more outward emotion. The tonicization of F minor introduces a declamatory expressive quality (suggested partly by the skips both in the bass and in the vocal part), which underlines the remote harmonic area. This emotional quality still prevails when the E♭–E♮ middleground motion is corrected to a descending foreground line E♮–E♭–D in mm. 16–17, displaced by the initial inward quality only when the tonic returns in m. 19. Yet a recollection of the preceding declamatory material remains in the left-hand figuration of m. 19, reminding us of the expressive intensification and tonal excursion that the E♭–E♮ motion started. The expressive significance of this ascent thus remains a memory, even after the music has returned to its affective point of departure.

The B section divides into three phrases. The first (mm. 22–27) recalls the song's opening material in major, prolonging the major-mode tonic and presenting ♮3̂ in the top voice (example 9.3). The emotion has here changed to joyful, and the major-mode environment creates a relaxed local expression, an emotional quality somewhat challenged, however, by the asymmetrical six-bar hypermeasure in mm. 22–28. A lead-in on the second quarter of m. 27 ushers in the second phrase (mm. 28–33), prolonging a B-major chord, a sonority that is in the middleground structure a ♭III♯ in the main key. But more locally, the chord suggests the function of the dominant of E minor, a key that remains illusory,

Example 9.3. "Der Wegweiser," mm. 22–40, voice-leading sketch.

however, since its tonic never arrives. The apparent E minor renounces the joyful expression that has governed the B section so far. The failure to confirm the key of E minor creates a yearning local emotional quality: the music reaches for something it cannot attain.

This B-major chord has motivic significance. Example 9.3a indicates that in m. 28 an inner-voice note is shifted to the uppermost voice. As a result, the top voice of the B-major chord is D♯, the third of the harmony. This pitch is enharmonically equivalent to the motivically significant E♭ strongly underlined in the A¹ section. But despite the same pitch class, the two pitches have different tendencies: the ascending aspiration of D♯ contrasts with the descending one of E♭.

In m. 33 the second and third phrases of the B section overlap (see the metrical analysis in example 9.3b). At the same time, D♯ is shifted back to an inner voice, and the structurally primary B returns to the top voice (example 9.3a). The third phrase (mm. 33–40) indicates that D♯ will not be resolved to E as one initially assumes: E minor will not be established as a local tonal center after all. Rather, in m. 35 the B-major chord is transformed into a minor harmony, and D♯ descends to D♮. As a result, D♯ does not fulfill its ascending tendency but rather the descending propensity of its enharmonic equivalent, E♭. Upward resolution is anticipated, however, and this creates the air of frustration in the music: the neighboring E♮s in mm. 28 and 30 actually do sound the pitch E, but only as an embellishing element, not as a structural resolution. This frustration further intensifies the music's expressive quality of yearning.

Once the ascending tendency of the D♯ has been denied, the music returns in m. 37 to the main key. The descent from D♯ to D♮ brings the music back onto the right track, so to speak, an impression enhanced by the metrical structure, where four-bar hypermeasures replace the asymmetrical six-bar units that have governed the B section so far (example 9.3b). The arrival at the G-minor chord in m. 37 is unprepared and shocking, with the stable top-voice B♮ transformed into B♭. The suddenness of the harmonic motion creates a horrified local expressive quality; the return of the tonic key is an almost frightening event. The significant motivic E♭ is heard once more in m. 38, this time without there being any doubt about its descending tendency; the pitch supports an augmented-sixth chord, the same sonority that introduced the motivic E♭ in m. 3. It thus turns out that the original, descending form of the motive is unavoidable, despite the attempt to rise from D♯ to E. The denial of the ascent and the inevitability of the descent can be associated with the events of mm. 11–16, where the descending E♮–E♭ motion in m. 16 cancels, as it were, the ascending E♭–E♮ of mm. 11–14. In mm. 38–39 a half cadence closes the B section. Now the music has a resigned expressive quality, with the traces of the preceding horror left behind; the music has accepted, as it were, that the joyful expression at the outset of the section was only a fleeting emotion that could not be sustained.

The motivic, tonal, metrical, and expressive layers of the B section all suggest a similar dramatic arch. The section's first two phrases introduce elements that contrast with aspects established in the preceding A^1 section: in the first phrase, G major contrasts with G minor (key areas), and the expression of the joyful thereby contrasts with the tragic, while in the second phrase, D♯ contrasts with E♭ (motivic design). Moreover, both phrases consist of six-bar hypermeasures that contrast with the predominantly four-bar units of the A^1 section. All of these elements ultimately turn out to be secondary: D♯ does not resolve upward, G minor replaces the major mode, the four-bar hypermeasures return, and the tragic overcomes the joyful. In addition, the apparent E minor is never cadentially confirmed; this tonal implication is also secondary. As a result, the B section creates a strong sense of unfulfilled aspirations: the music attempts to do something in contrast to the A section, but the attempt is in vain. The elements governing the song's beginning recur at the end of the B section; they cannot be avoided.

The coda, which follows the repetition of the A section in mm. 41–56, is in many ways remarkable. I have already mentioned that it is longer than any other coda in *Winterreise* and that, together with the coda of "Der Leiermann," it is the only one in which the singer is not silent. Moreover, it is more chromatic than

Example 9.4. "Der Wegweiser," mm. 55–83, voice-leading sketch.

almost any music written up to that time; one must wait for composers such as Liszt, Wagner, and Wolf to hear music in which chromaticism hides the sense of a tonal center to a comparable degree. The coda, whose voice leading is shown in example 9.4, consists of three phrases, the first two of which (mm. 57–68 and 69–77) begin with highly chromatic music and end in a cadence confirming the tonic key and the top-voice 1̂, a pitch first reached at the end of the A² section in m. 55. The third phrase (mm. 77–83) is a cadential progression that no longer challenges G minor as a tonal center.

Example 9.5. "Der Wegweiser," coda, recomposition.

The motivically significant bass note E♭, and its capacity either to ascend to E♮ or to descend to D, functions prominently in the formation of the coda's tonal instability. Example 9.5a, a recomposition of the beginning of the coda, clarifies the role of E♭. The coda begins in m. 57 with a predominant ♯IV⁷, which is transformed through a voice exchange into a German augmented-sixth chord (m. 59), a sonority that maintains the predominant function. If the augmented-sixth chord were to resolve as expected (shown in example 9.5a), then E♭ would descend in the bass to D, the root of a cadential dominant. Thus, the chromaticism at the beginning of the coda would fall, remotely but clearly, within a G-minor framework. But this is not what happens. Instead of descending, the bass note E♭ of m. 59 ascends to E♮. This unexpected motion, which evades the anticipated cadential progression, initiates a series of voice exchanges that momentarily seem to hide the tonal center (example 9.4).[4] Ultimately, these voice exchanges transform the ♯IV⁷ of m. 57 into a II⁷₇ (m. 64), and once the right path has been found again, the coda's first phrase ends with a strong cadence in mm. 66–67.

The chromaticism of the coda's second phrase, which repeats the motivic material of the first, is not as extreme, and the G-minor framework is clear throughout. Yet an unexpected ascent of a bass note, E♭, complicates the music here, too (cf. example 9.4 with 9.5b): the resolution of a chord assumed to function as an augmented-sixth chord (m. 73) is again avoided, postponing the cadential progression that closes the coda's second phrase. In the third and final phrase of the coda, an augmented-sixth chord is finally properly resolved, and the immediate repetition of the E♭–D motion underlines the finality of this descending step (example 9.4; the asterisks indicate the association between the sonorities in mm. 59, 73, and 78). The song's closing bars thus seal the primacy of the descending tendency of the E♭, a tendency that had been primary in the G-minor context of the song throughout but that the music had still challenged in several places.

These structural factors interact with the expression (example 9.4). The extreme chromaticism of the coda's first phrase suggests a horrified emotional quality (the music has lost its way, as it were), which gives way in the cadential progression of mm. 66–67 to a declamatory style, an announcement of the regaining of the tonal center and the right path. The second phrase is less chromatic and texturally more repetitive; accordingly, its expression is contemplative rather than horrified. The third and final phrase, with its steady, long chords combined with tonal clarity, brings back the song's initial inward expressive quality, now merged with a resigned quality. The expressive intensity thus gradually decreases from the high point of the first phrase via the peak of the second to the resigned conclusion in the third.

9.2. Text

Der Wegweiser

Was vermeid' ich denn die Wege,
Wo die andern Wandrer gehn,
Suche mir versteckte Stege
Durch verschneite Felsenhöhn?

Habe ja doch nichts begangen,
Daß ich Menschen sollte scheun—
Welch ein törichtes Verlangen
Treibt mich in die Wüstenei'n?

Weiser stehen auf den Wegen,
Weisen auf die Städte zu,
Und ich wandre sonder Maßen,
Ohne Ruh', und suche Ruh'.

Einen Weiser seh' ich stehen
Unverrückt vor meinem Blick;
Eine Straße muß ich gehen,
Die noch keiner ging zurück.

The Signpost

Why do I avoid the roads where other wanderers go and seek hidden paths through snow-covered rocky heights?

Yet I have done no wrong that I should shun people—what foolish yearning drives me into the wilderness?

On the roads are signposts that point toward the towns, and I wander ever farther, restless but seeking rest.

I see a signpost standing immovable before my gaze; I must travel a road from which no one has returned.

"Der Wegweiser" consists of four stanzas. The first two stanzas pose two questions and ask why the wanderer avoids all human company, even though he has done nothing wrong. In the second stanza, the wanderer observes that only foolish yearning drives him to seek lonely paths. The last two stanzas introduce the poem's central image, the signpost (*der Wegweiser*). Two kinds of signposts are juxtaposed: those pointing toward the towns (the third stanza) and a single one pointing to a road from which no one has ever returned—death (the fourth stanza).

The wanderer now faces a decision of paramount importance, for him as well as for the overall narrative of *Winterreise*. If since "Der greise Kopf" he has contemplated death and considered it a positive option, he now must decide whether to seek it actively, whether to follow the lonely signpost in the fourth stanza. If he follows the signposts pointing to the towns, he will return to society and other people. At this moment in *Winterreise,* the choice is obvious: the protagonist will relinquish all company, including his beloved. He is done with people, love, and human emotions. Death, which thus far has only been an image, now affects his actions; he feels compelled to follow the road leading to death: "I must travel a road from which no one has returned" (eine Straße muß ich gehen, / Die noch keiner ging zurück). The previous contemplation of death is about to be transformed into reality—or at least this is what the protagonist assumes.

Table 9.1a indicates the poem's narrative structure, which moves from state 1 via transformation (choice) into state 2. State 1 represents the present state of affairs, the avoidance of the company of people spoken about in the first three stanzas. The company of people is interpreted as O_1, and because of the protagonist's solitude, S and O_1 are disjoined. State 2 represents the hoped-for future, the attainment of death (O_2). Since the wanderer believes that he will find death, S and O_2 are conjoined. Indirectly, the poem suggests relinquishing the initial object of the entire cycle, the beloved: since the poem's final state gives up even the possibility of company, the future with the beloved becomes impossible.

The signposts in the poem are concrete signs, and they have been interpreted as two forms of the sender in table 9.1b. Sr_1 occurs in state 1, defining O_1; in other words, the signposts pointing to the towns represent the company of others, which the protagonist would find if he were to follow these signposts. Sr_2, on the other hand, occurs in state 2, defining O_2. This signpost directs the wanderer to a road that leads, he assumes, to death, a road he feels compelled to follow.

9.3. Musico-Poetic Aspects

The poem's concrete wandering, first on hidden paths and then down a road from which there is no return, is reflected imitatively in the music. The accompaniment of repeated eighth notes can be understood as imitating the steps

Table 9.1. "Der Wegweiser," underlying structure of the poem

a. Underlying narrative structure

state 1		state 2
present	choice	future
$(S \cup O_1)$	$\Rightarrow$	$(S \cap O_2)$

b. The signpost as sender

$Sr_1 \rightarrow O_1 \rightarrow R$ (state 1)

$Sr_2 \rightarrow O_2 \rightarrow R$ (state 2)

Actant	Reference
S	the protagonist
O_1	the company of people
O_2	death
Sr_1	the signposts pointing to the towns
Sr_2	the signpost pointing to a road from which there is no return
R	the protagonist

of the wanderer.[5] Also, the expressions of the poem and the music are related, and the tragic, which governs most of "Der Wegweiser," effectively corresponds to the expression of the poem. The only brief escape into the joyful is the G-major opening of the B section, a passage setting the beginning of the poem's second stanza in which the protagonist seeks consolation from knowing he has done nothing wrong (see the expressive genre in example 9.1).

The central image of the poem, the signpost, is related to its central theme: the juxtaposition of the company of people (O_1) and death (O_2). The poem has two forms of the signpost, interpreted in table 9.1b as Sr_1 and Sr_2. The former is secondary, pointing to the towns and people, while the latter is primary and unavoidable, pointing to the road from which there is no return, death. The company of people and death can be associated with the two stepwise progressions from the pitch E♭: the primary motion in the song's G-minor environment is a downward descent to D, and this can be seen as a reference to the primary O_2, whereas the secondary ascending motion to E♮ can be understood as pointing to the subordinate O_1. In other words, in both the music and the text, two signs are juxtaposed: in the music, the pitch class E♭/D♯, which can either ascend or descend, and in the poem, the company of people (Sr_1) and death (Sr_2). Both pairs are hierarchically organized: in the music, the descending direction is primary, while in the text, death is primary.

The temporal appearance of the musical and textual pairs of signs, however, is different. In the music, the juxtaposition of the two directions from the pitch class E♭/D♯ extends through virtually the entire song, whereas in the poem, the primary road of no return (O_2) is mentioned only in the final stanza (state 2 in table 9.1a). In spite of this temporal difference, I believe that the similarities among these musical and textual signs are sufficient to justify a musico-poetic interpretation. The musical motive, which can be heard throughout the song, can be seen as implying that the protagonist is constantly aware of the choice he is doomed to make. In other words, again the music affects the interpretation of the poem when the text is understood as part of the Lied; the music seems to suggest that the element revealed only in the poem's final stanza is considered by the protagonist throughout the entire song. Thus, the designation $(S \cup O_1) \Rightarrow (S \cap O_2)$ in table 9.1a, which shows a narrative transformation, could be understood in terms of a static underlying formula, $(S \cap O_2)$.[6] This poetic change subtly underlines the function of "Der Wegweiser" in the cycle as a whole; the conscious search for death emphasizes the role of this song as a clear turning point. Death is no longer merely thought about but actively sought.

Let us move from these general considerations to more local musico-poetic associations. The text's first stanza poses a question, and this sense of questioning is reflected in the music of mm. 11–20. The descending, primary E♭–D motion is heard at the outset of this passage, in mm. 11–12. But in the middleground, this descent is challenged by the ascending E♭–E♮ motion, which tonicizes F minor (example 9.2a). The remote tonicization and the ascending middleground progression echo the question in the text. The wanderer's uncertainty is reflected in harmonic remoteness, as it were. Even though in this part of *Winterreise* the protagonist is clearly seeking death (O_2)—after all, he has contemplated death ever since "Der greise Kopf"—he still questions the justification of his situation and has doubts about the choice he is making; in other words, he fears abandoning the company of people (O_1), even though at the same time he is seeking solitude. Similarly, the music questions the primacy of the E♭–D descent, associated with death, by displacing it with an E♭–E♮ middleground ascent leading to tonicization of the remote F minor. But much as the protagonist cannot—and does not want to—reverse the course of his journey, the E♭–D motion cannot be avoided; this progression returns in m. 16, when the text repeats the end of the question. Here, in a way, the music goes farther than the poem. While the text's first stanza ends in a question, the music is giving the answer, so to speak: the E♭–D motion (a sign referring to death) indicates that the reason for the wanderer's solitude (the topic of his question) is the desire for death, a reason explicitly stated in the text only at the poem's end. The local expression, with its increase in intensity and declamatory expressive quality, underlines the significance of the question and also indirectly the answer suggested by the music.

In the musical expression, the beginning of the B section brings a brief moment of the joyful. The protagonist now remarks that he has done nothing wrong that would require him to avoid the company of people; it is only a foolish yearning that drives him into the wilderness. In the abstract formalizations, there is no reason to avoid O_1 and seek O_2 instead. The joyful and relaxed expression reflects the knowledge that the protagonist cannot accuse himself of anything. In the stanza's final two lines, frustration is reflected in the music's motivic material. With the mention of the "foolish yearning" (*törichtes Verlangen*), the tragic expression returns with a somewhat yearning local quality that results from unsuccessful attempts to cadentially confirm E minor. At the same time, the music introduces an emphatic D♯, a pitch that is enharmonically equivalent to E♭ but that, owing to the locally apparent E-minor key, has a clearly ascending tendency. The text-music associations are strong. Just as the text questions the very reason for seeking solitude and ultimately death, or, formally, O₂, so the music challenges the descending tendency of E♭, the motive associated with O₂. Moreover, the music's yearning expressive quality, an outcome of the pitch D♯, which wants to move to E, sets the word *Verlangen* (yearning). Yet D♯ does not ascend but instead descends to D♮, so the primary descending tendency of E♭ remains operative. Likewise, the protagonist does not alter the inevitable direction of his path, even though the second stanza shows his situation to be unjust. At the B section's end, the singer remains silent while the piano alone brings back the tonic key, in mm. 33–39. Yet the rather horrified local expressive quality of m. 37 can clearly be associated with the speaker's emotions. In mm. 38–39 an emphatic augmented-sixth chord, which resolves to the dominant, repeats the introduction's initial form of the E♭–D motive. The sign referring to death thus returns, reminding us of the song's primary topic.

The third stanza, set in the A² section, mentions the important signposts for the first time, but only those pointing to the towns, not the one leading to the road from which no one has returned. The E♭–D motive of the bass in mm. 42–44 suggests that the wanderer walks past the signs, thus abandoning O₁ and seeking O₂. The musico-poetic connection here is similar to the one at the beginning of the song, where the same music sets the words in which the protagonist says that he avoids the paths that other travelers take—the paths to which the signs here point. The contrast between E♭–D and E♭–E♮ in mm. 46–54 sets the words that juxtapose restlessness and seeking rest. Again, E♭–D can be associated with the company of people (O₁), while E♭–E♮ refers to the peace provided by death (O₂).

The coda forms the heart of "Der Wegweiser"; it is here that the text makes it clear that the protagonist will follow the path from which there is no return. In other words, O₂ is now explicitly stated. It is significant that the *Ursatz* reaches its conclusion already at the end of the A² section. This completion signifies that there is indeed no return, since the structure has been closed. From an expressive perspective, the chromaticism and the stepwise bass lines of the coda can be associated with the *ombra* topos of the eighteenth century, used, according to Leonard G. Ratner, "to evoke the supernatural . . . and to bring forth feelings of awe and terror" (1980, 24). The *ombra* of the music matches the awe and terror the wanderer feels when he states his conscious decision to seek death. So far, he has only contemplated its possibility, but now he faces the actual choice.

In the coda, expression, tonality, motivic material, and word repetitions create a subtle web of associations. The poem's fourth stanza is set twice, and both settings include internal repetitions. The repetitions stress the final stanza's significance in the poem as well as in *Winterreise* as a cycle. The first setting of the stanza ends in m. 67 in the coda's first cadence. This passage includes the most extreme chromaticism in the song, intensified, as the recomposition of example 9.5a indicates, by the failure of the E♭ in m. 59 to descend to D. Poetically, since the ascending version of the basic motivic idea is heard, the memory of O_1 still lingers, although its renunciation has been declared in the text. The internal word repetition suggests that the wanderer is inexorably led to the recognition that he must take the path leading to death: the crucial words "eine Straße muß ich gehen" (I must travel a road) are heard twice, underlining the necessity.

The extreme chromaticism has its effect on the musico-poetic function of the expression in mm. 55–67. The local expressive quality is rather horrified, giving way, in the cadential gesture of mm. 66–67, to declamation (example 9.4). This suggests that the wanderer is terrified by his choice. Yet he is certain that it cannot be avoided, his confidence being reflected in the declamatory expression that reconfirms the top-voice $\hat{1}$, the pitch stressing the firmness of the closure at the end of the A^2 section. There is no escape from the protagonist's resolution. He further confirms his choice by repeating that he must travel the road. That the coda's first unit forms the song's dramatic high point (example 9.1) emphasizes the wanderer's determination.

The coda's second phrase (mm. 69–77) sets the fourth stanza once more, this time without internal repetitions. As example 9.5b indicates, the failure to descend from E♭ to D again intensifies the chromaticism. But this time the sense of G minor as a tonal center remains audible, so the chromatic detour is not as great as in the coda's first phrase. Since the tonal center can be heard throughout, the expressive quality is no longer horrified (as in the coda's first phrase) but rather is contemplative (example 9.4). The wanderer gradually acknowledges his decision, whose unavoidability is again confirmed by the declamatory cadential material in mm. 76–77. Finally, the coda's last phrase repeats the stanza's important final words, "die noch keiner ging zurück" (from which no one has returned). These words refer to O_2 alone, and all recollections of O_1 seem to have vanished: motivically, E♮ is no longer heard, and E♭ descends emphatically to D (example 9.4). Also the *ombra* topos has vanished, and in its place there is a partly chromatic descent in the bass, reminiscent of the rhetorical figure *passus duriusculus*, widely used by composers of earlier generations to refer to lamentation and death.[7] The expressive quality is inward and resigned (example 9.4): the wanderer no longer considers reasons to offset his determination to seek death. In effect, the coda's three phrases gradually accept more firmly the finality of the protagonist's decision, an interpretation conveyed by the word repetitions, tonal events, motivic material, and musical expression.

"Der Wegweiser" is one of the most important songs in the dramatic trajectory of *Winterreise*. Now, the protagonist recognizes that the path to death is inevitable. The decision to seek death is not an easy one, however; the difficulty is reflected in the complexities with the pitch E♭ and its downward motion to D, as well as in the extreme chromaticism of the coda. The songs that follow will describe the outcome of this decision. The next song, "Das Wirtshaus," is an immediate reaction to his choice. "Der Wegweiser" and "Das Wirtshaus" are associated through common motivic material, and the manner in which Schubert uses their shared motives reflects the consequences of the events of "Der Wegweiser." Thus, the two songs form a kind of pair in which a decision is taken to seek death, and then the outcome of this decision is portrayed.

10 Death Eludes the Wanderer: "Das Wirtshaus"

10.1. Music

With "Das Wirtshaus," the gloominess of "Der Wegweiser" (especially its concluding coda) gives way to solemn and religious-sounding music. This slow, through-composed song divides into three sections, preceded by an introduction (mm. 1–5) and followed by a coda (mm. 29–31) (example 10.1). The tonally closed first section (mm. 6–15) draws on the chorale-like texture established in the introduction. The second section (mm. 18–22, preceded by material from the introduction in mm. 16–17) is tonally less stable, beginning with a dissonant seventh chord and ending in a half-cadential dominant. The third section (mm. 23–28) is rhetorically the most emphatic, and the dramatic high point occurs here. Moreover, the expression temporarily changes from the joyful, which has dominated up to this point, to the tragic. The tonal events of the third section are more complex than before, including remote tonicizations of A♭ major and C minor. As in most of the songs of *Winterreise*, the coda is based on the material of the introduction, so the Lied ends in the same expression with which it began.

The solemn character at the beginning creates a pious, expressive quality (example 10.2), the slow-moving, chorale-like harmonies suggesting a religious atmosphere.[1] Metrically, the introduction begins as if it consisted of a four-bar phrase ending in a half cadence in m. 4, an impression created by an apparent cadential $^6_4$ chord on the third quarter beat in m. 4. However, this six-four sonority does not resolve to the expected $^5_3$. Instead, the bass note C in m. 4 turns out to be a passing tone within a prolongation of a predominant IV, and the expected four-bar unit is thereby transformed into a five-measure phrase, which eventually attains the expected dominant in m. 5 (example 10.2b). The dramatic course thus first suggests a goal (a half cadence in m. 4) whose arrival is then evaded, a process that makes the trip to the concluding dominant longer than the listener first assumes. In the local expressive quality, this unexpected deferral briefly replaces the primary pious quality with a surprised expression.[2]

The introduction is motivically related to the preceding song, "Der Wegweiser." The significant IV, prolonged in mm. 4–5, is prepared in m. 3 by a secondary dominant in which E♭, the first chromatically altered pitch in the song, has been added to the tonic. Since this pitch and the descent from E♭ to D were such significant elements in "Der Wegweiser," the return of the same pitches at

Example 10.1. "Das Wirtshaus," an overview.

the very beginning of "Das Wirtshaus" draws a motivic connection between the songs. But the environment in which the E♭–D motion now occurs is different. In "Der Wegweiser" E♭ is a diatonic pitch (6̂), while in "Das Wirtshaus" it is a chromatic one (♭7̂). As a result, in the former song E♭ is part of the diatonic framework, while in the latter it is outside the underlying F-major diatony. Also, the expression is different. In "Der Wegweiser" the E♭–D motion occurs in the tragic emotion, while in mm. 3–4 of "Das Wirtshaus" it is heard in a kind of pious, chorale-like expression of the joyful.

The E♭–D motion also occurs prominently in the song's first section (mm. 6–9; see the staff above the graph in example 10.2b). Now the E♭ is preceded by an E♮, a preparation significant in two respects. First, the E♮ paving the way to the E♭ is part of a dominant sonority, so the ascending tendency of the leading tone is (at least momentarily) denied by the descent. Second, the addition of E♮ forges an ever clearer motivic association with "Der Wegweiser": now the music also introduces the pitch that in the earlier song provided the alternative ascending motion from E♭ to E♮. The E♮–E♭–D motion is heard twice. The first occurrence is very local, taking place in m. 6 within a I^{5-6} progression preparing a II (example 10.2b).

Example 10.2. "Das Wirtshaus," mm. 1–11, voice-leading sketch.

The brief tonicization of G minor (the predominant II) in m. 7, initiated by the Eb, affects the music's expression: the reigning joyful is briefly replaced by a shade of the tragic (example 10.2b). This fleeting tragic expression and the tonicized G minor draw further references to the preceding "Der Wegweiser": the E♮–Eb motion of m. 6 is an almost exact quotation of m. 16.

The second occurrence of the E♮–Eb–D motion is more emphatic. The cadential dominant of the phrase in mm. 6–9 arrives in the middle of m. 8. Instead of an immediate resolution, however, the dominant is prolonged in the first half of m. 9. At the outset of this measure, an Eb is sounded emphatically on a metrically strong beat and in the bass. Structurally, this pitch is a chromatic passing tone within a third-progression descending from E to C (example 10.2b); that is, it is a purely decorative element, its local emphasis notwithstanding.[3]

The song's brief second section consists of a single phrase. It begins with a two-bar subphrase (mm. 18–19) whose varied repetition (mm. 20–22) touches on the minor mode and the tragic expression (example 10.3). Eb again appears prominently. In the middleground, the repeated subphrases feature a neighboring $\frac{5\text{-}6\text{-}5}{3\text{-}4\text{-}3}$ progression prolonging the tonic (example 10.3a). On the surface, the seventh Eb that prepares the neighboring $^6_4$ sonority has been added to the opening tonic, so the consonant point of origin (a $^5_3$ sonority with an octave F) has been elided (see the single staff in example 10.3b). As a result, Eb is significantly emphasized on the surface while retaining a purely decorative structural function at a deeper level. The Eb therefore assumes rhetorical significance beyond

Example 10.3. "Das Wirtshaus," mm. 18–22, voice-leading sketch.

its voice-leading function. The music seems even more eager to stress E♭, allowing this motivically significant pitch to affect the music's sonic quality considerably. The fact that both of the subphrases end on a back-relating dominant—that is, one without a tonal resolution—leaves the tonal process ultimately incomplete. It is as if the music twice asked a question, the second time even more forcefully, owing to the tragic shades of expression. Accordingly, the expressive quality changes from the pious to the declamatory (example 10.3b).

The song's complex third part (mm. 23–28) immediately changes the entire musical character by sounding an F-minor sonority in m. 23 whose tragic ex-

Example 10.4. "Das Wirtshaus," mm. 23–28, voice-leading sketch.

pression is a kind of corroboration of the tragic shades of the preceding measures. Even though the F-minor chord is a local center (a modally inflected structural tonic), it functions more globally as the initiating harmony of an auxiliary cadence tonicizing the ♭III, an A♭-major chord (example 10.4).[4] The music's dramatic effect is powerful here. The F-minor sonority first seems to confirm the tragic implications of mm. 21–22. The auxiliary cadence momentarily denies these implications, however, leading the music instead into a joyful major sonority, the tonicized A♭-major chord. This major sonority underlines the expression's undecided local quality: neither the tragic nor the joyful seems to be fully established as the locally governing expression. Ultimately, the tragic appears victorious, and the A♭-major triad is just a brief midpoint in the harmonic I–♭III–V♭ progression leading to a minor-mode dominant in m. 25. The tonicized A♭-major sonority thus provides no lasting escape from the tragic expression.

The V♭ of m. 25 functions as the song's dramatic high point. The uncertain tragic that began the song's third section now changes to a depressed quality (example 10.4b), as if to suggest that the tragic has gotten the upper hand and powerfully displaced the joyful and pious expression of the song's opening. In the middleground voice leading, the V♭ supports the background 2̂ (example 10.4a). At a deeper level, the dominant is transformed in m. 28 into a major chord, which resolves to the closing tonic supporting the background 1̂. Prior to the conclusive arrival at the final tonic in m. 28, a 1̂/I is heard in the middle of m. 26. Even though this arrival at the tonic momentarily sounds conclusive the instant it appears, the continuation almost immediately revokes this impression. An A♭ instantly transforms the chord into a minor sonority leading back to the minor-mode dominant in m. 27. We are back to where we were in m. 25, and the fleeting sense of arrival at the tonic is subverted. The progression to the tonic is then repeated with small variants, this time arriving at the tonic to complete the background structure.

Example 10.4 shows my interpretation of the first motion to a tonic as a parenthetical event—a progression that does not affect the deep-level voice leading. I take the dominant chords before and after the parentheses (in mm. 25 and 27) as structurally connected, thus arguing that the events within the parentheses do not affect the global course of the music. This is indeed the general characteristic of musical parentheses: the musical events before and after the parentheses are directly linked, despite the intervening material.[5] We have also seen earlier in *Winterreise*, in mm. 33–37 of "Die Krähe," an instance in which repetition of material led to a parenthetical insertion (see example 6.4). There are two significant differences between the parenthetical repetitions in "Die Krähe" and those in "Das Wirtshaus," however. First of all, in "Die Krähe" the material is interpreted as parenthetical when it reappears, whereas in "Das Wirtshaus" the first occurrence is understood as parenthetical. Second, in "Die Krähe" the tonic arrives only after the parenthetical material, whereas in "Das Wirtshaus" the tonic is also heard in the parenthetical passage.[6] Both of these features strongly suggest that the structure could indeed close in m. 26. Yet the larger context challenges this possibility, indicating that the music must still repeat the previous material in order to complete its global course and resolve the musical tensions. The tonic in m. 26 thus turns out to be premature, and the subsequent material forces it to relinquish its attempt to assume a primary structural function.[7]

The music within the parentheses features significantly in the expression (example 10.4b). After the tragic affect that has been increasingly emphasized since m. 20, the parenthetical material attempts to regain the joyful expression in m. 26, an attempt that locally suggests a relieved expressive quality; momentarily, the music believes it has escaped the tragic, as it were. The return of the V⁵ in m. 27, however, and the subsidiary structural function of m. 26 indicate that the time for the return of joy has not yet arrived. Only the attainment of the concluding tonic in m. 28 confirms the joyful expression. Ultimately, the coda brings back the pious, joyful mood that begins the song; after long detours, we are back where we started.

The complex tonal events of mm. 23–28 continue to elaborate the motivically significant pitch E♭ (see the staff above the voice-leading sketch in example 10.4b). This pitch is heard in m. 24 as the fifth of the tonicized A♭-major chord and more emphatically in the ensuing bar as the third of a C-minor triad. The minor-mode dominant is an unusual harmony in a major key, a chord that has a ♭7̂ instead of the leading tone. Now this pitch takes part in an important motivic network. In mm. 25–28 the tension between E♭ and E♮ (between minor-mode and major-mode dominant chords) is acute. The first attempt to correct E♭ to E♮ in mm. 25 and 26 is not successful, because the C-minor triad returns after the parenthetical passage.

It is as if the music attempts to resist the ascending tendency of the leading tone by sticking to the ♭$\hat{7}$. But ultimately, E♮ is primary: it replaces E♭ when the structural dominant is finally resolved to the concluding tonic in m. 28. So E♭ ascends to E♮ after all (see the staff above the voice-leading sketch in example 10.4b). E♭ is briefly recalled in the coda (mm. 29–30), but the primacy of E♮, heard in the closing cadence in mm. 30–31, is clear. As the F-major key has suggested throughout, E♭ is and remains a decorative element, all the emphasis given it notwithstanding.

10.2. Text

Das Wirtshaus

Auf einen Totenacker
Hat mich mein Weg gebracht.
Allhier will ich einkehren:
Hab' ich bei mir gedacht.

Ihr grünen Totenkränze
Könnt wohl die Zeichen sein,
Die müde Wandrer laden
In's kühle Wirtshaus ein.

Sind denn in diesem Hause
Die Kammern all' besetzt?
Bin matt zum Niedersinken,
Bin tödlich schwer verletzt.

O unbarmherz'ge Schenke,
Doch weisest du mich ab?
Nun weiter denn, nur weiter,
Mein treuer Wanderstab!

The Inn

My way has brought me to a graveyard. Here I will take lodgings, I thought to myself.

You green funeral wreaths must be the signs that invite tired travelers into the cool inn.

Are all the rooms in this house then taken? I am so tired I could collapse; I am fatally wounded.

Oh pitiless inn, do you nonetheless turn me away? Well, onward then, still onward, my trusty walking staff!

As discussed in the previous chapter, "Der Wegweiser" signifies a turning point in *Winterreise;* the protagonist stops merely contemplating death as something positive and consciously decides to seek it out. The first two stanzas of "Das Wirtshaus" reflect the wanderer's relief after making this difficult decision; he be-

Table 10.1. "Das Wirtshaus," underlying structure of the poem

a. Underlying narrative structure

state 1		state 2
illusion, hope		reality
$(S \cap O)$	$\Rightarrow$	$(S \cup O)$

b. The inn (cemetery) as sender

state 1		state 2
illusion, hope		reality
$Sr_1 \rightarrow (S \cap O)$	$\Rightarrow$	$Sr_2 \rightarrow (S \cup O)$

Actant	Reference
S	the protagonist
O	death
Sr_1	the inn (the cemetery) with free rooms
Sr_2	the inn (the cemetery) with no free rooms

lieves that he is about to meet death, symbolized in the poem by the cemetery. Yet the poem's third stanza suggests that the relief might be premature. Its first two lines ask whether all the rooms are taken, while the last two attempt to justify why the protagonist should be allowed in. But he is turned away, as becomes evident in the final stanza. The death he has chosen in "Der Wegweiser" does not come, so the wanderer is forced to continue his desolate journey.

Table 10.1a indicates the narrative structure of "Das Wirtshaus." The first two stanzas are represented by state 1, indicating the conjunction of S and O (death). This state represents only illusion and hope, however, and it is questioned in the third stanza. This questioning is interpreted in table 10.1a as a transformation (a double-lined arrow) leading to state 2, the reality shown in the final stanza, in which S and O are disjoined. As table 10.1b indicates, the motion from state 1 to state 2 is brought about by the changing information provided by the sender, represented in the poem by the inn. In state 1 the protagonist hopes that there are free rooms, and the inn with free rooms is considered Sr_1. In reality, however, there is no vacancy, and the inn with no rooms is interpreted in state 2 as Sr_2.

10.3. Musico-Poetic Aspects

The overall expression and character of the music of "Das Wirtshaus" suits the content of the poem very well. The somewhat religious musical atmosphere can be associated with the cemetery as a place, on the one hand, and with the death anticipated by the protagonist, on the other. The music's expressive genre, in turn, corresponds closely to the poem's narrative structure (the two are aligned in example 10.1). Both begin in a positive state, joyful in the music and S

∩ O in the poem. This state does not last, however. In the music's third part and the poem's fourth stanza, the tragic and S ∪ O replace the previous joyful and S ∩ O, a replacement anticipated in the music's second part and the poem's third stanza. In the poem's last two lines, the protagonist accepts that his journey will continue, an acceptance suggested in the music by a return of the opening expression, which ends the song on a somewhat more positive emotion than the poem, to be sure.

The music's motivic material is again closely related to the textual structure. Above, I noted that the motivically significant E♭ is associated with the preceding song, "Der Wegweiser." I would argue, furthermore, that the association extends to the musico-poetic relationship. As we saw in section 9.3, in "Der Wegweiser" the descending E♭–D motion can be understood as referring to death, and E♭ seems to retain the same referentiality in "Das Wirtshaus." But the tonal environment is now different: while E♭ is a diatonic pitch in the G-minor tonality of "Der Wegweiser," it is a chromatically inflected note in the F major of "Das Wirtshaus." In other words, E♭ functions in the latter song as an embellishing element foreign to the underlying diatony. This difference in function reflects the distinct roles that death plays in the texts of each song. In "Der Wegweiser" death is a real option that ultimately is chosen; likewise, E♭ is part of the song's underlying diatony, its tonal reality, as it were. In "Das Wirtshaus," by contrast, death is only an illusion, and hence, E♭ is not part of the basic tonal framework.

E♭ appears in two guises in "Das Wirtshaus." On the one hand, it is heard as the seventh of a V^7 of IV, the most common use of ♭$\hat{7}$ in the major mode. (Occasionally, it is also heard in a rather similar function, as the seventh of a VII^7 of II.) On the other hand, E♭ appears alongside the leading tone E♮, in most instances as a chromatically altered minor third of the dominant sonority, a chord juxtaposed with the diatonic major harmony. Both uses of the ♭$\hat{7}$ have characteristic expressive aspects: V^7 of IV retains the primary expression of the joyful, while the minor-mode dominant is associated with the tragic. I will argue, furthermore, that the first is associated with the acceptance of reality, the admission that death will not come (state 2 in table 10.1), while the second struggles to retain the illusion of death (state 1), a task that is ultimately futile. The tragic expression of the minor-mode dominant highlights the gloominess of this struggle.

The introduction features E♭ as part of a V^7 of IV and of a VII^7 of II (example 10.2b), so that E♭ is first heard in the form referring to reality (a function that will become apparent only later). The piano thus seems to be aware of the reality before the protagonist (or at least before he admits what is real). As so often in *Winterreise*, the introduction seems to refer to a reality that the protagonist then challenges. In the introduction the reality, namely, the continuation of the journey, also appears in a somewhat imitative manner. The anticipated four-bar unit is expanded into a five-measure phrase, so the introduction has to continue past the goal that was initially assumed. The impression is very close to the protagonist's words in the poem's final stanza, where he observes that the journey must continue. This five-measure phrase is not initially expected, hence, the surprised local expressive quality in mm. 4–5 that foretells the song's outcome.

E♭ is heard for the first time in the main body of the song in m. 6, where it transforms the dominant chord into a minor sonority (understood retrospectively as IV of G minor). It simultaneously touches on the tragic expression, which is further stressed in m. 7 by the tonicized G-minor sonority (a predominant II). (When this progression is repeated in m. 12, E♭ is even more emphatic, owing to its high register.) Now that the singer has joined in, the motivic E♭ occurs in the form that refers to the struggle to find death, to the illusion prevailing at the poem's beginning, here set to music. The tragic expression introduced by the pitch is in turn associated with the impossibility of getting a room at the inn, that is, a resting place in the cemetery.

The second occurrence of E♭ in m. 9 combines, as it were, the two guises of this pitch (example 10.2b). Locally, the chord functions as a V_2^4 of IV, which is resolved to a IV^6 on the second eighth note of the measure. It thus refers to reality. More globally, E♭ occurs within a prolonged dominant; the characteristic E♮–E♭ progression, associated in m. 6 with the minor-mode dominant, is present, even though the V♭ itself is not. As a result, the illusion of death is alluded to indirectly. This duality reflects the duality in the poem. In the text set in mm. 8–9, the protagonist observes that he will take lodgings at the cemetery. There is thus a contrast between the real environment (the cemetery, which ultimately provides no rest) and the protagonist's inner thoughts ("Hab' ich bei mir gedacht" [I thought to myself]). Of these, the cemetery is primary; likewise, in the music, the prolonged V is the principal sonority.

The pitch E♭ as part of a V^7 of IV is kept active in the short piano interludes of mm. 10–11 and 16–17, which recall the first instance of this note in the song. Thus, the references to reality prevail in the music. This function is highlighted in the song's third part, mm. 18–22, where the significance of E♭ as part of the V^7 of IV is emphasized by the omission of the octave, the consonant point of origin from which the seventh descends (example 10.3b). The poem's third stanza, set in these measures, is crucial for the overall narrative. It is here that the protagonist asks (in the stanza's first two lines) if all the rooms are taken, then argues (in the last two lines) that he should be allowed to stay. In other words, in the underlying structure, the stanza represents the transformation indicated in table 10.1 by the double-line arrow. Likewise, it is here that the form of E♭ referring to reality is heard for the first time, and powerfully, in the main body of the song.

The protagonist attempts even now to resist reality, as is conveyed by the progression leading to the song's third part. On the surface, the seventh chord in m. 18 is preceded by a back-relating dominant. These two chords are not structurally connected through prolongation, but their succession directly juxtaposes E♮ and E♭. The E♭ of m. 18 therefore retains a trace of the E♮–E♭ progression, a challenge to reality, even though the function of the chord is unequivocally tonic with an added seventh (or a V^7 of IV), a reference to reality. The formal similarity of the text to the music in mm. 18–22 underlines the musico-poetic association: the division of the poem's third stanza into a two-line question and a two-line plea, both of which remain semantically open, is reflected in the music's division into two declamatory subphrases, both ending in tonally open, back-relating dominants (example 10.3). The tragic shades of the second subphrase underline the emotional tone of the protagonist's plea.

In the fourth stanza, heard in the music's third part (mm. 23–28), the protagonist must accept that his journey does not end here, that the cemetery provides no rest. This unwelcome conclusion is reflected in the music's tragic expression. The idea of the journey simply continuing onward is conveyed by the repetition of the poem's significant last two lines. The impression of continuation is further highlighted by the musical parentheses. The first tonic chord in m. 26, which is heard within the parentheses, is not yet conclusive, so the tonal goal is not achieved here. Rather, the music must continue to seek its goal, much as the wanderer must utter the final lines twice and go on with his apparently unending journey.

In the song's third part, the poem's emotional climax (the fourth stanza) coincides with the music's dramatic high point, as well as with the most powerful appearance of the motivically significant E♭. Now the protagonist asks if he will indeed be rejected, and he ultimately accepts his fate. E♭ is heard in the form referring to illusion, as the third of the minor-mode dominant. As the staff above the voice-leading sketch of example 10.4b indicates, the tension between E♭ and E♮ is acute. Much as the protagonist tries to convince the inn to give him lodging, E♭ attempts to displace the diatonic E♮. But both attempts are ultimately futile. In the poem, the protagonist does not find peace but must continue his journey, while in the music, E♮ and a major-mode dominant ultimately replace E♭ and the C-minor triad.

The acceptance of the unavoidable reality is a more nuanced process in the music than in the poem. In the latter, the protagonist simply states that he must continue the journey. In the music, on the other hand, the difficulty in accepting his fate is clearly audible. The repetition of the poem's last two lines and the musical parentheses suggest that the acceptance is indeed a process, not an instantaneous event. Motivically, the struggle between E♭ and E♮ underlines the difficulty in reaching acceptance, because the first time E♮ appears to overcome E♭ (m. 26) turns out to be a premature resolution of the tension: E♭ returns in m. 27, after the parentheses, so the struggle continues.

Yet m. 26 contains the seeds of acceptance. At an immediate level, the measure has the same sonority that will eventually close the global structure, suggesting the primacy of state 2 in table 10.1. More indirectly, the cadential figuration of m. 26 recalls m. 9, where the two guises of E♭ are presented at the same time. It is as if the return of this figuration at the very moment the protagonist consciously recognizes the unavoidable continuation of the journey suggests that he has been aware of the outcome all along. In the structurally conclusive cadence (m. 28), E♭ returns, this time as part of a secondary dominant of the supertonic; it is resolved to D when II⁶ arrives (example 10.4b). Thus, the guise of the motivic pitch, which is associated with reality, returns just as the closure of the background structure is set to arrive, poetically sealing the reality and the journey's continuation. E♭ is still heard twice in the coda, both times as part of a secondary dominant of a predominant, that is, in the form referring to reality. No traces of the E♭–E♮ conflict appear in the coda, much as no trace of the illusion remains at the end of the poem.

"Das Wirtshaus" is an important song in *Winterreise*. The preceding song, "Der Wegweiser," was a culmination of a process in which the protagonist gradually prepared himself to declare his determination to seek death. "Das Wirtshaus," however, provides a frustrating conclusion to this desire: there are no rooms at the inn; the death so desired does not come. This association between "Der Wegweiser" and "Das Wirtshaus" is enhanced by the significance of the common motivic element, an E♭ that either descends to D or is related to E♮. But the motive functions differently in each song, drawing a musical parallel to the poetic notion of the initially emerging hope for death and the frustration that arises from not fulfilling this hope. In "Der Wegweiser" the E♭–D motion is part of the underlying tonal framework, thus operating within the tonic key or the reality of the song, so to speak, whereas in "Das Wirtshaus" the motion is an embellishing gesture and accordingly does not occur in the diatony of the song, that is, within its tonal reality.

The remaining three songs of *Winterreise* reflect on the frustration arising from not fulfilling the death wish. Their widely diverging reactions will be examined in the last analytical chapter.

11 Reflecting on the Inability to Find Death: "Mut," "Die Nebensonnen," and "Der Leiermann"

The last three songs of *Winterreise* show the protagonist reflecting on the situation in "Das Wirtshaus," where death, consciously chosen in "Der Wegweiser," eluded him. This final analytical chapter traces the various forms taken by the protagonist's frustration in these closing songs.

11.1. "Mut"

"Mut" directly juxtaposes the tragic and a rather exuberant, joyful expression; many of the phrases begin in the minor mode but end in major. Extended repetitions shape the song's course; this is immediately evident in mm. 1–36, which sound the same music twice (in mm. 1–18 and 19–36; a repeat sign replaces the written-out repetition in example 11.1).[1] Formally, the material that is repeated consists of an introduction (mm. 1–4 and 19–22) and the first main part of the song, shown by a boxed number in example 11.1 (mm. 5–18 and 23–36). The second part (also a boxed number in example 11.1) likewise includes large-scale repetition, which divides the part into two phases, the first of which occurs in mm. 37–48. The second phase (mm. 49–60) begins as if it were going to repeat the first an octave higher. There are changes, however, the most significant being a tonicization of B♭ major in mm. 51–54 (not heard in the first phase), after which the music resumes its earlier course.[2] The closing coda (mm. 61–64) consists of exactly the same music as the introduction.

In the main body of the song (from which the introduction and coda have been excluded), there are four perfect authentic cadences in the tonic key, closures whose significance is enhanced by the immediate repetition of each: mm. 15–16 (repeated in mm. 17–18), mm. 33–34 (repeated in mm. 35–36), mm. 45–46 (repeated in mm. 47–48), and mm. 57–58 (repeated in mm. 59–60). The first two cadences close the repeated units of the first part, while the last two cadences close the two phases of the second part. The four cadences are related to the tension permeating the song, which grows out of the juxtaposition of minor, the primary mode, and the contrasting major. Each of the four cadences ends in a

⌐ = B♭–A–G ; ✻ = B♭ / B♮

| | 1 | 5 7 12 14 | 16 | 37 38 | 45 46 | 49 50 | 51 55 56 | 57 58 | 61 |
| | 19 | 23 25 30 32 | 34 | 43 44 | | | | | |

$\hat{3}$ — $\hat{2}$ — $\hat{1}$

$\begin{matrix}5\text{———}♭6\text{—}5\\ \#\text{———}♮\text{—}\#\end{matrix}$

I♭ ———————— ♮   V   I♮   V   I♮—♭

Form:	intro.	1		2				coda
Expressive genre:	tragic	tragic vs. joyful		joyful		joyful (mingled with tragic)		tragic
Expressive quality:	declamatory	uncertain vs. confirming		rejoicing		uncertain	confirming	declamatory
Dramatic curve:								high point
Textual structure:	(S ∪ O)	(S ∪ O) vs. (S ∩ O)						(S ∪ O)

Example 11.1. "Mut," an overview.

major-mode tonic. Yet they all close a structural unit that starts in the minor, with third-progressions descending from the *Kopfton* B♭ heard at the song's outset (example 11.1; the brackets indicate the third-progressions).

The third-progressions concretize the tension between minor and major: when their concluding 1̂s arrive, the opening top-voice B♭ (a minor third) has been replaced by inner-voice B♮s (a major third). The concluding major sonorities are given further emphasis by the immediate cadential repetitions. The third-progressions are nested, each one spanning a larger musical unit than the previous, the largest ultimately constituting the *Urlinie*. (Since the song's first part consists of a repetition of the same music, this is shown only once in example 11.1.) As a result, there is an impression of a four-part trajectory that attempts to transform the opening minor chord into a major sonority, each unit of this trajectory being more extended than the last. The replacement of the minor-mode tonic with a major sonority is further enhanced by the dominant chord that begins the song's second part. There is therefore no structural minor-mode tonic at all in this part, so the music might imply that the major ultimately outweighs the minor. But it does not. The coda repeats the music of the introduction, ending in a minor-mode tonic whose top voice 1̂ closes a third-progression descending from B♭ (see the brackets in example 11.1). The coda thus indicates that when the song ends, we are back where we started, inescapably in minor. This denial of the attempts to displace the minor can be understood as the song's high point, a moment that nullifies the music's previous aspirations.

The juxtaposition of minor and major defines the song's expressive genre (example 11.1). After the tragic introduction, the tragic and joyful are juxtaposed in the song's first part, which consists of two phrases (mm. 5–11 and 12–18). The first ends on a back-relating dominant, a tonicized major-mode dominant, while the second closes in the first of the song's perfect authentic cadences in the tonic major. Both phrases thus include mixture, a move from the minor diatony to major. The song's second part, on the other hand, is almost exclusively dominated by the joyful and the major mode, with only one fleeting reference to the tragic and minor, in m. 50. But this fleeting minor-mode coloration considerably affects the music's subsequent course; the pitch B♭, the signal for the minor, is later tonicized in mm. 51–54, so it now appears in a joyful major-mode environment.

The song's overall expression aligns with its structural course. As the third-progressions descending from the opening 3̂ (B♭) become more extended, the significance of the opening tragic weakens (with the exception of the brief allusion to the tragic in m. 50). In other words, as the major-mode tonics that close the third-progressions are temporally further removed from the opening minor-mode tonic, the recollection of the initial tragic becomes fainter. The local expressive quality, in turn, moves along with the phrase structure (example 11.1). In the song's first part, all phrases begin in minor and with a somewhat uncertain expressive quality, as if asking a question. But they all end in a major-mode cadence and with a confirming expression. Thus, the certainty of the major locally denies the uncertainty of the minor. The second part then begins without any hint of minor, and the expressive quality is one of rejoicing. The minor colorations of mm. 50 ff. bring back the uncertainty, but this hesitancy is soon displaced by the confirming expression of the final, structural cadence. Yet the minor ultimately has the upper hand, the structural major-mode closure notwithstanding: the coda conclusively and unavoidably reconfirms the minor and the tragic with a declamatory expression, so the song ends without any traces of the joyful.

The significance of the major mode can also be seen in the music's motivic material. Throughout, B♮ occurs as a neighbor note above A (see the staff above the graph in example 11.1). As a result, in the local motivic design the initial indicator of the tragic (the *Kopfton* ♭3̂) is replaced by the chromatic variant of the same scale degree that now refers to the joyful (♮3̂). But B♮ is a decorative element every time; it never prolongs the minor-mode *Kopfton* or displaces it structurally. Also, the only reference to the tragic in the song's second part is related to this motivic network. In m. 50 the neighbor note above A is the minor-mode B♭ for the first time, and, consequently, the embellishing neighboring chord is a G-minor sonority. But the music immediately denies the tragic implications of the top-voice B♭. This pitch occurs again as a neighbor note in mm. 51–54 (with greater structural emphasis), but this time as the top voice of a tonicized B♭-major chord. Hence, a major sonority now supports it within a joyful expression. It is as if the music attempted, in mm. 50–54, to resist the tragic expression of B♭ that has governed since the song's beginning. But ultimately this expression cannot be avoided, and B♭ is again heard in the coda, this time an unequivocally tragic expression.

Mut

Fliegt der Schnee mir in's Gesicht,
Schüttl' ich ihn herunter.
Wenn mein Herz im Busen spricht,
Sing' ich hell und munter.

Höre nicht, was es mir sagt,
Habe keine Ohren.
Fühle nicht, was es mir klagt,
Klagen ist für Toren.

Lustig in die Welt hinein
Gegen Wind und Wetter!
Will kein Gott auf Erden sein,
Sind wir selber Götter!

Courage

When the snow flies in my face, I shake it off. When my heart speaks in my breast, I sing loudly and gaily.

I do not hear what it says; I have no ears. I do not feel its laments; lamenting is for fools.

Merrily out into the world, against wind and weather! If there is no God on earth, then we ourselves are gods!

The text of "Mut" reflects the protagonist's frustration that, in "Das Wirtshaus," death eluded him. Now he tries to refute the devastating reality he has just faced. The poem consists of three stanzas. The first includes two two-line units whose odd-numbered lines 1 and 3 state a real situation (snow in the wanderer's face and his heart speaking to him), whereas the even-numbered lines 2 and 4 deny the reality. The second stanza again juxtaposes even and odd lines, continuing to elaborate on the denial of the heart's message or the protagonist's feelings. The speaker refuses to hear what the heart says and declares that lamentation is for fools. The third and final stanza takes the next step: now the speaker claims to be cheerful, not caring about reality, denying even the existence of God. But this cheerfulness, of course, is only on the surface; underneath, the protagonist has been forced to confront yet another disappointment on his long journey, a disappointment that cannot be so easily ignored.

Table 11.1a formalizes the poem's underlying opposition. On the one hand, there is reality, state 1, in which the subject (the protagonist) and the object (the escape from reality) are disjoined. In other words, the reality (snow and despair) cannot be avoided. On the other hand, there is illusion, state 2, where reality has been denied; S and O are therefore conjoined. In the poem, the protagonist

Table 11.1. "Mut," underlying structure of the poem

a. Structural opposition

state 1		state 2
reality		illusion
cannot be denied		attempts to confirm
(S ∪ O)	vs.	(S ∩ O)

b. Underlying static state

(S ∪ O)

Actant	Reference
S	the protagonist
O	escape from reality

claims to have established state 2, denial of reality, but in fact he has not, as indicated by the primary static state underlying the poem (table 11.1b).

The poem's juxtaposition of two states draws clear parallels to the music's juxtaposition of minor and major (see the textual structure shown in example 11.1). The primary state of minor refers to the main state 1, while the embellishing major refers to the secondary state 2. In the poem the protagonist's rhetoric gradually becomes more intense, a feature also reflected in the music. The first stanza admits that the snow and the wanderer's emotions are real (the snow is shaken off, and the sounds of the heart are drowned out by loud singing). In the second stanza, the heart's emotions are again mentioned, but the speaker immediately claims that he does not pay them any attention. This opposition of first exposing and then denying reality is reflected in the phrase structure, expressive quality, and modal mixture in the song's first part. Lines 1 and 3 of the first two stanzas (state 1) are set in minor (mm. 5–7, 12–14, 23–25, and 30–32), and in these measures the expressive quality is uncertain. Lines 2 and 4 (state 2), on the other hand, are set in major (mm. 8–9, 15–16, 26–27, and 33–34), and now the expression is confirming. Furthermore, in these measures the neighbor note B♮ is heard as an embellishing element. The music thus attempts, in quite a concrete manner, to deny the minor and B♭ and confirm the major, just as the poem tries to escape reality.

In the third stanza, set in the song's second part, the heart's emotions are no longer mentioned. Likewise, the minor mode does not appear in the music (except in m. 50, to be discussed presently). The strong cadence in m. 46 could well end the background structure, and this is indeed what one initially expects when m. 49 begins to repeat both the music and the text of mm. 37 ff. It is as if the protagonist attempts to convince himself that the cheerfulness he is asserting is justified. But it is not: reality shows itself in the brief minor-mode hints and a glimpse of the tragic in m. 50, the suggestion of the primacy of state 1 in table

11.1a. Yet the significance of the minor mode (and state 1 of the poem) is still denied, and in mm. 51–54 the music reinterprets the B♭ as the top voice of a joyful major sonority, much as the protagonist repeats the apparently cheerful final
stanza describing state 2. But the major mode, the joyful, and state 2 are all secondary, and the song closes with the minor-mode coda in which B♭ recalls the
Kopfton 3̂. The coda's perfect authentic cadence in minor ultimately confirms the
song's tonal reality, at the same time indicating that the wanderer's cheerfulness
was only an illusion.

11.2. "Die Nebensonnen"

After "Mut," the character of the cycle again drastically changes with
the slow "Die Nebensonnen." The song is in ternary form (A¹–B–A²) with only
minimal thematic material: the A sections repeat the introduction's four-bar
phrase, and this same thematic material also governs the B section's mm. 20–23.
The A¹ section consists of two phrases (mm. 5–8 and 10–13), of which the latter
is emphasized by VI prolonged in mm. 10–12 (example 11.2). This VI ties the A¹
section's two phrases into one harmonic I–VI–V–I progression. At the beginning
of the B section, the tonic chord is transformed into a minor sonority, a change
that alters the expressive genre from the joyful to the tragic (example 11.2).[3] In
m. 20 a C-major chord (♮III) is tonicized, hinting again at the joyful expression
but within the locally governing minor-mode diatony. The dominant closing the
first branch of the interrupted background structure arrives in m. 25, so the ♮III
functions as a third that subdivides the fifth between I and V into two thirds. The
tragic expression is resumed in m. 22 when the minor-mode tonic key returns
(with the A-minor sonority of m. 22 functioning as an apparent rather than a
structural tonic, however). The brief A² section constitutes the second branch of
the interrupted structure, repeating once again the same thematic four-bar unit
heard in the introduction and sounded twice more in the A¹ section.

"Die Nebensonnen" recalls the chorale texture and the somewhat religious
quality of "Das Wirtshaus," the song preceding the outburst of "Mut." But the
melodic gestures are now shorter, leading to a somewhat different expressive
quality from the earlier song. Instead of the two-measure melodic gestures of
"Das Wirtshaus," "Die Nebensonnen" mostly consists of one-bar melodic seg-
ments (♩ | ♩ ♩ ♩.). Owing to the shorter gestures, the expressive quality, shown
in example 11.2, now combines the pious quality (the chorale texture) with more
active declamation (the one-bar melodic segments).

The B section has two kinds of texture. First, mm. 16–19 give up the sara-
bande-like rhythm, which has dominated so far, for two-bar thematic units,
which replace the previous one-bar segments. In the local expression, the larger
gestures and minor mode exemplify a lamenting quality (example 11.2). After
this, the initial texture returns in m. 20. This time, however, the harmonic environment is unstable, so the stability associated with the pious expression does not
return; only the declamatory quality is left. This novel treatment of the governing

| | 3 | 5 | 7 | 10 | 13 | 16 | 20 | 22 | 23 | 25 | 26 | 29 |

$\hat{3}$ $\flat\hat{3}$ $\hat{2}$ ‖ $\hat{3}$ $\hat{2}$ $\hat{1}$

I   (VI   V   I)   I♮   ♮III   V ‖   I   V   I

Form:	intro.	A^1		B		A^2		+ coda
Expressive genre:	joyful			tragic (mingled with joyful)		joyful		
Expressive quality:	pious / declamatory			lamenting	declamatory	pious / declamatory		
Dramatic curve:					high point			
Textual structure:		$(Sr_1 \rightarrow R)$ vs.		$(Sr_2 \rightarrow O_1 \rightarrow R)$		$\Rightarrow (Sr_3 \rightarrow O_2 \rightarrow R)$		

Example 11.2. "Die Nebensonnen," an overview.

thematic idea, together with the increase in intensity, highlights the passage; accordingly, the song's high point appears here. With the return of A major and the opening thematic material in the A^2 section, the combination of the pious and declamatory expressive qualities returns.

Die Nebensonnen

Drei Sonnen sah' ich am Himmel stehn,
Hab' lang und fest sie angesehn;
Und sie auch standen da so stier,
Als wollten sie nicht weg von mir.
[5] Ach, meine Sonnen seid ihr nicht!
Schaut andern doch in's Angesicht!
[7] Ach, neulich hatt' ich auch wohl drei:
Nun sind hinab die besten zwei.
[9] Ging' nur die dritt' erst hinterdrein!
Im Dunkeln wird mir wohler sein.

Mock Suns

I saw three suns in the sky; I gazed at them long and hard. And they too stood there so fixedly, as if unwilling to leave me. [5] Ah, you are not my suns! Look into other people's faces! [7] Ah, recently I too had three suns; now the two best have set. [9] If only the third would follow! I would feel better in the dark.

The poem consists of ten lines that form one undivided entity; thus, there are no independent stanzas (hence, the identifying numbers have been added). The poem can be divided into three temporal planes. The first six lines describe the present: the protagonist is gazing at three suns, observing that they are not his. These lines move from neutral description (lines 1–4) to the tragic observation that the suns are not the speaker's (lines 5–6). Temporally, the next two lines (7–8) look back; the protagonist remarks that he too once had three suns, but the two best have set. At the same time, the three suns are given value: they are something positive; specifically, they are related to love.[4] That two of the wanderer's three suns have set indicates that his love has been lost. The three suns he sees are not his, so love is now for others, not for him. The last two lines (9–10) look to the future and express the hope that the last of the protagonist's suns will also set, thus releasing him from the memory of the three suns and the beloved. The setting of the final sun refers to darkness and, at least indirectly, to the underlying theme of *Winterreise*'s part 2, death. "Die Nebensonnen" can thus be seen to sum up, just before the end of the cycle, the wanderer's course: the gloomy present (lines 1–6), the happy past (lines 7–8), and the hope for a future released from misery (lines 9–10).

The poem's emotional course subdivides the ten lines in a manner that differs slightly from this temporal division. The first four lines are a neutral description of the present, the three suns. The next four (lines 5–8) express mourning, both because the three suns are not the speaker's (lines 5–6) and because the protagonist has lost his own suns (lines 7–8). The last two lines represent hope for the future.

Table 11.2 shows the poem's underlying structure, which I interpret as consisting of two states. The first juxtaposes present and past: on the one hand, there are the three suns at which the protagonist gazes; on the other hand, there are the three suns he once had. The suns are interpreted in the poem as various guises of the actant sender; that is, they function as a source of information. The present suns (Sr_1) are given value only when they are compared to the former suns the wanderer once had (Sr_2); therefore, Sr_1 and Sr_2 are interpreted as taking place within one larger state. This value is positive: the suns refer to love, interpreted as O_1, the first form of illusion contemplated by the speaker throughout *Winterreise*. In the second state, the hoped-for setting of all three of the wanderer's suns (Sr_3) would bring peace, so Sr_3 is interpreted as death, the second form of illusion prevailing in the cycle.

The formal outlines of the music follow the poem's emotional course, discussed above, which divides the text into 4 + 4 + 2 lines. The A^1 section sets the first four lines, which describe the three suns (Sr_1). The B section sets the

Table 11.2. "Die Nebensonnen," underlying structure of the poem

state 1			state 2
present	past		future
	illusion		illusion
negative	positive		positive
$(Sr_1 \rightarrow R)$	vs.	$(Sr_2 \rightarrow O_1 \rightarrow R)$ $\Rightarrow$	$(Sr_3 \rightarrow O_2 \rightarrow R)$

Actant	Reference
Sr_1	the three suns at which the protagonist gazes
Sr_2	the protagonist's three past suns
Sr_3	the protagonist's suns, all of which have set
R	the protagonist
O_1	love
O_2	death

next four lines, which introduce sadness. The content divides lines 5–8 into two two-line units. In lines 5–6 the protagonist remarks that the three suns are not his; the tragic is expressed in the poem for the first time. At the same time, the major-mode tonic is transformed into a minor sonority, transforming the music's expression from joyful to tragic. The music's expressive quality is here one of lamenting, an apt way to reflect the speaker's emotions. In lines 7–8 the protagonist first observes that he too once had three suns (Sr_2), but he has lost the two most valuable.

The music's major/minor juxtaposition subtly reflects the poetic duality between joyful memory and gloomy present. When the protagonist mentions his former suns in mm. 20–21, Sr_2, the music is in the tonicized C major, in the joyful expression. But the C-major chord takes place in the underlying A-minor diatony of the B section, functioning as a ♮III, so the expression of the major chord is conditioned by its minor-mode context (example 11.2). Likewise, in the poem, the recollection of the joyful past takes place within the tragic present. The tragic expression and the A-minor key area return in m. 22; when the speaker says that he has lost the two best suns, he turns from past recollections to the present. The significance of mm. 20–25 as a juxtaposition of the wanderer's joyful past with the gloomy present is enhanced by the song's dramatic high point occurring here. The concluding A^2 section returns to the primary A major. Here, the protagonist turns his gaze, as he does so often in part 2 of *Winterreise,* to the future, hoping to find there darkness and death. The hope that the final sun (Sr_3) will set is reflected in the music's joyful expression, which Yonatan Malin has described as "redemptive" (2010, 108).

The song's local expressive quality underlines this trajectory. The chorale-like texture and pious quality associate the song's beginning with "Das Wirtshaus," in which the wanderer hoped to experience a dignified death. Now, however, the pious expressive quality is merged with the declamatory texture; as the speaker knows that his decision to seek out death did not lead to the hoped-for conclusion, his statements are more heavily underlined rhetorically. After the lament in the B section, where the repeated word *ach* reflects the intensity of the protagonist's emotions, the initial expression returns with the onset of the A^2 section.[5] Now the speaker once more turns his gaze to the future, and the combination of pious and declamatory qualities conveys that he is still yearning for a dignified death. The intensity of his desire is underlined by the declamatory expressive quality.

One may argue, somewhat speculatively, that the suns are referred to in the song in an indirectly imitative manner. As we have seen, the introduction and the A sections repeat the same four-bar thematic idea several times, and this motivic material is referred to as well in mm. 20–23 of the B section. At the beginning, the thematic idea is heard exactly three times (mm. 1–4, 5–8, and 10–13), perhaps reflecting the three suns mentioned in the A^1 section. The same idea is heard in mm. 20–23 when the protagonist recalls his past three suns. But two of them have set, leaving only one; consequently, the thematic idea is heard only once. The one sun is still referred to in the A^2 section, where the music sounds the thematic idea once. In other words, the number of repetitions of the four-bar thematic idea, which permeates most of the song, reflects the number of suns spoken about in the poem. The coda repeats the same thematic material, suggesting that the third sun has not set, as the protagonist had hoped. At the song's end, state 2 in table 11.2 remains an illusion. The song's repetitive thematic material thus has musico-poetic significance.

11.3. "Der Leiermann"

"Der Leiermann," the final song of *Winterreise,* is one of the cycle's strangest. The musical material is sparse and repetitive; most notably, the piano's bass part consists of a drone, an open fifth A–E, in every single bar. The song has two strophes that repeat the same music (mm. 9–30 and 31–52).[6] This main body is framed by an introduction (mm. 1–8) and a coda (mm. 53–61).

The harmonic events are also severely limited: the entire piece consists of alternating tonic and dominant harmonies above the drone (example 11.3). The dominant appears in two guises, both heard in the introduction, either as a back-relating dominant (mm. 4 and 5) or as a harmony resolved to the tonic (mm. 7 and 8). These two guises underlie two motivically significant gestures (usually spanning two bars), which dominate most of the song (see the staff above the graph in example 11.3). On the one hand, there is a C–B motion in which the back-relating dominant supports the B of a local interruption-like structure. (Strictly speaking, there is no actual interruption, since A is constantly in the bass.) On the other hand, there is a third-progression C–B–A, whose concluding B–A motion is supported by a V–I progression (again with A as a pedal in the bass). Significantly, the closing A of this third-progression is only implied, since A consistently appears only in an inner voice. (The one exception occurs at the

$\sqcap$ = C–B ; $\overset{\frown}{\sqcap}$ = C–B–A

3 4 6 7	9 11 13	19	21	23 24	25 29			53	56	60 61			

$\hat{3}$ ⌐ ⌐ ⌐ 15 17 $\hat{3}$ $\hat{2}$ $\hat{1}$

mm. 31–52 = mm. 9–30

Form:	intro.	1		2	coda
Expressive genre:	tragic				
Expressive quality:	numb / yearning				
Dramatic curve:		(no high point)			
Textual structure:		(S → O → R)	⇒	(S ∪ O)	

Example 11.3. "Der Leiermann," an overview.

very end of the song.) The avoidance of the closing A, the $\hat{1}$ in the tonic key, creates an unfulfilled quality. Yet the song does not avoid a top-voice A altogether; the pitch is heard emphatically in the top voice in mm. 25–26 (and in the repetition in mm. 47–48), but it provides no sense of completion, prolonging the previously implied A rather than completing a middleground third-progression from C above (example 11.3).

All of these features create two intertwined qualities characteristic of this strange song: on the one hand, the music gives a clearly static impression, the sense of immobility resulting from the repetitive thematic and harmonic material and the drone; on the other hand, there is a feeling of incompleteness, because the music arrives at no strong closures or conclusions until the very end. This incompleteness primarily results from the back-relating dominants, which leave the harmonic situation unresolved, and the avoidance of top-voice A's that would complete the third-progressions descending from C. Together, these two features affect the song's expression (example 11.3). The sense of motionlessness throughout unites a tragic expression with a local quality of numbness, an outcome of the inability to escape the drone. And owing to the avoidance of a strong, upper-voice $\hat{1}$ until the very end, numbness is combined with yearning.

The coda brings a slight intensification, yet without displacing the numbness. Now A is established clearly as a top-voice pitch in mm. 53–55. But in these bars A prolongs an implied pitch that is reached in the main body of the song, so it

Reflecting on the Inability to Find Death 151

does not complete the C–B–A progression to provide structural closure by displacing the C, which has dominated so far (example 11.3). Indeed, C is again reached in m. 56, but this time only in the piano part; here the singer has e^2, an embellishing pitch not belonging to the underlying C–A framework. This is the singer's final note, so he ends outside the primary C–A third. The vocal line thus fails to achieve closure, and the yearning quality remains. The last two bars in the piano part are significant, since now the music suggests, for the only time in the song, a sense of completion: for once, in m. 61, the top-voice third-progression arrives in the foreground on A. Thus, in mm. 56–61 there is a $\hat{3}$–$\hat{2}$–$\hat{1}$ motion, the *Urlinie* of the song (if one wants to say that there is one). As a result, the very end of the song finally provides a sense of closure and fulfillment after the stasis and feeling of incompleteness that have prevailed up to this point. But the sense of closure is the weakest conceivable: it takes place after the singer has said all he has to say, and the $\hat{2}$ is not supported by a dominant pitch in the bass. Structural closure thus arrives without providing a true sense of resolution.

Der Leiermann

Drüben hinter'm Dorfe
Steht ein Leiermann,
Und mit starren Fingern
Dreht er was er kann.

Barfuß auf dem Eise
Wankt er hin und her;
Und sein kleiner Teller
Bleibt ihm immer leer.

Keiner mag ihn hören,
Keiner sieht ihn an;
Und die Hunde knurren
Um den alten Mann.

Und er läßt es gehen
Alles, wie es will,
Dreht, und seine Leier
Steht ihm nimmer still.

Wunderlicher Alter,
Soll ich mit dir gehn?
Willst zu meinen Liedern
Deine Leier drehn?

The Hurdy-Gurdy Man

Over there, beyond the village, stands a hurdy-gurdy man, and with numb fingers he plays as best he can.

Barefoot on the ice, he totters here and there, and his little plate always remains bare.

No one wants to listen to him, no one looks at him, and the dogs growl around the old man.

And he lets everything go on, as it will; he turns, and his hurdy-gurdy is never still.

Strange old man, shall I go with you? Will you play your hurdy-gurdy to my song?

The poem consists of five stanzas subdivided as 4 + 1. The first four describe an old man, a beggar, playing a hurdy-gurdy. He pays no attention to his environment, nor does anyone take notice of him. He is outside the human community; only the dogs growl around him. The old man seems to be untouched by all human emotions, either positive or negative. He just plays his hurdy-gurdy, apparently perpetually, without any contact with what goes on around him. Even though it is not stated directly, the protagonist is the witness who makes these observations. In the poem's final stanza, the speaker becomes active, asking if he may join the old man.

Table 11.3 shows the underlying structure of the poem, which consists of two states. The former spans the first four stanzas. In this state the old man is interpreted as the sender, while the protagonist is the receiver. In other words, the protagonist (S) is observing the old man (Sr), thereby receiving information. The old man's numb state seems desirable to the protagonist at this stage in his journey; it is a state in which misery is no longer felt. Thus, table 11.3 indicates that Sr defines O: the old man exhibits a state without pain. In the final stanza the protagonist declares a desire to reach such a state himself. So the poem moves from the protagonist observing the old man and his state ($present_1$) to the protagonist expressing the wish to achieve a similar state ($present_2$). But he does not reach this goal in the poem; instead, he simply asks if it could be achieved, so subject and object are disjoined in the second state in table 11.3.

The old man's numb state differs markedly from the rather dignified death the protagonist contemplated earlier, particularly in "Das Wirtshaus"; this numbness is mundane and ungraceful. But since a dignified and somewhat religious death

Table 11.3. "Der Leiermann," underlying structure of the poem

state 1		state 2
$present_1$		$present_2$
$(Sr \rightarrow O \rightarrow R)$	$\Rightarrow$	$(S \cup O)$

Actant	Reference
Sr	the hurdy-gurdy man
R	the protagonist
O	a state without misery
S	the protagonist

was not attained in "Das Wirtshaus," the speaker is content even with such an in-elegant state of peacefulness; he is ready to accept any conclusion that would free him from his constant pain and misery. Yet, in the end the poem provides no resolution: it closes with the wanderer asking questions but receiving no answers. Even this miserable, wished-for state remains an illusion, and the subject is once again disjoined from the object.

The song's A–E drone forms an obvious instance of imitation: it mimics the sound of a hurdy-gurdy. The repetition of the drone in every measure refers in turn to the fact that the old man's hurdy-gurdy is never still. More indirectly, the almost complete lack of harmonic activity and the repetitive thematic and mo-tivic material can be seen as imitating the old man's static and numb state, which seems, in some sense, to stand outside of time—the state the protagonist ulti-mately wishes to reach as well.

In addition to imitation, the poem's structure seems to be reflected in the music. As table 11.3 shows, state 1 of the poem's underlying structure defines the object, something to which the subject attaches value, whereas state 2 indicates that the subject remains disjoined from the object. The motivic material shown on the staff above the graph in example 11.3 can be associated with the object and the attempts to reach it. The top voice tries over and over again to descend from C to A without success: either the progression is interrupted (leading only to B), or the concluding A is omitted on the surface (replaced by an E). In other words, both the poem and the music define an object (a peaceful state and a third-pro-gression, respectively) that is contemplated but not realized. Yet in mm. 25–26 and 47–48 the music features an emphatic top-voice A, only it does not com-plement the third-progression. We can understand this A as referring to the in-creasing clarity with which the object is defined in the first state in table 11.3; in other words, both the poem and the music clarify the goal (O in the poetic structure and A as the explicitly stated goal of a third-progression in the music) without reaching it.

In the coda mm. 53–58 set the poem's significant fifth stanza, where the pro-tagonist asks if he can join the old man (state 2 in table 11.3). Mm. 53–55, in which the protagonist asks the first of his two questions, directly refer to aspects of the incomplete third-progressions in the main body of the song, a musical factor associated above with the poem's object. In m. 53 the singer begins on e^1, the pitch which earlier replaced A, the goal note of the incomplete third-pro-gressions. Now A appears, fleetingly at first in m. 53 and then more stably in m. 55, when the question is completed. In the turn of mm. 54 and 55, there is even a small embellishing third-progression C–B–A, a recollection of the music's counterpart to the poem's object. In effect, the musical elements associated with the poetic object surface when the protagonist ventures to ask the first of his con-cluding questions. But S and O remain disjoined in the poem's second state (table 11.3). Similarly, this A prolongs the pitch arrived at in the main body of the song (although it is only implied there), so it does not complement the third-progres-sion associated with the object. The disjunction of S and O becomes even clearer with the second question (mm. 56–58), in which A is not present at all; rather, the singer's line centers on E (both e^1 and e^2). Poetically, the object is not attained, much as the music is unable to secure A as the conclusion of its third-progression.

The song's final measures feature a clear third-progression, but only after the singer's part has ended. The interpretation of the poetic function of this structural closure is complex. It can be given a purely musical interpretation. In Schubert's time a musical work was expected to have a clear cadential closure, and the $\hat{3}$–$\hat{2}$–$\hat{1}$ descent of mm. 60–61 provides a tonal closure, albeit a weak one. But in my view, such a reading should be complemented with a musico-poetic interpretation. One might argue that the completion of the third-progression only after the singer has ended his part could indicate that the object is beyond the reach of the subject, that the peace the protagonist seeks remains an illusion, even at the cycle's very end. Alternatively, the fact that the completion of the third-progression ultimately does arrive, providing a sense of closure not heard earlier, could be interpreted in a more positive light, suggesting that, after the protagonist has asked his final question, he gets the answer he hopes to hear. Both readings are possible. Since the end of the song gives us no definitive information, the interpretation ultimately depends on individual interpreters. Schubert's cycle thus closes with an undecidable musico-poetic situation, much as Müller's cycle ends in a question.

The three concluding songs of *Winterreise* provide no consolation for the wanderer. The denial of a dignified death and peace in "Das Wirtshaus" leads to an emotional outburst in "Mut," in which the wanderer wants to deny reality, a futile task. "Die Nebensonnen" reminds him of his journey, summing up the hapless present, the joyful past, and the hope of finding peace in the future. "Der Leiermann" is the last step. The speaker prefers the numb state of the old hurdy-gurdy man to his present misery—any state that would free him from his pain is preferable to the present. But neither the poem nor the song provides a true conclusion, and the wanderer is left in a state of uncertainty. His anguish thus prevails even at the moment the cycle ends.

Part 3. Cycle

12 The Song Cycle as a Genre: Some Recent Views

This chapter examines recent views of the song cycle, describing various perspectives on the issue of unity (or the lack thereof) suggested in the literature. My aim is to provide a general context for my interpretation of *Winterreise* as a cycle.

In section 2.1 I examined early nineteenth-century views of the emerging genre of the song cycle and demonstrated that the writers of the time almost unanimously based the unity of song cycles on poetic factors, with music usually playing no role in their assessments of a cycle's cohesion. In our time, the situation is different. At least in the Anglo-American literature, musical features are almost invariably commented on along with textual aspects whenever the unity of song cycles is discussed. The musical coherence is sought primarily in thematic and motivic cross-references, large-scale harmonic unfolding (connections among the keys of individual songs), or a combination of these. In order to give an overview of such approaches, I will describe some studies of song cycles in a general manner without relating their ideas to my own views just yet. As will become apparent in the next chapter, I do not share all the views represented in these writings, at least if applied to *Winterreise*. (A more general discussion of song cycles is outside the scope of this book.)[1]

The composer whose song cycles' unity has been most widely described (and at times denied, as will be seen) is Robert Schumann. For this reason, I will concentrate on the commentaries about his song cycles. Even though I concede that Schumann's cycles differ in various ways from Schubert's (including *Winterreise*), I still believe that today's analytical views of the song cycle can best be clarified by discussing the literature on Schumann; there is simply a larger body of thorough analytical (and methodological) literature addressing the issue of coherence in his song cycles than there is for Schubert. Yet first, a brief comment on the historical context of Schumann's cycles is in order.

When Schumann composed his song cycles in the 1840s, musical coherence and, most importantly, associations among the keys of a cycle's individual songs were increasingly being commented upon in published reviews (Turchin 1981, 224–30). A cycle's unity was no longer considered solely textual, as reviewers in Schubert's time had usually maintained. In addition, Schumann himself makes it clear that the Lieder of his day differed from those written earlier. In his review of Robert Franz's songs, op. 1, published in 1843, Schumann set forth the new aesthetic, based on a new kind of poetry: "Thus arose that more artistic and profound style of song of which earlier composers could of course know nothing, for it was due to the new spirit of poetry reflected in music." Indeed, Schumann went on to state that "perhaps the *Lied* is the only genre in which a remarkable improvement actually has occurred since Beethoven's time" (1983, 242). He also noted the role of Schubert's songs in paving the way to the new Lieder but maintained that Schubert had not achieved this new kind of song. The historical context in which Schumann composed his song cycles clearly differs from that of Schubert, the temporal proximity notwithstanding. But this historical difference does not mean that there should necessarily be methodological differences in discussing the inner organization of Schumann's and Schubert's song cycles. Indeed, the extended literature on Schumann's cycles provides useful background for discussing *Winterreise.*

In his study of Schumann's *Dichterliebe,* Arthur Komar (1971, 63–66) describes seven qualities that may unify a song cycle. Komar does not suggest that these should all be found in every unified cycle; rather, the qualities provide a framework for interpreting unity in a cycle. The first quality is a general one, while the next three deal with either motivic cross-references among individual songs or small-scale continuity between adjacent songs: (1) similarity of style in both the music and the poems of the songs; (2) similarity and cross-references among thematic, harmonic, and rhythmic figurations; (3) certain pitch configurations occurring untransposed in various songs; (4) the pairing of adjacent songs through motivic repetition or harmonic associations (e.g., a fifth relationship between the keys). These four qualities do not refer to all songs in any given cycle and thus do not address the topic of an overarching, global unity.

Komar's remaining three points directly address the overall organization of a song cycle: (5) the keys of the songs constitute a coherent key scheme; (6) there is a general plan that embraces all of the songs in their given order, providing a rationale for the ordering of nonadjacent songs; (7) a single key governs the entire work. In analyzing *Dichterliebe,* Komar (1971, 77–81) uses these overarching organizational principles to interpret key relationships. At the broadest level, he argues that the entire cycle is governed by one tonic, A major. In his view, the tonic of each song is related to this center, constituted by unified linear motions in the bass and depicted with a Schenkerian-oriented bass-graph extending through the entire cycle. More locally, the adjacent songs are associated, Komar argues, through recurring voice-leading procedures connecting their respective tonic chords.

Apart from the general first point and number 4 (which concentrates on associations between two adjacent songs only), Komar's statements can be grouped into two subcategories. On the one hand, points 2 and 3 refer to motivic and other associations among individual songs. This is a recurring feature in literature also more generally; motivic cross-references have played a significant role in many recent analyses of the unity of song cycles. Such cross-references are usually seen as creating associations among several songs of a cycle, although without providing a foundation for the logic of the overarching course of the whole. On the other hand, points 5, 6, and 7 refer specifically to the overall organization and attempt to explain the function played by each song, given its specific location within the cycle. Many analyses of song cycles have sought a basis for unity in the principles underlying the series of keys of the individual songs. Such studies do not necessarily suggest, as Komar does in his analysis, that prolongational hierarchy underlies the key connections; as will be seen, scholars have also sought harmonic unity in other organizing principles.

While Komar's discussion of motivic associations and overall harmonic unfolding as sources of unity is in accordance with much of the recent literature on this genre (although a variety of analytical approaches have been applied), his essay departs in one significant respect from the vast majority of studies: he pays practically no attention to the text. Usually, scholars look for interactions between a song cycle's poetic aspects and its musical features, often tracing associations between the overall courses of the two. David Neumeyer, for example, has stressed the significance of combining voice-leading and narrative viewpoints in discussing the unity of song cycles; he argues that "the combination of the harmonic-tonal with narrative-dramatic aspects should potentially allow an adequate interpretation of organic structure which either aspect alone could not achieve" (1982, 97).

In his essay on *Dichterliebe*, Berthold Hoeckner (2006) finds a close correspondence between the unfolding of the cycle's music (mainly large-scale harmony based on the keys of the songs) and the poems (the narrative trajectory). The poetic structure thus plays an important role in Hoeckner's analysis. Unlike Komar, Hoeckner does not seek harmonic unity in prolongational voice leading. Rather, he relates the chain of the songs' keys to a table of key relationships published in Gottfried Weber's *Theory of Musical Composition* (1846). The keys of adjacent songs follow Weber's table closely, with only small deviations. There is one large departure from this table, however: the move from the B♭ major of song no. 12 to the E♭ minor of no. 13, a motion that falls significantly downward in the table instead of moving step by step as the songs had done up to that point. Hoeckner finds this departure significant for both music and narrative: "This fall is a 'collapse' in the truest sense. . . . As such, it is a cornerstone of my analysis, a central piece in the puzzle of the interlocking tonal and narrative paths" (2006, 76). In other words, when tracing the parallel paths of the tonal course and the narrative trajectory, Hoeckner interprets song no. 13 as representing a significant turning point in both music and text.

Hoeckner's emphasis on one song from the perspective of both music and text (and to a lesser degree his emphasis on some other songs in the cycle) suggests a step beyond mere assessment of unity. He is not only claiming that both the music and the poems of *Dichterliebe* form unified wholes that proceed in tandem but also arguing that there are moments in the musical and poetic unfolding that function as turning points from the perspectives of both the music and the text. As these turning points emphasize certain events, they articulate dramatic arches, and thus Hoeckner discusses the cycle's dramatic nature in conjunction with its structural unity.

Patrick McCreless's (1986) study of Schumann's *Liederkreis,* op. 39, to poems by Joseph von Eichendorff, examines motivic cross-references among the songs together with the cycle's harmonic course (the keys of the songs) and poetic organization. McCreless argues that the poems of *Liederkreis* do not form a narrative trajectory but rather are connected through common imagery and symbolism. Yet he sees their order as significant; the affective relationships among the songs divide the cycle symmetrically into two groups of six poems. "Most of the songs of the first half project a *Stimmung* of happiness, while most in the second project one of 'grief and affliction.' . . . Furthermore, in each half there is a song of doubt or uncertainty" (1986, 12–13). In examining the cycle's tonal structure, McCreless is not referring to unity as an outcome of prolongational hierarchy (like Komar) or cyclical ordering of the keys (like Hoeckner). Rather, he is arguing that the tonal structure, like the poetic cycle, is symmetrical: "Not only are the first and last songs in the same key . . . but also the key sequence of the last three songs constitutes a retrograde of that of the first three" (15). As a result, McCreless argues, the symmetry forges a connection between the cycle's poetic unfolding and its tonal course.

Dividing the cycle into two parts, each consisting of six songs, McCreless also discusses the function of motives. At a general level, he makes a distinction between two types of motivic relationships: "unordered" and "ordered." Unordered relationships refer to cross-references generally; here the location in which the instances of the motives occur is not significant. Ordered ones, on the other hand, refer to motivic instances whose moment of occurrence is significant; in other words, when ordered motivic associations take place, it is not only the cross-references per se that are important but also their temporal placement. As a result, ordered motivic cross-references play a specific function in defining the organization of the whole. In a song cycle the ordered motivic relationships are "those that exhibit either a clear role in articulating the musical grouping of the songs— that is, relationships that delineate, say, symmetry or adjacency, beginning or closure—or a clear text-associative role" (McCreless, 1986, 14). McCreless argues that some of the motivic cross-references in *Liederkreis* are ordered, thereby articulating the cycle (along with the textual unfolding and the tonal structure) into two halves.[2]

Charles Rosen's (1995, 116–236) complex, extended, and thought-provoking discussion of the song cycle examines the genre within its historical context. But rather than seeking background in what was written in the early nineteenth century on song cycles or on songs more generally, Rosen begins by examining the function of landscape, nature, and memory in Romantic literature and painting. Specifically, he describes the function that past and present (or memory and perception) played in Romantic aesthetics. According to him, past and present were not mutually exclusive but simultaneously present. In other words, in looking at a landscape (or writing about it or painting it), the artist also understood the past that led to the present. The same notion of the coexistence of present and past (specifically memory), Rosen argues, governs Romantic song cycles; that is, they operate simultaneously on various time scales (as do Romantic poetry and landscape painting). Past and memory (and occasionally future) merge with the present in song cycles.[3]

In discussing those musical aspects that he sees as contributing to the unity of song cycles, Rosen, like many other writers, mostly refers to relationships among keys and musical cross-references. Yet such musical issues do not seem to be his main concern, and at times he makes no attempt to relate all (or even most) of a given cycle's songs to overarching harmonic or cross-referential schemes. In examining cycles by Beethoven, Schubert, and Schumann, Rosen is more interested in his broad historical (or ideological) framework, drawing to a large extent on the coexistence of different time scales—layers that occur, Rosen argues, both in the text and in the music. It is this dialogue between present and memories of the past (and also at times the future) that, in conjunction with more technical musical factors, creates the unity of each cycle. Within this rather unspecified framework, individual cycles may cohere in various ways and to different degrees, and the source of unity may at times be difficult to specify. Rosen discusses these difficulties in examining *Dichterliebe,* a cycle that "refuses all the easy ways out" (1995, 212). Within this cycle, he identifies the musical factors creating unity: the closeness of the keys of adjacent songs, thematic cross-references, inconclusive endings of individual songs requiring resolution at the beginning of the next song, and the repetition of the closure in the twelfth song at the cycle's end. Yet Rosen argues that the unity of *Dichterliebe* transcends such specifically musical features, and the cycle, despite its unity, is ultimately open-ended.

Coherence, Rosen maintains, is a prerequisite if compilations of songs are to be understood as cycles: many early song collections should not be considered cycles, since "none of them has the unity, cohesion, or power of Beethoven's and, later, Schubert's cycles: they are only loosely related groups of songs that do not even pretend to a more impressive status" (1995, 125). However, in Rosen's view, the unity of Romantic song cycles follows no predetermined plan. Rather, each work constitutes its coherence in an individual manner: "The song cycle is the embodiment of a Romantic ideal: to find—or to create—a natural unity out of a collection of different objects without compromising the independence or the disparity of each member. By a 'natural' unity I mean one which is not imposed in advance by convention or tradition: the large form must appear to grow directly from the smaller forms, and this preserves their individuality" (212). Rosen does not believe that the unity of a song cycle is something one could, or even should, thoroughly demonstrate through music-analytical means. Rather, unity is an outcome of an ongoing process, emerging as the cycle unfolds and intuited by the listener.

So far, I have discussed studies that take the coherence of song cycles as their starting point, although, to be sure, different writers understand this notion very differently. But unity is not always taken for granted; recently, David Ferris (2000), Beate Julia Perrey (2002), and Leon Plantinga (2001) have all challenged the very idea of coherence in Schumann's song cycles. Both Ferris and Perrey have published far-reaching monographs on Schumann's cycles: Ferris on *Liederkreis,* op. 39, Perrey on *Dichterliebe.* Even though the conclusions and methodological starting points of these two studies differ—at times significantly—they share certain premises and are based on some common historical ideas.

Both Ferris and Perrey take the early Romantic concept of the "fragment" described, above all, by Friedrich Schlegel and Novalis as one of their primary starting points.[4] To oversimplify, the Romantic fragment is based on the literary and philosophical idea of incompleteness, open-endedness, and incoherence. The fragment consists of irresolvable contradictions, often eluding any attempts at finality.[5] Of the two books, Perrey's is the more radical departure from conventional ideas about song cycles. Largely drawing on the concept of the fragment, she sets out to offer "some aesthetic parameters for a theoretical and hermeneutic model by which one can reconstruct the formal relationship between text and music in Schumann's *Dichterliebe* which renders the cycle's intrinsic semantic ambiguity meaningful in its very negation of unity, completeness, or what is usually understood as a 'logical sequence of events'" (Perrey 2002, 5). Perrey indicates that the early Romantics were against the idea of a finished work of art, so she suggests that the lack of continuity, an aspect she emphasizes in *Dichterliebe,* grows out of the prevailing ideology at the beginning of the nineteenth century. Perrey seeks background for her argument in certain twentieth-century philosophers, above all, Theodor Adorno and Hans-Georg Gadamer, in addition to Romantic theorists such as Friedrich Schlegel and Novalis.

Although the title of Perrey's book mentions *Dichterliebe,* the study seems to be concerned with issues of Lieder in the mid-nineteenth century generally, the poetry of Heinrich Heine, and Schumann's conception of song. All of these aspects are examined in the literary-historical context mentioned above. The book does provide close readings of selected songs from *Dichterliebe,* but the songs are primarily approached as individual entities rather than as parts of the cycle. Indeed, the most extensive discussion on musical cross-references occurs between a song from *Dichterliebe* ("Ich hab' im Traum geweinet") and one composed ten years later ("Der schwere Abend," op. 90, no. 6) (Perrey 2002, 148–62).[6] And in discussing the significance of the keys of the cycle—an issue important (as we have seen above) in many studies suggesting the unity of song cycles—Perrey refers to an abstract distance from the "simple, unadorned C major" (Schumann's own description) rather than to relationships among the keys of *Dichterliebe*'s individual songs (145–46).

To be sure, Perrey occasionally does speak about the cyclical features of *Dichterliebe.* Such features are analyzed when she discusses several occurrences of a diminished-seventh chord in various songs, a sonority she interprets as a "metaphor of the amorous." This chord "becomes a sonorous sign, surpassing at certain significant moments in *Dichterliebe* its traditional function as a passing chord" (Perrey 2002, 178). In addition, the last song (specifically, its concluding piano postlude) creates cyclical connections, she argues. But when elucidating these associations among individual songs in her context of early Romantic aesthetics, Perrey sees even such connections as occurring in isolation, beneath the surface. As a result, *Dichterliebe* ultimately seems to consist for Perrey of a set of fundamentally unrelated songs, although they are associated by their shared aesthetic foundation and poetic theme, much as single Romantic fragments were considered unconnected to each other. In brief, the cyclic qualities Perrey finds in *Dichterliebe* do not grow out of issues such as coherence, unity, and, least of all, organicism.

Ferris also draws on the notion of fragment when proposing a view of the Romantic song cycle as a genre generally and of Schumann's *Liederkreis*, op. 39, specifically. Like Perrey, Ferris too denies the idea of organicism in song cycles, speaking instead about openness—in the case of *Liederkreis*, especially about weak openings and open endings of individual songs. He also traces historical evidence for his view, arguing that Schumann and his contemporaries did not consider song cycles to be unified wholes but rather looser collections (Ferris 2000, 5–7, 195–203).[7]

Even though Ferris challenges the notion of unity in Schumann's *Liederkreis* (and in Romantic song cycles more generally), he is still sympathetic to the idea of connections among the individual songs of a cycle:

> The nineteenth-century song cycle is not primarily "an integrated musical whole,"
> to use Arthur Komar's formulation, but a collection of parts. If we want to understand the ways in which these parts interrelate and cohere, then it is more fruitful to
> begin from the individual part and work toward the whole than it is to go the other
> way around. What we need, in order to do this, is some model that can replace, or
> at least radically modify, the metaphor of formal organicism. And this is where
> the ideas of the Schlegels, as refashioned in the writings of Schumann and his colleagues, can be of great usefulness. (2000, 91)

The starting point of analysis, then, should be the individual songs, not the cycle as a unified whole. Whatever connections emerge—in Ferris's analyses the same sets of compositional ideas and repeated formal strategies, for example—will emerge from understanding the individual parts: "What makes the cycle such a compelling musical genre is the fact that it is made up of individual parts that are suggestive and imply a variety of potential interconnections" (2000, 226). This notion of the primacy of individual songs is close to Charles Rosen's views, discussed above. But the two writers' opinions on the coherence of the cycles differ. Rosen emphasizes the significance of unity, while in Ferris's view cycles are and remain open, despite possible interconnections between individual songs.

In sum, many writers have attempted to show that the Schumann cycles constitute unified wholes. The unity has primarily been traced through three factors: first, motivic repetitions (which McCreless further identifies as unordered or ordered); second, large-scale harmonic structure, whose unity has been sought (in the studies referred to above) in prolongational voice leading (Komar), harmonic cycles (Hoeckner), or symmetry among keys (McCreless); third, text, which has been seen as either forming a narrative (Hoeckner) or unified by a common topic (McCreless). Furthermore, it has often been suggested that some songs function as turning points, or culminations, in the overall unfolding of the cycles (Hoeckner, McCreless, and Rosen). On the other hand, some recent studies have challenged the very notion of unity in Schumann's song cycles, suggesting instead that they should be understood as fragmentary and open (Ferris, Perrey, and Plantinga).

In discussing these studies, I have concentrated on their theoretical approaches rather than details of their analytical findings. In this way, I have attempted to highlight the various analytical and theoretical perspectives they provide for describing the nineteenth-century song cycle. It should be emphasized, however, that the studies examined in this chapter do not necessarily endeavor to present a general and comprehensive definition of the song cycle. As a result, it would misrepresent the authors' intentions to overinterpret their ideas as attempts to define the nineteenth-century song cycle as a genre. Yet I believe that together these discussions on specific Schumann cycles give a relatively comprehensive picture of recent music-analytical views. It is now time to leave Schumann, and the song cycle generally, and consider cyclical aspects of *Winterreise*.

13 *Winterreise* as a Cycle

I will now relate the second part of *Winterreise* to the four perspectives on the large-scale organization of song cycles outlined in the last chapter: textual unity (13.1), large-scale harmonic organization (13.2), musical cross-references (13.3), and whether song cycles should be understood as unified wholes at all (13.4). I will also comment on some published analyses of *Winterreise*. Even though these four areas often appear in the literature on song cycles (as we saw in the preceding chapter), here I propose novel methodologies for approaching them. The poetic cycle is approached from the perspective of hierarchically layered narrative, suggested by Roland Barthes (13.1); the overall harmonic organization is analyzed through concepts of neo-Riemannian theory (13.2); musical cross-references are seen as growing out of various kinds of musical factors, not just pitch motives (13.3); and aspects creating a sense of discontinuity are seen as being in direct interaction with factors creating unity (13.4).

13.1. *Winterreise* as a Topical and a Narrative Cycle

The textual organization of early nineteenth-century song cycles can be divided into two basic categories, which were presented in section 2.1: cycles concentrating on a certain theme without a linear narrative, that is, topical cycles, and cycles constituting a logically constructed narrative, that is, narrative cycles.[1] Considering *Winterreise* solely as either a topical or a narrative cycle would, in my view, narrow its dramatic effect. Instead, I argue that *Winterreise* includes aspects of both.

The main topic of *Winterreise* initially seems clear enough: lost love and the protagonist's longing, the *Sehnsucht* so characteristic of the early phases of Romantic literature. As discussed in section 1.2, scholars such as Thrasybulos G. Georgiades and Susan Youens have suggested that the poems show the speaker constantly reflecting on his emotions, which ultimately stem from the loss of his beloved. In short, the poems present variations on the persistent theme of longing. In the cycle's second part, the focus of this study, the longing is mainly for death, although the loss of love is frequently mentioned as the source of the speaker's misery.

Since longing is the central topic of *Winterreise*, there is a relationship between the longing subject (S) and the object for which he longs (O). The object assumes two guises: on the one hand, the love that has been lost, the initial source

Table 13.1. Textual organization in the second part of *Winterreise*

Songs	"Der greise Kopf" (no. 14) and "Die Krähe" (no. 15)	"Letzte Hoffnung" (no. 16)	"Im Dorfe" (no. 17), "Der stürmische Morgen" (no. 18), "Täuschung" (no. 19)
Textual oppositions S = speaker, O_1 = love, O_2 = death	$S \cup O_2$	$(S \to O_1) \Rightarrow (S \to O_2)$	$S \cup O_1$ (nos. 17 and 19), $S \to O_2$ (no. 18)
Narrative framework (kernels)	The thought of death emerges.	Death may replace love as the primary goal of longing.	The preceding kernel continues.
Narrative situations (satellites)	The protagonist considers death as a positive option while lamenting that it does not come.	The protagonist notes that finding death requires abandoning all hope of regaining love. He feels a sense of relief.	The protagonist considers the outcome of "Letzte Hoffnung," the idea of abandoning the hope of regaining love. He shows different reactions.

Songs	"Der Wegweiser" (no. 20)	"Das Wirtshaus" (no. 21)	"Mut" (no. 22) and "Die Nebensonnen" (no. 23)	"Der Leiermann" (no. 24)
Textual oppositions S = speaker, O_1 = love, O_2 = death	$S \to O_2$	$S \cup O_2$	$S \cup O_2$	$S \cup O_2$
Narrative framework (kernels)	The decision to seek death.	The inability to find a dignified death.	The preceding kernel continues.	The decision to seek a numb state (a graceless death).
Narrative situations (satellites)	The decision to seek death.	The protagonist is not able to have a dignified death.	The protagonist reflects on his inability to find a dignified death, showing different reactions: frustration (no. 22) and nostalgia and contemplation of the past (no. 23).	The protagonist accepts the numb, graceless nature of death, heading for it without knowing if it can be found.

of the subject's misery (O_1), and, on the other hand, death, which is central in part 2 (O_2). These two forms of the object are fundamentally invariant, even though the actual content of the individual poems might not directly refer to love or death. In Greimassian terminology, applied earlier in the analyses of the songs and explained in section 4.1, there are invariant underlying actants (O_1 and O_2), which locally may be represented by a variety of actors. To take but two examples: In "Im Dorfe" love and its loss (O_1) are not explicitly mentioned, yet they clearly form the poem's object, although, strictly speaking, the speaker merely says, "I am finished with all dreams." But in the context of *Winterreise*, these dreams cannot be understood as anything other than the false hope of love. Likewise, in "Der Leiermann" death (O_2) is not expressly mentioned. But the old hurdy-gurdy player represents a state in which no emotions are felt, and at the cycle's end, such a state should be understood as death, spoken about since "Der greise Kopf."[2]

Table 13.1 clarifies certain textual aspects of songs 14–24. The second row shows the topical layer of the songs: the underlying opposition between the longing subject and the longed-for object as well as the various guises this opposition takes in individual poems. "Der greise Kopf" and "Die Krähe" introduce the concept of death as a positive option.[3] However, this significant notion arrives without any preparation. The preceding poem, "Die Post," is clearly related to the first form of the object, the lost beloved: the speaker refers to her, to the town where she lives, which he left in the first song ("Gute Nacht"), as well as to the fact that he has lost her (he apparently receives no letter from her). The significance of the new theme—death—is enhanced by the fact that it is contemplated in two poems, which are further unified by the protagonist's inability to find death in either of them ($S \cup O_2$).

"Letzte Hoffnung" provides a larger context for the theme of death, broached in the preceding songs; in other words, the theme remains the same, but it is now contextualized. As we saw in chapter 7, this song plays a subtle role in the cycle. If the poem is read on its own, it seems to end in deep depression, reflecting the loss of hope and ultimately the acceptance that the beloved has been lost (that O_1 is unobtainable). But when the musico-poetic associations are taken into consideration, the serene, almost religious quality of the song's end precludes an interpretation of deep despair. The musical expression therefore suggests that the interpretation of the poem should be revised when the musico-poetic associations are considered. I have argued that giving up the hope of reuniting with the beloved (O_1) at the poem's end simultaneously introduces the possibility of peace, which death would bring (O_2), a poetic reading suggested by the music at the song's end. The second row of table 13.1 shows this transformation in schematic form.

Songs 17–19 form a single unit, as discussed in chapter 8, in which the protagonist considers one particular aspect of his longing: abandoning all hope of regaining past happiness (O_1). Even though death is not mentioned in any of these poems, it is implied. Particularly in "Der stürmische Morgen," the coldness of heart can be understood as a more or less direct reference to death (hence, the underlying opposition of that song is interpreted in table 13.1 as $S \rightarrow O_2$). The protagonist is still somewhat uncertain, however, of how to react to the newly emerged notion of death and to the idea of abandoning love for good; thus, the expression of songs 17–19 varies greatly.

In "Der Wegweiser" this uncertainty turns into certainty: here, the speaker consciously decides to seek death. The theme of longing for death is thus still present (formalized in the second row of table 13.1 as $S \rightarrow O_2$), and now this longing is uttered with conviction, not just contemplated as an option. Yet the conviction does not lead to the hoped-for conclusion. "Das Wirtshaus" shows that death does not come as the speaker hopes. This situation ($S \cup O_2$) is contemplated in the concluding songs 22–24. As a result, the theme of death and the longing for it remain the topical focus, even at the very end of the cycle. The expressive differences among the last three songs indicate the variety of emotions with which the protagonist reacts to the knowledge that, even at the end, he is unable to find death and the peace he thinks it will bring to him (O_2).

As the second row of table 13.1 indicates, songs 14–15 (which introduce death as a positive option) and songs 21–24 (which close the cycle) consist of the same kind of underlying opposition: the protagonist is unable to attain death ($S \cup O_2$). In other words, from the perspective of the principles defining a topical song cycle, these two groups of songs represent the same topic and even the same kind of underlying relationship between the longing subject and the longed-for object. Yet the contexts in which these two groups of songs occur are very different: songs 14–15 represent the emergence of death as a positive option, while songs 21–24 describe the speaker's emotions on recognizing his inability to find it. In order to understand the function of the two different contexts of the invariant topic of longing, we have to consider the cycle's narrative characteristics along with its topical features. Indeed, certain narrative aspects have already been implied in the above discussion of the cycle's topical nature.

In section 1.2, which discusses the poetic cycle at a general level, I divided poems 14–24 into four states: "death as a positive option" (poems 14–15), "reflecting on the idea of death and renouncing love" (poems 16–19), "the choice of death" (poem 20), and "the inability to find death" (poems 21–24). I suggested further that this sequence of states provides a foundation for a narrative layer. I did not, however, consider in detail how such a narrative would actually be formed. It is now time to examine how these states can create a goal-directed trajectory.

It is often stated that a narrative does not emerge unless its constituent events are causally connected. A mere sequence of incidents does not necessarily create a narrative; there must be causal relationships.[4] Seymour Chatman has stated this point clearly:

It has been argued, since Aristotle, that events in narratives are radically correlative, enchaining, entailing. Their sequence, runs the traditional argument, is not simply linear but causative. The causation may be overt, that is explicit, or covert, implicit.... In classical narratives, events occur in distributions: they are linked to each other as cause to effect, effects in turn causing other effects, until the final effect. And even if two events seem not obviously interrelated, we infer that they may be, on some larger principle that we will discover later. (1978, 45–46)

As we saw in section 1.2, some commentators on *Winterreise* argue that the cycle has no narrative unity. These writers may indeed hold this strict view of narrative; that is, they may feel that there is no goal-directed, causally constituted progression as required by this narrow definition of narrative unity. John Daverio, for example, has maintained that in *Winterreise* the "poems can in no way be taken to chart a progressive, linear development toward a goal" (2010, 372), and Barbara R. Barry has argued that "while its [*Winterreise*'s] main direction is clear enough, it is not a continuous journey where each part is causally linked to the preceding one, but is essentially episodic, because the links are emotional rather than logical" (2000, 188).[5] I concede that, on the surface, the poems of songs 14–24 do not form the kinds of unequivocal causal connections that unambiguously constitute a narrative trajectory fulfilling the requirements outlined above. Nevertheless, I believe that these poems are underpinned by causal associations that generate a unified, goal-directed process.[6]

Roland Barthes (1977, 93–95) has discussed the constitutive elements of narrative, making a hierarchical distinction between "kernels" and "satellites."[7] These terms may help us to understand how songs 14–24 form a unified narrative trajectory. Kernels are the fundamental narrative moments that form the logical and causal trajectory of an overall plot. No kernel can be deleted without destroying the narrative logic. The kernels advance the plot by raising questions, introducing options, and providing answers and closures. Satellites, on the other hand, are of lesser significance for the global narrative. They are attached to individual kernels (rather than to the overall trajectory), embellishing and elaborating on them. Hence, they are not fundamental to the global narrative and could, in principle, be deleted without changing the underlying plot. Barthes himself wrote:

> Returning to the class of functions, its units are not all of the same "importance": some constitute real hinge-points of the narrative . . . ; others merely "fill in" the narrative space separating the hinge functions. Let us call the former *cardinal functions* (or *kernels*) and the latter, having regard to their complementary nature, *satellites*. For a function to be cardinal, it is enough that the action to which it refers open (or continue, or close) an alternative that is of direct consequence for the subsequent development of the story, in short that it inaugurate or conclude an uncertainty. . . . Between two cardinal functions, however, it is always possible to set out subsidiary notations which cluster around one or other kernel. . . . These satellites are still functional, insofar as they enter into correlation with a kernel, but their function is attenuated, unilateral, parasitic; it is a question of a purely chronological functionality . . . whereas the tie between two cardinal functions is invested with a double functionality, at once chronological and logical. (1977, 93–94)[8]

The third and fourth rows of table 13.1 show the narrative framework (kernels) and the local narrative situations (satellites) as these occur in songs 14–24, respectively. In 14–15 the thought of death emerges, constituting the first kernel. The thought is invested with uncertainty: the protagonist laments that death does not come, but at the same time he does not relate the idea of death to a larger context—least of all, to his lost love, the driving force of his journey thus far. The next kernel (song 16) provides the context and thus is a logical next step in the narrative. In other words, the context for death is a causal reaction to the emerging idea of death. The protagonist now observes that death may replace love as the primary goal of longing and that to accept this change he will have to relinquish the hope of regaining love. (This interpretation of "Letzte Hoffnung" is again based on a reading of the poem that has been affected by its musical setting.) This kernel extends through songs 16–19. Songs 17–19 are satellites attached to the kernel introduced in song 16; in these songs the protagonist shows different reactions to the idea of death replacing lost love as the object of his longing. In other words, songs 17–19 are directly related to the kernel (song 16), but they do not form part of the underlying primary narrative trajectory. Moreover, they seem rather detached from each other, avoiding any causal connections.

"Der Wegweiser" (no. 20) introduces a new kernel: the protagonist now consciously decides to seek death. The connection to the preceding kernel is again causal: the speaker recognizes that death is now the primary object of his longing, displacing the beloved. In other words, the uncertainty of the preceding kernel is resolved in this new one. But the next, penultimate kernel, which is introduced in "Das Wirtshaus," indicates that the protagonist cannot find death. This kernel is again causally related to the preceding one, providing the consequence of his search for death. Songs 22–23 form satellites attached to this kernel. They exhibit different reactions to the inability to find death: frustration in "Mut" and nostalgia and, indirectly, recollection of the beloved in "Die Nebensonnen."

The death that cannot be found in "Das Wirtshaus" is of a special nature: the poem's setting in a cemetery together with the expression in Schubert's music suggest that the death referred to in this song has a dignified, religious quality. The sacred connotations of the graveyard and the solemn, pious music imply that the death the wanderer hopes to find (but ultimately cannot) has a noble (and peaceful) character. The final kernel of *Winterreise*, "Der Leiermann," changes this situation. Now the speaker wishes to join the old man. The death referred to here is abject—numb and graceless; no traces of dignity remain. This kernel is again causally related to the preceding one: since the wanderer was unable to find a dignified death in the preceding kernel, he is now ready to accept even the graceless death described in "Der Leiermann." The final song, however, provides no resolution to the protagonist's destiny; we do not know the answers to the questions he asks at the end of "Der Leiermann." As a result, the cycle arrives at its end without providing an unequivocal closure to resolve the earlier textual tensions. The final poetic kernel thus opens new uncertainties, which remain unresolved.[9]

In sum, *Winterreise* (and its part 2 in particular) includes elements of both a topical and a narrative cycle. However, at times each of these organizational principles is somewhat concealed, at least locally. On the topical side, there are poems that do not explicitly mention the loss of love or death, the two objects of long-ing that dominate the cycle. Yet I have argued that even these poems can be seen to reflect indirectly either O_1, O_2, or their juxtaposition. On the narrative side, there are moments in which discontinuity seems to feature prominently, espe-cially in songs 17–19. But if we approach such moments of discontinuity from the perspective of a hierarchical narrative organization, we can understand them as growing out of the juxtaposition of various satellites attached to a common ker-nel. Both topical and narrative organizations thus persist through songs 14–24, even though their organizational principles are at times hidden.

13.2. Large-Scale Harmonic Organization in Part 2 of *Winterreise*

The search for tonal unity in *Winterreise* encounters a specific problem not found in other song cycles. As we have seen, five songs appeared in the first edition in keys that are different from those in the manuscript (table 1.1). There-fore, anyone proposing an interpretation of the cycle's overall tonal organization must first decide whether to follow the key scheme in the manuscript or that of the first publication. As shown in section 1.1, scholarly opinion on the merits of each source varies greatly. Some writers argue that the manuscript forms a more plausible whole, while others maintain that the first edition does so. Still oth-ers suggest that the different keys do not appreciably alter the cycle's overall im-pression. In this section I will primarily consider the published keys but will also briefly comment on those found in the manuscript. I will argue that the original keys create a somewhat different musical effect from those in the first edition, but I will also suggest that the large-scale musico-poetic associations still remain very similar in both.

Barbara R. Barry (2000), Richard Kramer (1994), and Edward D. Latham (2009) have discussed the large-scale tonal organization of *Winterreise* from a prolongational perspective. Furthermore, all three relate their overall tonal in-terpretations to the unfolding of the text. These three analysts interpret D minor as the governing tonic throughout. Latham (who bases his study on the keys of the first edition) argues that only the opening song represents the tonic chord, while the other songs, twenty-three in all, prolong the back-relating dominant. So he reads an overarching $\hat{3}$–$\hat{2}$ ‖ progression in the top voice, supported by a harmonic I–V ‖ motion. This reading seems problematic to me: the proportions alone between the primary tonic and the embellishing dominant (one versus twenty-three) seem to challenge its explanatory validity.

The proportions seem more justifiable in Barry's interpretation. In her view, the entire first part prolongs the tonic, while the second part begins with an ex-tended predominant, which then leads to the dominant, arrived at in the last song (but anticipated in song 22). Yet this assessment of tonal unity, with its im-plication that a D-minor chord retains its function as the matrix throughout the cycle, also appears rather difficult to justify. In addition, Barry's handling of the keys raises further problems: in her analysis she mixes songs in keys of the manuscript with songs in keys of the first edition without explaining her choices. The only comment she makes on this issue is that "'Wasserflut' was originally written in F sharp minor, and in *some later editions* transposed to E minor" (Barry 2000, 193; emphasis added).

Kramer's overall prolongational reading, based on the keys in Schubert's manuscript, is the least specific of the three, which, in my view, lends it more credibility.[10] He observes that the "sense of tonic, perceived in *Winterreise* . . . is an elusive quality, more an invisible magnetic force that, by association and implication, draws the poetry of the cycle into something cohesive. This is not the closed, 'finished' tonal game of a Mozart quartet" (Kramer 1994, 187). Yet he also sees D minor extended as a point of reference throughout the cycle (even though it is not, in his view, literally prolonged), an assessment I cannot perceptually follow.

Some scholars have found harmonic coherence in *Winterreise* without claiming a prolongational framework. Christopher Lewis (1988, 58–66) divides the cycle's narrative into three parts: songs 1–9, 10–16, and 17–24. (It is worth mentioning that Lewis does not follow Schubert's division of the cycle into two parts.) He then suggests that all three parts have somewhat similar narrative trajectories, as well as tonal curves that resemble one another. Lewis bases his analysis on the keys in Schubert's manuscript.

There are also commentaries on *Winterreise* that question the view of an overarching tonal unity. Charles Rosen (1995, 203–204), for example, has maintained that the cycle lacks a large-scale harmonic scheme, and Walter Everett has argued that "no significant tonal structure can be found to govern a unified system of keys of individual songs" (1988, 5). Avoiding such strict assessment, Susan Youens (1991, 95–104) finds harmonic associations among the tonics of the individual songs without suggesting a thorough-going, underlying tonal scheme. Barbara Turchin (1987, 14) primarily refers to harmonic associations between adjacent tonics, further suggesting that similarity of poetic content affects the closeness of successive tonics. I agree with these scholars that it is not plausible to infer either a large-scale prolongational structure or a single governing tonic in *Winterreise* or, specifically, in its second part. But I would not go as far as Rosen in arguing that there is no large-scale harmonic scheme in part 2; nor do I feel, like Youens, that tonal organization is found only in small groups of songs. Instead, I argue that there is indeed a large-scale harmonic plan extending through the entirety of part 2 but that this plan is not fundamentally prolongational, nor does it rely upon one governing tonic as its center. Rather, this harmonic plan grows out of the immediate harmonic relationships between adjacent songs. In this respect, my view resembles Turchin's. Furthermore, I suggest that this harmonic plan is intimately connected to the poetic narrative of the cycle.

Example 13.1c shows the tonics of the individual songs in the second part of *Winterreise* (the tonics are those of the first edition; the whole notes refer to minor keys; the double whole notes refer to major keys). There are three kinds of relationships between adjacent tonic pitches: they may be the same; there may be a leap (a third or a descending fourth); or there may be a stepwise motion.

o = minor key

𝄆 = major key

⌢ = common tones

⎿__⏌ = stepwise bass (no common tones)

keys in the manuscript

a)

(13) 14 15 16 17 18 19 20 21 22 23 24

b)

kernel (s a t e l l i t e s) kernel

c)

common tones between adjacent songs
(except 16–17)

no common tones between adjacent songs
(except 23–24)

Example 13.1. Keys of the songs in part 2 of *Winterreise*.

These connections between adjoining tonic pitches lead to two large categories of relationships between contiguous tonic chords: either the two harmonies have common tones or they do not (example 13.1b). Common tones occur in cases when either the tonic pitch is retained or the two consecutive tonics are connected by a leap, whereas the two adjoining tonic chords do not share pitches when their roots are connected by stepwise motion. There may be one to three common tones, and instances of each can be found in songs 13–24.

At a general level, the existence of common tones is a powerful means of drawing associations between consecutive chords. Indeed, in triadic music, shared pitches have often been considered a way of creating close associations among sonorities. Recently, neo-Riemannian studies on transformations among triads have emphasized the significance of shared pitches among triads. There are two neo-Riemannian principles that seem pertinent here: first, the idea of "parsimonious" or "smooth" voice leading, where one or two pitches of a triad remain invariant while the others move by step; second, the view that the triads connected through such transformational procedures are not related to any governing tonal center.[11] The first of these principles suggests two kinds of relationships between successive tonic chords of the individual songs of *Winterreise*: on the one hand, tonics that are closely related (i.e., they have common tones), and on the other, tonics that are more distant from each other (i.e., they have no common tones). The second neo-Riemannian principle, namely, the avoidance of a tonal center, enables discussion of the large-scale course of individual song tonic chords without reference to a governing primary center.

These neo-Riemannian principles differ substantially from the kind of harmonic logic and syntax suggested by the Schenkerian analyses of individual Lieder in chapters 5–11. The two theories are not used to show connections between the same musical elements, so the theories have no direct interaction in this study. I have used Schenkerian analysis to describe individual song structures in a multilayered manner; in other words, how local events are related to deeper-level procedures and ultimately to the *Ursatz* expanding through entire songs. Local and global layers are therefore inseparably intertwined, and a single governing tonic sonority unifies the layers. On the other hand, my use of neo-Riemannian ideas, as shown in example 13.1, indicates motion from the tonic chord of one song to the tonic of the next without suggesting any further hierarchy. I am thus not arguing that there are large-scale prolongational units consisting of the tonics of several songs, nor am I positing neo-Riemannian connections between the tonic chords of nonadjacent songs. (There is one exception to the latter, however, to be discussed presently.) Unlike in Schenkerian structure, the harmonic connections remain local, so to speak, and there is no one center (either chord or pitch) that functions as a global point of reference.[12]

As the commentary beneath example 13.1 indicates, the second part of *Winterreise* can be divided, from the perspective of large-scale harmonic unfolding, into two large overlapping units. First, in songs 13–19 there are common tones between the adjacent tonic harmonies (with one exception, songs 16–17); thus, the harmonic relationships between successive tonics suggest smooth links and continuity. Second, in songs 19–24 there are no common tones (again with one exception, in songs 23–24), so these songs imply greater harmonic variety and distance.[13] The abstract chordal relationships shown in example 13.1 are also heard on the musical surface. Apart from the opening of "Letzte Hoffnung," songs 13–24 all begin and end with the tonic chord; in other words, the same harmonic motions appear on the surface (when moving from one song to the next) as well as in the abstract row of tonic chords.[14]

Songs 13–16 create a unified group in which all tonic chords have two pitches in common (G and E♭). These smooth harmonic motions can be related to the important narrative events taking place. "Die Post" (no. 13) still recalls the opening situation, the lost beloved (or O_1 in the Greimassian formalization), while "Der greise Kopf" and "Die Krähe" (nos. 14 and 15) introduce the theme of death

(O_2 in the Greimassian formalizations). Finally, "Letzte Hoffnung" (no. 16) juxtaposes the two themes, providing a context for O_2 (the necessity of abandoning O_1), which was not provided in songs 14 and 15. The unity of this narrative trajectory is underlined by the consistency of the harmonic progression: all adjacent tonic chords have either two pitches in common or, in the case of songs 14 and 15, which introduce the concept of death, all three pitches in common. As a result, the smooth motion from one tonic chord to the next proceeds with the same consistency with which the poetic narrative unfolds.

There are also common tones between adjacent tonic chords in the ensuing songs, 17–19, so these too form a group in which the motion from one tonic to the next is smooth. But there are no common tones between the tonic chords of the initial song of this group ("Im Dorfe," no. 17) and the closing song of the preceding group ("Letzte Hoffnung," no. 16); rather, the tonic here moves a half step down, from E♭ to D. The harmonic unity within songs 17–19, as well as their harmonic detachment from the preceding songs, can again be related to the organization of the poetic cycle. As the third row of table 13.1 indicates, poems 14–16 all include primary narrative elements, kernels of the narrative trajectory. (Poem 13 also forms a kernel, although this is not shown in table 13.1.) Poems 17–19, on the other hand, may be understood as satellites attached to the kernel of poem 16 in that they do not advance the underlying plot. In the same way that poetic satellites are not related to the course of the kernels, the tonics of songs 17–19 are detached from the harmonic framework established by songs 13–16; these keys do not continue the smooth connections found in songs 13–16. As a result, the harmonic gap supports the poetic situation in which the primary narrative trajectory does not move forward.

There is again a stepwise motion from the A-major tonic in "Täuschung" (no. 19) to the G minor of "Der Wegweiser" (no. 20). This second stepwise motion in part 2 of the cycle occurs at a moment when the poetic structure returns from the satellite excursions of poems 17–19 to the next narrative kernel in "Der Wegweiser." In other words, those songs whose poems form satellites are detached from the larger musical context by stepwise motion between tonics both before and after songs 17–19 (the only stepwise motions so far in part 2). This detachment of songs 17–19 from both the preceding and the following tonics suggests a large-scale connection (albeit somewhat speculative), shown on the lower staff of example 13.1b. In the same way that the principal narrative connections occur between the kernels of poems 16 and 20, so the G-minor tonic of "Der Wegweiser" (whose poem introduces a new kernel) is smoothly related to the E♭-major tonic of "Letzte Hoffnung" (whose poem includes the preceding kernel). In other words, the tonic triads of songs 17–19 are interpolated within a smooth transformational triadic continuum of songs 13–20 in the same way as their poems consist of satellites interpolated within the narrative trajectory consisting of the kernels.[15]

Songs 13–20 therefore seem to follow the principle by which songs whose poems include kernels are connected by the common tones of their tonic triads; in other words, the smooth connections create links among the triads. This principle is abandoned after "Der Wegweiser," however. The ensuing "Das Wirtshaus" (no. 21), which comprises the penultimate kernel of the poetic cycle, is in F major, a step below the G minor of "Der Wegweiser," with no common tones between the two tonics. Indeed, from here on, there are common tones only between the tonics of the last two songs. Thus, with "Der Wegweiser" the second part of *Winterreise* moves from adjacent tonics that predominantly have common tones to tonics whose roots move most often by step (example 13.1c).

This change of harmonic strategy plays a significant role in the overall organization of part 2 and can be related to the course of the poetic cycle. Up to "Der Wegweiser," the narrative in part 2 has proceeded in a relatively straightforward manner, and in some sense (oddly, in such a thoroughly tragic cycle as *Winterreise*), its course has at least indirectly followed the desires of the protagonist. The narrative kernel of "Die Post" includes a recollection of the events of the cycle's first part, the loss of love (O_1), which forms the sad, unavoidable starting point of the wanderer's journey. In the next kernel, introduced in poems 14 and 15, the idea of death (O_2) emerges as a possible way out of the misery (see the third row in table 13.1). In the ensuing kernel ("Letzte Hoffnung"), the protagonist realizes that to find death, he must first accept the loss of love, while in the following kernel ("Der Wegweiser"), he decides to seek death and thus abandon love. So far, this narrative has been directed toward the conclusion, the attainment of death ($S \cap O_2$). If this final state were to arrive, the course of part 2 would fulfill the protagonist's hopes (although he becomes fully conscious of these hopes only gradually). But the next kernel, which comes in "Das Wirtshaus," signifies, of course, the inability to find death ($S \cup O_2$). As a result, the state that actually arrives is not the one prepared by the preceding narrative trajectory.

This change of direction is reflected in the change of strategy by which the tonic chords are associated with each other. The direction of the wanderer's path has changed, and so has the principle connecting the successive tonic chords. The avoidance of closely related tonic harmonies after "Der Wegweiser," in contrast to the smooth connections that prevailed up to this point in part 2, is an apt reflection of the protagonist's confusion and frustration. His journey no longer has a goal (a goal that was initially unconscious, to be sure). Likewise, the harmonic motions are distant, without connecting common tones. The protagonist does not know how to proceed, and, analogously, the music has lost its smooth connections between adjacent tonics. Only the last two songs have common pitches (and even the same tonic). This can be related to the idea that, after the initial confusion created by the penultimate kernel (governing songs 21–23), the cycle now introduces the final poetic kernel: the speaker is ready to accept even the benumbed state of the old hurdy-gurdy man, a state far removed from the dignified death he had hoped for still in "Das Wirtshaus." So the protagonist again has a goal, and the common tones between the two successive tonic chords signify a renewed sense of narrative directedness. But the cycle ends here, and no conclusion is reached. Poetically, "Der Leiermann" is a kernel that raises new tensions instead of resolving the existing ones.

The harmonic situation and musico-poetic associations are slightly different if the keys of the manuscript are considered instead of the keys of the first edition (example 13.1a), yet the larger picture remains unaltered. When "Mut" appears in A minor, as it does in the manuscript, the harmonic motion in songs 21–23 includes common tones among the tonics, creating a continuum through these songs. This could suggest, poetically, that the smooth harmonic connections among the tonics of these songs (the penultimate kernel and the two satellites attached to it) reflect the protagonist considering the outcome of "Das Wirtshaus." The lack of common tones between "Die Nebensonnen" and "Der Leiermann" in B minor, in turn, could highlight the arrival of the final kernel by the striking change of key. In other words, the harmonic strategy in moving from song 23 to song 24 (with no common tones) differs from that encountered in songs 21–23 (which do have common tones). In sum, like the keys of the first edition, the keys of the manuscript emphasize the arrival at the final kernel in "Der Leiermann," but the means of creating this emphasis are different.

13.3. Musical Cross-References in Part 2 of *Winterreise*

In section 4.2 I discussed a distinction between motivic relationships (understood in a specifically Schenkerian sense) and freer musical associations. Both occur in *Winterreise*. Walter Everett (1988, 1990) and Walther Dürr (2004) have spoken about the significance of strictly defined motives. Everett's perspective is Schenkerian, so the motives he discusses occur in part in the middleground. He examines many songs in detail and traces how recurring motivic ideas (the $\hat{6}$–$\hat{5}$ progression, in particular) occur in individual songs with consistent musico-poetic associations. Dürr in turn refers to various instances in several keys where a half step, f^2–e^2, features prominently. Dürr's comments are intentionally preliminary; they concern just a few songs and provide no comprehensive picture. Youens, on the other hand, has spoken about freer connections among specific, clearly recognizable figures that appear in various songs. Primary among these is the "journeying figure," which consists of four repeated nonlegato pitches or chords. In Youens's view, this figure is "a recurring accompanimental motive with a significance derived from the text that can be found throughout *Winterreise*, although not in every song" (1991, 83–84). As with Everett's interpretation of the $\hat{6}$–$\hat{5}$ motive, she suggests that repeated figures (the "journeying figure," in particular) can be heard in several songs with unvarying poetic associations.

At a general level, Everett's and Youens's discussions of motivic connections in *Winterreise* include many perceptive comments. Everett concentrates on a very common element in tonal music, namely, the $\hat{6}$–$\hat{5}$ progression, which is found repeatedly throughout the tonal repertory. When it appears in the minor, this progression is often associated with grief and tragic emotions, associations Everett also makes. Youens in turn associates the "journeying figure" with the walking of the protagonist in a clearly imitative manner. But she does not claim that this figure plays a highly significant role in the cycle's organization. Both Everett and

Youens associate the motives they discuss with textual themes that recur in many of the poems, thereby illuminating cyclical aspects of *Winterreise*.

Because Everett and Youens connect given motives with certain recurring themes, the associations illuminate the topical (rather than the narrative) quality of the cycle. In other words, if we consider the distinction made by Patrick McCreless between unordered and ordered motives (discussed in section 12.2), these musical cross-references would make unordered musico-poetic connections; the specific location of the motivic occurrences is not of primary importance. Below, I will primarily discuss *ordered* musico-poetic cross-references, situations in which the exact location of the cross-references is considered important. As a result, such ordered motivic and other musico-poetic cross-references take the overall course of the cycle into consideration: since the locations of individual motivic occurrences are considered significant, the motives will be associated with the large-scale temporal unfolding of the poetic and the musical cycle.

In this respect, the ordered cross-references resemble the overall narrative and large-scale harmonic organization discussed in the preceding sections: all three approaches attempt to describe song cycles and their cyclical features from the linear or temporal perspective. Yet there are also differences among the three. The examination of the overarching poetic narrative and large-scale harmonic organization attempts to interpret the function played by each poem and the key of each song in the cyclical unfolding. Ordered cross-references, on the other hand, take the larger context into consideration without attempting to establish a network of motives that would account for every song. As a result, the following discussion will not try to establish motivic associations among all of the songs in a way that shows an overarching motivic trajectory. I believe that such a trajectory does not exist in *Winterreise*.

Table 13.2 indicates the musical elements to be discussed. The list is by no means complete; I have included only the main musical factors that have been addressed in the analyses of the individual songs in part 2. The musical elements are numbered 1 to 8 for easier reference. No. 1, modal mixture, is the most common, occurring in nine songs out of eleven, while no. 8, the juxtaposition of E♭–D and E♭–E♮, is heard in only two songs. These musical elements include clear motivic ideas (e.g., no. 5) and freer musical associations (e.g., no. 4). In the following discussion, I will not make a distinction between strict motives and freer associations; both create cross-references, and these, rather than their precise essence, concern us here.

The first musical element in table 13.2, a mixture of major and minor, appears in all but two songs, "Der stürmische Morgen" and "Der Leiermann." (It is significant that there is no mixture in these songs. I do not believe that it is by chance; I will return to this issue in chapter 14.) As the analyses of individual songs have indicated, in all instances mixture can be understood as referring to the juxtaposition of illusion (associated with major) and reality (associated with minor). Indeed, several scholars have pointed out that such poetic connections are often found in Schubert's songs, so this association is not limited to *Winterreise*. Hans Heinrich Eggebrecht (1970, 96–98) and William Kinderman (1986,

Table 13.2. Musical cross-references in songs 14–24

Element number	Musical element	Poetic reference
1	modal mixture (songs 14, 15, 16, 17, 19, 20, 21, 22, 23)	juxtaposition of illusion (major) and reality (minor)
2	completion of the *Urlinie* in the piano part (songs 14, 15, 17, 18, 24)	inability of the protagonist to affect his own fate (in song 17 a related idea of uncertainty)
3	unison (songs 14, 15, 16, 18)	inability of the protagonist to affect his own fate
4	repetition of closing cadential material (songs 14, 15, 16, 17, 21)	unwillingness to accept reality (in songs 16 and 17, a related idea of hesitancy in accepting the emerging new hope)
5	$\hat{6}$–$\hat{5}$ (songs 14, 15, 20)	death as a longed-for state
6	enharmonicism (songs 14, 15, 16, 20)	duality generally and juxtaposition of illusion and reality in particular
7	quasi-religious chorale texture (songs 16, 17, 21, 23)	peace brought by death
8	juxtaposition of E♭–D and E♭–E♮ (songs 20, 21)	decision to seek death and the inability to find it

65–75) have argued, at a general level, that major and minor function in many Schubert songs as symbols of illusion and reality. Carl Schachter (1999a, 299–303) has examined in detail the juxtaposition of major and minor in "Ihr Bild" from *Schwanengesang* and interpreted the mixture as reflecting the contrast between illusion and reality.

Owing to its generality in part 2 of *Winterreise*, mixture can be understood as primarily creating unordered musico-poetic associations (to use McCreless's term) with the topical quality of the cycle. In other words, since mixture occurs in the majority of songs, it mostly seems to refer to the opposition between reality and illusion as a general topic rather than to specific states in the overall narrative trajectory. Yet there are also more specific mixture-related musical cross-references that suggest ordered associations. The clearest of these is when a new formal section of a major-mode song begins with a minor-mode tonic chord, a device encountered in three songs: "Täuschung" (m. 22), "Das Wirtshaus" (m. 23), and "Die Nebensonnen" (m. 16). In "Täuschung" and "Das Wirtshaus" the modally inflected tonic is an apparent tonic that begins an auxiliary cadence (examples 8.3 and 10.4), whereas in "Die Nebensonnen" the tonic represents a modally inflected structural tonic (example 11.2).

These different structural functions of outwardly similar musical events reflect the narrative situation in each poem. As discussed in section 13.1, "Täuschung" is the last of the narrative satellites (songs 17–19) attached to the kernel of "Letzte Hoffnung" (table 13.1). All of these satellites provide different perspectives on the situation outlined in the kernel. In "Täuschung" the protagonist admits that he is consciously following delusion and avoiding reality. Thus, the song transforms the minor-mode tonic (a reference to reality) into a contrapuntal sonority rather than allowing it to function as a structural element. Likewise, in "Das Wirtshaus" the protagonist attempts to resist reality—the fact that death eludes him, that there is no vacancy at the inn. Again, the transformation of a minor-mode tonic chord into a contrapuntal element can be seen as an attempt to resist reality. In "Die Nebensonnen" the situation is different. Now the protagonist does not try to avoid reality; rather, he hopes that the third sun will also set, that death will come to claim him. Because he does not actively resist what he knows to be real, the minor-mode tonic (the reference to reality) is not interpreted as a contrapuntal element. Especially in "Das Wirtshaus" and "Die Nebensonnen," however, the musico-poetic function of the mixture is more complex and nuanced, as discussed in chapters 10 and 11. Furthermore, in each of these songs, the aspect examined here takes part in an internal, many-sided web of associations. But I believe that the rather straightforward cross-references created by these minor-mode tonic chords (whether apparent or structural), as well as the consistency with which they refer to the cycle's poetic content, draw significant cyclical associations and ordered musico-poetic cross-references. The sonic importance of this device is further enhanced by its appearance in mm. 27 ff. and 72 ff. of "Die Post," the opening song of part 2.

A specific use of mixture in an individual song can also create ordered connections. "Letzte Hoffnung" is a turning point in *Winterreise*. After beginning to contemplate death in "Der greise Kopf" and "Die Krähe," the protagonist now places death in a larger context, specifically considering it along with the loss of the beloved. As I argued in chapter 7, the internal musico-poetic associations of "Letzte Hoffnung" suggest that the protagonist gradually becomes aware that accepting the loss of love is prerequisite to desiring death. This gradual process of moving from contemplation of reality (the loss of love) to considering illusion (the possibility of death) is reflected in the juxtaposition of minor and major: in the background, a major-mode tonic chord is prolonged throughout "Letzte Hoffnung," while on the surface, the major-mode tonic key firmly displaces the minor only close to the end. In other words, mixture plays a significant role in the musico-poetic associations of this important song. And since "Letzte Hoffnung" is a turning point in the overall narrative of the cycle, mixture here creates ordered cross-references to other songs featuring mixture.

The second musical element of table 13.2, the completion of the *Urlinie* in the piano part, is more specific than the first. This device suggests that the singer loses his role as the center of the musical focus: he fails to execute the primary top-voice events precisely at the moment the listener has the impression that the song is about to reach its close. The singer is thus unable to complete the music's global structure and bring the drama to an end. This element can also be understood as a referential sign. The narrator's lack of power over his own destiny is a central theme in *Winterreise:* first, the wanderer is unable to be reunited with his beloved; then in the end he is unable to die—death too eludes him. The secondary structural role that the voice part plays in instances where the *Urlinie* descends in the piano is an apt image of this poetic inability: the singer is unable to take part in the inevitable course of the background voice leading, much as the protagonist cannot change the course of events.

The specific musico-poetic associations of the *Urlinie*'s descent in the piano part differ slightly among the songs referred to in table 13.2. In "Der greise Kopf" and "Die Krähe" the protagonist's inability to reach his goal is quite clear: he cannot find death, which he is considering in the poems (cf. chapters 5 and 6). In "Im Dorfe" the passive role of the singer in the structural closure refers primarily to uncertainty and only indirectly to his inability to affect the course of events. "Im Dorfe" is the first of the satellites attached to "Letzte Hoffnung" (table 13.1). In these satellites the protagonist contemplates the inevitable loss of love and the emerging thought of death—in "Im Dorfe" specifically whether to accept the loss of love and seek death. In section 8.1 I suggested that in this song the protagonist is in principle ready to accept the inevitable, yet he still hesitates. These doubts are reflected in the singer's evasion of the concluding background î: he avoids the final closure and resolution.

In "Der stürmische Morgen," the second of the satellites attached to "Letzte Hoffnung," the speaker grieves over his situation, the knowledge that death would also eliminate any chance to experience tender emotions (section 8.2). But he cannot change his destiny and still keep warm human feelings. Likewise, the voice does not take part in the completion of the *Urlinie* (or, in this instance, even in the course of the background top voice). Finally, in "Der Leiermann" the whole cycle ends with the descent of the *Urlinie,* but only in the piano. With this song the protagonist stops recounting the tale of his journey by asking questions about his future; his final destiny is thus beyond his control. For the ordered musico-poetic cross-references, it is significant that the cycle closes with the *Urlinie* descending in the piano part. This event emphasizes that, even at the end, the protagonist cannot determine his own course, as he has been unable to do throughout his journey.

The third musical element of table 13.2 (unison) is thematically linked to the second element: here, too, the poetic reference is to the protagonist's inability to affect his own fate. Now the vocal part loses its independence through its reliance on the piano.[16] This textual sign is most clearly audible in "Der stürmische Morgen." Apart from mm. 10–13, the vocal line follows the piano throughout. The unison underlines the speaker's desperate outcry, a reaction to the preceding poetic kernel introduced in "Letzte Hoffnung" (table 13.1). Now he resists the present situation, namely, that abandoning love also means abandoning his emotions in general. But his destiny has led him to this state, and he cannot avoid it; likewise, in the D-minor sections of the song, the vocal part cannot do anything other than follow the piano in unison.

This dramatic use of unison has been subtly prepared in the preceding songs, which poetically anticipate this outcry. In "Der greise Kopf" there is a distinctive unison texture in mm. 25–28 when the protagonist observes how far he still has to go to reach the grave; in other words, he must now admit that the death he longs for eludes him, a situation he cannot alter. In "Die Krähe" unison governs mm. 6–12, 25–28, and 37–38, in which the protagonist contemplates the crow as a possible omen of death. But he is unable to affect the bird's flight; metaphorically, he cannot alter his destiny. The changes in relationship between the vocal part and the piano (discussed in chapter 6) reflect the changing views, or hopes, of the speaker. Finally, in "Letzte Hoffnung" unison is heard briefly (but significantly) in two places, mm. 12–13 and 21. In these measures the wanderer first gazes at the leaf and then wonders whether it will fall, unable to affect the destiny of the leaf or, poetically, of himself. Here the unison (associated with the inability of the protagonist to influence his own fate) contrasts with the profoundly different chorale texture at the end, which suggests the emergence of a new hope, the hope for death. This textural contrast underlines the poetic significance of the unison and the cross-references it creates.

The fourth musical element in table 13.2, the repetition of closing cadential material, refers to the protagonist's unwillingness to accept reality. Just as the speaker wants to avoid the inevitable, the music attempts to resist or alter the final tonal closure.[17] In each case, the poetic significance of the repeated cadential progression is enhanced by a musical reiteration accompanying a word repetition. The precise technical foundation on which the repetition is based differs slightly in each case. In "Der greise Kopf" the top-voice $\hat{1}$ that completes the first cadential progression in a major-mode tonic (m. 39) appears in an inner voice, so it does not complete the *Urlinie* (example 5.3). Thus, the major-mode tonic (referring to illusion) is not conclusive, and only the second cadential progression closes the background structure in m. 42 in a minor-mode tonic (referring to reality). In "Die Krähe" the music reaches the structural dominant in m. 32 (example 6.4). This is not immediately resolved, however; rather, the path leading to it is repeated before the concluding tonic and $\hat{1}$ arrive in m. 38. By postponing the cadential arrival, the music attempts to resist the inevitable arrival of the concluding tonic, just as the protagonist resists reality in the poem.

In "Letzte Hoffnung" the first cadential attempt in mm. 37–38 ends on a VI (instead of the tonic), which forms part of an unfolding in the bass (example 7.4). The second cadential progression then reaches the closing tonic in m. 43. In section 7.3 I suggested that this deferral of the conclusion reflects how the protagonist gradually becomes aware of the positive aspect of death (O_2) after having first lamented the inevitable loss of love (O_1). In "Im Dorfe" the repeated cadential material first leads to an inner-voice $\hat{1}$ (m. 40) and only in m. 46 to the structurally conclusive $\hat{1}$ (example 8.1). In section 8.1 I argued that the repetition reflects the speaker's reluctance to relinquish all thoughts of the beloved. Finally, in "Das Wirtshaus" the first cadential arrival at the tonic in m. 26 takes place within a parenthetical insertion, while the concluding structural tonic is attained in m. 28 as a conclusion to the second cadential progression (example 10.4). In section 10.3 I suggested that this musical factor indicates that the protagonist first resists his inability to find death, ultimately accepting (in the concluding cadence) the inevitability of his situation and the continuation of his journey. Despite their different technical foundations, these repetitions of cadential progressions make, in my view, significant musico-poetic cross-references that rather directly relate to the poetic narrative.

The fifth musical element in table 13.2, a 6̂–5̂ motion, can be associated with death as deeply desired. It connects two important narrative moments (table 13.1), one in which the thought of death emerges ("Der greise Kopf" and "Die Krähe") and another in which the speaker declares his intention to seek death ("Der Wegweiser"). These cross-references are thus clearly ordered. The musico-poetic associations of the 6̂–5̂ motion are somewhat different in the two narrative moments. In "Der greise Kopf" and "Die Krähe," whose poems make it clear that death has not yet come, this motivic progression refers to reality, to death as only an illusion. In "Der greise Kopf" the speaker is still young, and death remains far away (section 5.3). In "Die Krähe" it turns out that the crow does not function as an omen of death after all (section 6.3).

In both songs the 6̂–5̂ motion is associated with another cross-referential motive, enharmonicism, musical element no. 6 in Table 13.2. In these songs, the 6̂ (A♭) is enharmonically reinterpreted as a ♯5̂ (G♯). This pitch functions as a chromatic passing tone, which ascends to A♮, a chromatically altered version of 6̂. In both songs the G♯–A♮ motion is heard at the moment when the speaker expresses hope that death is at hand (mm. 11–12 in "Der greise Kopf" and, indirectly, in mm. 36–37; mm. 19–22 in "Die Krähe"). In other words, when the sign referring to reality (6̂) is enharmonically reinterpreted (♯5̂), the poetic reference also changes from reality to the illusion that death is near. Through this G♯–A♮ progression, a C-major diatony (locally suggested by the tonicized G major and the tonic major in "Der greise Kopf" and the tonicized F major in "Die Krähe") briefly replaces the C-minor diatony. As a result, the enharmonic reinterpretation also refers to the first musical element in table 13.2 (modal mixture), which juxtaposes reality with illusion.

The musico-poetic associations of the 6̂–5̂ motion are somewhat different in "Der Wegweiser," where the protagonist declares that he will consciously seek death (section 9.3). In this song, where death is a real option, the 6̂–5̂ progression is associated with death (O₂). Occasionally, however, 6̂ (E♭) does not descend but ascends to E♮, the chromatically inflected 6̂. This secondary, ascending motion can be associated with the company of people spoken about in the poem and, indirectly, with the thought of the beloved (O₁); the wanderer does not follow the signposts leading to the towns, declaring instead that he will no longer seek the company of people, including his beloved. As in "Der greise Kopf" and "Die Krähe," 6̂ in "Der Wegweiser" is associated with enharmonicism. In mm. 27–34 D♯ (♯5̂), the enharmonic equivalent of E♭ (6̂), is heard prominently. Yet ultimately, D♯ descends to D♮ in the same way that 6̂ descends to 5̂ in G minor; D♯ does not ascend to E♮, as the listener might have expected in this new context. In this part of the narrative of *Winterreise*, O₂ (death symbolized by the 6̂–5̂ motion) is primary, so the ascending tendency of ♯5̂ (associated with the company of people) is relinquished.

As we just saw, enharmonicism (the sixth musical element in Table 13.2) occurs fleetingly in "Der greise Kopf," "Die Krähe," and "Der Wegweiser." But in "Letzte Hoffnung" it is of primary significance; indeed, two enharmonic pairs feature prominently throughout the entire song (as shown in chapter 7). I have argued that the flat-side members of the two pairs (G♭ and C♭) function as signs referring to the outer reality, whereas the sharp-side members (F♯ and B♮) refer to the speaker's inner thoughts (section 7.3). Ultimately, the two worlds are fused in the poem: the outer world (the fall of the leaf) lends new consciousness to the inner world (the notion that abandoning love leads to death). Likewise, at the song's end (mm. 35–43) both the sharp- and flat-side members of the enharmonic pairs set the same words for the only time.

Musical element no. 7 in table 13.2, the quasi-religious chorale texture, associates the endings of "Letzte Hoffnung" and "Im Dorfe" with "Das Wirtshaus" and "Die Nebensonnen." Each of these moments features prominently in the cycle's overall narrative (table 13.1). At the end of "Letzte Hoffnung," the thought of death as an escape from misery is clarified and contextualized in the protagonist's mind. This thought is emphasized (and indeed suggested in the first place, as discussed in section 7.3) by the solemn texture at the song's end. "Im Dorfe" in turn begins the three-song group of satellites in which the narrator considers the newly emerged idea of hope from various angles. The associations brought up by the chorale texture enforce the narrative idea, lending considerable support to death being a positive option once the loss of love has been accepted.

When in "Das Wirtshaus" the wanderer anticipates that his desire for death will be fulfilled (in vain, as he will soon learn), the music recalls the texture that initially announced this desire. Further associations are created by the words that, at the end of "Letzte Hoffnung," mention the grave and, in "Das Wirtshaus," the cemetery. In "Die Nebensonnen," a satellite attached to "Das Wirtshaus," the wanderer reflects on the outcome of the earlier song, how death eludes him. The song follows the frustration expressed in "Mut," and the return to the chorale texture of "Das Wirtshaus" underlines the poem's return to the desire for death, symbolized by the setting of the third and final sun. The fusion of pious and declamatory expressive qualities (discussed in section 11.2) mirrors the protagonist's rhetorical intensity, which now merges with religious thoughts associated with death.

The eighth and final musical element, the juxtaposition of E♭–D and E♭–E♮ in "Der Wegweiser" and "Das Wirtshaus," is directly related to the fifth element, the $\hat{6}$–$\hat{5}$ motion in "Der Wegweiser," discussed above. The eighth element appears in only two songs, but it is so significant for the overall narrative of the cycle that it merits close examination. In "Der Wegweiser" the primary descending motion refers to death (O_2), which the protagonist now consciously chooses, while the secondary ascending version refers to abandoning human company, including that of the beloved (O_1). In "Das Wirtshaus" the descending version also refers to death. E♭ is now a secondary, chromatically inflected element, however; E♮ is the leading tone of the song's F major and thus the primary version of $\hat{7}$. E♮ therefore ultimately replaces E♭, most significantly near the song's end, in mm. 23–28.

Likewise, in the poem death eludes the wanderer, who is forced to continue his journey.

The musico-poetic cross-references discussed above have mainly concerned songs whose poems form kernels in the cycle's narrative structure (table 13.1). This makes the ordered nature of these cross-references clear. In other words, musico-poetic cross-references primarily occur in songs whose poems advance the underlying narrative trajectory, while there are fewer cross-references among the satellites, whose poems are attached to the kernels without suggesting a progression of the underlying narrative. As a result, the exact locations where the cross-references occur are of great significance for the organization of *Winterreise*'s part 2; the network of elements further emphasizes the importance of those songs that function as significant turning points in the cycle, thus clarifying the overall narrative. Furthermore, apart from elements 7 and 8, all of the musical cross-references were introduced in "Der greise Kopf" and "Die Krähe," the two songs that represent the kernel in which the poetic theme of death is first introduced. The music's cross-referential network thus emerges at the very moment the theme of death is introduced in the poems. It is also consistent that elements 7 and 8 are not introduced in songs 14 and 15: element 7 refers to dignified death, while 8 underlines the conscious decision to seek death with all of its consequences. Temporally, these two ideas follow the emergence of the idea of death, with the associated musical factors appearing only later.

13.4. A Coherent Whole or a Collection of Fragments?

We saw in section 12.1 that in writing about Schumann, David Ferris, Beate Julia Perrey, and Leon Plantinga challenged the idea of song cycles as a coherent whole. These scholars have argued that Schumann's cycles should not be understood as unified entities but rather as fragmentary and open. As a result, they see discontinuity, rather than coherence, as the guiding principle of the cycles. Cyrus Hamlin (1999) has suggested a similar view of *Winterreise*. Although his commentary mainly addresses the text, Hamlin clearly challenges the idea of musical coherence as well. Charles Rosen (1995) has likewise maintained that *Winterreise* includes no narrative action, large-scale harmonic scheme, or clear motivic cross-references. He seems to deny the existence of the very features on which the coherence of song cycles has usually been based. At the same time, Rosen maintains that unity is the prerequisite of a song cycle, an assessment that suggests that *Winterreise* too must have some kind of coherence.

Both Ferris and Perrey take the Romantic concept of the literary fragment as their starting point in viewing the organization of Schumann's cycles. They argue that many individual numbers in song cycles have weak openings (such as beginning in the middle of an ongoing process) as well as inconclusive endings. While these descriptions seem quite appropriate to many of Schumann's songs (perhaps, most famously, to the opening song of *Dichterliebe*, "Im wunderschönen Monat Mai"), such accounts do not correspond very well to the songs of *Winterreise*. Apart from the opening of "Letzte Hoffnung," all of the Lieder analyzed in this study begin on a clearly stated tonic chord and have a structurally conclusive perfect authentic cadence at or near the end (with the exception of "Der Leiermann" and, on the level of the immediate musical surface, "Im Dorfe"). In effect, Schubert's songs do not exhibit in a marked manner the kinds of features on which Ferris and Perrey largely base their assessment of Schumann's cycles as being fragmentary in nature.[18]

Yet I believe that discontinuity does play a significant role in *Winterreise*.[19] I make this claim despite the fact that, so far in this chapter, I have discussed only those features that emphasize the cycle's coherence: topical unity, narrative trajectory, large-scale harmonic organization, and musico-poetic cross-references. The moments of discontinuity in *Winterreise* arise from both poetic and musical factors: in the poetry, primarily from dissociation from the topics of adjacent poems, and in the music, from remote key relationships or sharply differing expressions in adjacent songs. I will begin by discussing the poetic discontinuities and then address those in the music. My goal is to show how the impression of discontinuity interacts with factors that create coherence, aspects discussed so far in this chapter. Rosen has also spoken, on a general level, about the coexistence of the apparently incompatible issues of unity and discontinuity in song cycles, stating that it "smacks a little of having one's cake and eating it, too" (1995, 212). I would argue that in *Winterreise* Rosen's assumed contradiction is only an illusion.

In section 13.2 I argued that part 2 of *Winterreise* forms a layered narrative trajectory consisting of primary kernels and their attached embellishing satellites. The kernels constitute the underlying narrative. I believe that this hierarchical interpretation also helps to address the issue of poetic discontinuity. The layered view is therefore not just a technical justification for the claim that *Winterreise* has narrative coherence, a view that many scholars have challenged. Rather, I believe that it also helps to explain two aspects of the poetic cycle that intuitively might seem to be mutually exclusive: the sense of coherence and large-scale unity, on the one hand, and the impression of local discontinuities, on the other.

Moments of poetic discontinuity are particularly evident in the two groups of songs that constitute satellites attached to previously introduced kernels, songs 17–19 and 22–23 (table 13.1). Here, one may temporarily get the impression that the textual arc loses its unity. In songs 17–19 the poetic themes include the seemingly unrelated topics of leaving a village ("Im Dorfe"), contemplating a storm ("Der stürmische Morgen"), and agreeing to being deceived ("Täuschung"). Even though the narrative course of each of the three poems shows clear discontinuity vis-à-vis the others, the larger context provides the logic underlying this local impression. The poems are satellites attached to the kernel introduced in "Letzte Hoffnung" and show different perspectives on the underlying narrative state presented there. The disparity among the satellites reflects the complexity of the kernel; the lack of cohesion among the poems at the local level is justified by the more global context. The protagonist has to consider carefully whether or not he will accept death as the principal goal of his longing. In order to reach a conclusion, he goes through a range of emotions and reactions, which are then reflected in the apparent discontinuity among the poems.

A similar impression of discontinuity appears at the end of the cycle (in songs 22–23). Yet I believe that same kind of explanation can be given here: the local disparity among the poems is an outcome of juxtaposing different satellites vis-à-vis the same kernel (introduced in song 21). The final kernel (song 24) then returns to the topic of death mentioned in the preceding kernel ("Das Wirtshaus"). As a result, the diversity of poetic topics is an outgrowth of the tension between the local satellites and the underlying kernels. This variety at the cycle's conclusion has an important consequence: it precludes any sense of unequivocal closure at the end.

The two sets of poetic satellites (songs 17–19 and 22–23) also function prominently in instances where musical discontinuity occurs. As example 13.1 shows, the keys of songs 17–19 are detached from the smooth progression (harmonic motions retaining common tones) governing songs 13–16: there is a stepwise bass motion (E♭–D) between songs 16 and 17, a progression leading to a succession of two remotely connected tonics. The harmonic detachment underlines the motion from the preceding poetic kernels (which constitute the underlying narrative trajectory) to the embellishing satellites. The tonic chords of the satellites form a unit consisting of smooth harmonic progressions. Thus, songs 17–19 form a harmonically unified group, a factor enhancing their similar poetic functions. But the musical expression creates a clear discontinuity among the three. Most important, the almost violent expression of the brief "Der stürmische Morgen" seems to detach it from its environment. As a result, the incoherence of expression in these three songs challenges their harmonic unity. This musical situation suits the poetic drama very well. The harmonic unity emphasizes that the three songs have a similar function in the large-scale poetic structure; all are satellites attached to the same kernel. At the same time, the expressive discontinuity indicates that here the protagonist expresses various, widely differing reactions to the idea that emerged in "Letzte Hoffnung," the preceding kernel.

Example 13.1 indicates that, after "Täuschung" (no. 19), smooth harmonic motion between adjacent tonics all but vanishes. (This is the situation with the keys in the first edition but not in the manuscript, as indicated in example 13.1a.) The harmonic discontinuity can be associated with the narrative confusion. From "Der greise Kopf" to "Der Wegweiser," the narrative has proceeded in a consistent manner (table 13.1). The thought of death (O_2) emerges and is contemplated, and finally, in "Der Wegweiser," the protagonist consciously decides to seek it. The logical next step in the narrative would be death's arrival ($S \cap O_2$). But this does not happen, so the speaker and his goal, death, remain disjoined ($S \cup O_2$). The harmonic discontinuity can be seen as reflecting the confusion and frustration at the cycle's end, as well as the failure of the penultimate kernel to provide the desired answer (table 13.1). This harmonic discontinuity is supported by the music's expressive contrasts. Most important, the expression of "Mut" departs considerably from its environment, which seems poetically justified. This song is the first satellite attached to the kernel of "Das Wirtshaus," in which it becomes evident that the much-desired death does not arrive. Now the protagonist cries out in frustration, and this extreme emotional outburst justifies the expressive discontinuity. The expressive contrast between the last two songs is great, but now the tonic chords share two pitches (including the tonic itself). The smooth harmonic motion underlines the arrival at the final kernel in "Der Leiermann," while the expressive contrast emphasizes that the graceless death referred to here is not the dignified goal the wanderer has been anticipating.

In this chapter I have argued that part 2 of *Winterreise* forms a unified whole whose coherence grows from thematic unity among the poems, the narrative trajectory, the large-scale harmonic scheme, and musico-poetic cross-references. One should be cautious, however, about drawing simplistic conclusions about *Winterreise* that diminish the cycle's subtlety. *Winterreise* eludes easy and clear-cut categorizations. In section 13.1 we saw that the cycle is neither exclusively topical nor exclusively narrative but includes aspects of both. Section 13.2 demonstrated that the keys in part 2 do not form a tonally unified whole in the sense that we can speak of a governing overall tonic or prolongational entities consisting of the tonics of consecutive songs. Yet there is a clear logic to the unfolding of keys, a logic that is related to the textual narrative of the poems. In section 13.3 we saw that there are no direct motivic recollections comparable to those in Beethoven's *An die ferne Geliebte*, for example, or in Schumann's *Dichterliebe*. Yet there are other types of cross-references that enhance the overall narrative of the cycle. Finally, in section 13.4 I suggested that the cycle includes moments of both poetic and musical discontinuity, yet such apparent fragmentariness takes place within a deeper-level unified scheme.

14 Epilogue: The Meaning of Death in *Winterreise*

Now that we have analyzed in detail songs 14–24 as well as the cyclic aspects of part 2 of *Winterreise,* we can return to the questions left unanswered in chapter 2 at the beginning of our journey: How should we understand the notion of death in *Winterreise,* and how can we justify this specific view historically? As discussed in section 2.2, death (and suicide in particular) was a common theme in late eighteenth- and early nineteenth-century German literature. We saw that in the literature preceding *Winterreise,* death might be understood either in a concrete sense (as a description of a physical event) or in a symbolic manner. I referred to Goethe's *Werther* as an instance of the former and to Friedrich Schlegel's *Lucinde* as an example of the latter. This duality was related to different ways in which the function of language could be understood. Eighteenth-century writers required language to be used in a precise manner (the "signifier" is unequivocally related to the "signified"), while the Romantics suggested that words may, or indeed should, be used in a way that avoided universally understood meaning (a given "signifier" is detached from any single "signified").

With the Romantics, a symbolic understanding of death does not necessarily include an end point. Rather, as we saw in section 2.2, writers such as Schlegel and Novalis argued that death signifies a change in the mode of existence, paradoxically, a kind of continuation of life in a different guise. I quoted a fragment by Novalis that states this clearly: "Death is the Romanticizing principle of our life. . . . Life is strengthened through death" (1997, 154). Death is, in a way, in the service of life: it can provide meanings beyond the reach of our mundane, finite, and earthly existence. Thus, it can be associated with the infinite and the eternal.

In section 2.3 I suggested that in *Winterreise* the notion of death should be understood in a symbolic way rather than as a description of a concrete physical event. Starting with "Der greise Kopf," the protagonist declares his desire to die, deciding in "Der Wegweiser" to seek death intentionally, a goal that, however, remains unobtainable. If we consider suicide as it appears in *Werther,* for example, the decision to die should (or at least could) lead to the protagonist killing himself. But in *Winterreise,* death remains beyond the reach of the protagonist. Suicide, and by extension physical death, does not seem to correspond to the poetic content of the cycle unless we assume that the protagonist lacks the courage to take his own life. It therefore seems that *Winterreise* is not speaking about a concrete, physical death. In other words, death does not necessarily mean the end point of the wanderer's existence but might signify a change in the nature of this existence.

Several poems provide a key for giving death a specific symbolic interpretation: death can be understood as referring to a state in which the protagonist no longer feels the misery caused by the loss of his beloved. Death is accordingly not the end of the wanderer's physical existence but a state in which his wretched memories no longer haunt him. Pairing death with ending the grieving for a lost love can be found at the close of another major song cycle, Schumann's *Dichterliebe,* to poems of Heinrich Heine. Its final poem, "Die alten, bösen Lieder" (The old, evil songs), consists of six stanzas, the first five of which describe a coffin whose dimensions are so immense that the poem clearly has an ironic air. The sixth and final stanza finally tells us the reason for the gargantuan size:

> Wisst ihr warum den Sarg wohl
> So gross und schwer mag sein?
> Ich senkt' auch meine Liebe
> Und meinen Schmerz hinein!
>
> Do you know why the coffin must be so large and heavy? I also sank my love and my grief therein.

As the love about which the protagonist speaks in *Dichterliebe* was great, so its grave must be big enough to encompass all sorrow. The poem's ironic tone suggests that the coffin is indeed sufficiently large: since the speaker is capable of humor, he will likely be able to leave the misery of his lost love behind. This view is also conveyed by Schumann's music: the final song is followed by a dreamy, almost otherworldly piano postlude in the major mode, quoting the postlude of "Am leuchtenden Sommermorgen" (In the bright summer morning).

In *Winterreise* the symbolic pairing of death with forgetting the beloved has more negative implications. Here, this pairing could be seen as referring to a state in which one is no longer able to feel any emotions, a state in which the heart is frozen, to use the expression Müller himself employed. References to such a state of numbness, to the loss of human qualities without physically dying, can also be found in poetry contemporaneous with *Winterreise.* Joseph von Eichendorff's "Die zwei Gesellen" (The two journeymen) describes two youths wandering about the world.[1] The first gets married, and the mother of the bride buys him a house and a farm, while the second is seduced by a siren's song, which pulls him into an abyss from which he escapes only as an old, exhausted man. The poem's final stanza introduces the narrator, who laments the destiny of both: the first youth has succumbed to a bourgeois existence, while the second faces a situation in which all that remains is, in Bernadette Malinowski's reading, "a loss of self and identity, a loss of creative power and language" (2004, 158). Both wanderers are still alive, but the poem's narrator suggests that neither is capable of living a life of human dignity.

At various stages of his journey, the protagonist of *Winterreise* refers to a state of numbness. He suggests that if he were to forget love and his beloved, it would mean that his tender emotions would be frozen. This idea is stated clearly in the final two stanzas (4 and 5) of "Erstarrung" (Numbness):

Soll denn kein Angedenken
Ich nehmen mit von hier?
Wenn meine Schmerzen schweigen,
Wer sagt mir dann von ihr?

Mein Herz ist wie erstorben
Kalt starrt ihr Bild darin:
Schmilzt je das Herz mir wieder,
Fließt auch ihr Bild dahin.

Shall I then take no remembrance from here? When my sorrows are stilled, who will speak to me of her?

My heart is as if dead, her image cold and rigid within. If my heart ever thaws again, her image too will melt away.

These stanzas speak of the coldness of the heart and the frozen image of the beloved. They imply that thinking of the beloved unavoidably leads to pain; if the misery ends, love too will vanish. In the final stanza, such a state of numbness is compared to death.[2] It is significant that the word *erstorben* (dead) is Schubert's addition; Müller's original text used the word *erfroren* (frostbitten). With this change, Schubert probably wanted to draw attention to death: the words *erstorben* and *erfroren* sound so similar that it seems unlikely the sonic difference would have been the reason for the alteration.[3] In "Auf dem Flusse" (On the river) the wanderer compares the dynamic, running river in the summer to the same river in the winter, now still and covered with ice. In the poem's final stanza, he associates the frozen river with his own heart, thus again referring to his emotions as being covered with immovable ice.[4]

In these two poems (both of which are from part 1 of *Winterreise*), such a numb state is considered negative: the cold heart, incapable of feeling love, is portrayed as depressing. Yet at the same time, numbness would provide peace and escape from misery and thus grant release from the present wretchedness.

When death is introduced in "Der greise Kopf" and "Die Krähe," these poems seem to be dealing with the possibility of a physical death. The former speaks about old age, which would bring death closer, while the latter refers in quite a macabre manner to the protagonist's body as the crow's prey. But as I have suggested in section 13.1, in these two songs the speaker does not yet contextualize the thought of death, the idea emerging here; most important, the death is not related to the lost love, the main topic of the cycle's first part. That contextualization takes place in "Letzte Hoffnung," and the ensuing three poems (the satellites in the narrative trajectory) provide various reflections on the thought of abandoning love and aiming at death. "Der stürmische Morgen" is the most desperate of these reflections, and the poem's distressed quality is enhanced by the almost violent music. Here the cycle returns to the notion of the cold heart referred to in part 1; the protagonist must now admit that if he continues to seek death, he will also lose his capacity to feel warm emotions or to love. In "Der stürmische Morgen" death, therefore, is not a physical event but a state in which valuable human qualities have been lost. This brief outburst is followed by the nostalgia of "Täuschung," however, so its expressiveness has no immediate effect.

"Das Wirtshaus" is of primary importance. This song depicts the consequences of the speaker's decision in "Der Wegweiser" to seek death while ultimately indicating that death will elude him. If death were understood solely in its physical form, then this powerlessness would most likely refer to the protagonist's inability to commit suicide. The last two songs challenge such a straightforward interpretation, however. In "Die Nebensonnen" the speaker refers for the last time (and here only indirectly) to the beloved. In other words, he has not been able to forget her or to freeze his heart. As a result, death (if understood as a state in which wretchedness is not felt) remains unattainable in "Das Wirtshaus": the thought of love still lingers in the speaker's mind. To put it another way, in this religious-sounding song, the wanderer seeks a dignified death (a state in which he would not feel the misery of lost love yet could still retain his tender emotions), but this turns out to be impossible. The last song, "Der Leiermann," shows a state of complete numbness. The old man pays no attention to his environment. He is not physically dead (he constantly plays his hurdy-gurdy), but he exhibits no other signs of life or any signs of human affection. At this stage of his journey, the wanderer is ready to accept even this abject state, one void of all human emotions. He asks if he can join the old man but receives no answer.

If interpreted with this view in mind, namely, that death refers to the lack of emotions rather than to a physical dying, "Der stürmische Morgen" plays a very important role, which is clear only in retrospect. The idea of death as an escape from misery is contextualized in "Letzte Hoffnung" when the speaker understands that in order to find death, he must first abandon the hope of regaining love. (Schubert's music suggests this reading more clearly than Müller's poem.) As we just saw, the inability to meet up with death in "Das Wirtshaus" and the indirect reference to the beloved in "Die Nebensonnen" show that the wanderer is initially unable to relinquish his tender emotions because he cannot give up the thought of the beloved. "Der stürmische Morgen" fits this trajectory well. Its brief outburst indicates what losing the capacity for positive human affections really means, but its brevity suggests that the protagonist is not, at that stage, ready to accept these consequences. Only in "Der Leiermann" is he prepared to admit the inevitability of the undignified, numb state to which the loss of positive emotions leads.

The end of *Winterreise* thus suggests that the protagonist initially tries to find a dignified death, a state reflected in the quasi-religious musical character of "Das Wirtshaus" (a characteristic first announced at the end of "Letzte Hoffnung" at the moment the contextualized idea of death emerges). In such a state, the protagonist could forget the misery of lost love but at the same time keep his dignity. Only when this kind of death turns out to be an unobtainable dream does he begin to consider seriously, in "Der Leiermann," the numb state void of any emotions. Such an emotional state is already envisioned in "Der stürmische Morgen," and the association between "Der Leiermann" and "Der stürmische Morgen" is enhanced by a musical cross-reference between the songs: as discussed in section 13.3, these are the only songs in part 2 that include no mixture of major and minor. In other words, only in these two songs is the major mode, often associated with illusion, absent. The connection between these songs—the avoidance of modal mixture, a departure from a norm that dominates the second part of *Winterreise*—creates an ordered musical cross-reference, an association showing a tonal environment free of the illusion of the parallel major. The musical pairing of the two songs underlines their poetic function; accordingly, the motion from the thought of a dignified death to numbness is clearer in Schubert's music than in Müller's poems. As so often in *Winterreise,* the music shapes the way the poems are understood.

This view of death as a state in which misery is not felt can be contextualized with a fragment published by Novalis in 1797–98: "Death is a victory over the self—which, like all self-conquest, brings about a new, easier existence" (1997, 24). Novalis's fragment seems to suggest that one has to conquer oneself in order to find an easier existence. In "Das Wirtshaus" the protagonist is not yet able to make this conquest. He clearly states that he seeks death (understood here, as explained above, as a state in which he feels no misery). But the death he envisions here is dignified; it still retains human affections, as is indicated by his recollection of the beloved in "Die Nebensonnen." Such a death cannot be found, however. Only in "Der Leiermann" is the speaker ready to accept all loss of humanity, a totally numb state devoid of any emotions. But the cycle ends before we know what happens: Does he take the final step toward such a state, or does he simply declare his willingness to do so?

But at this point my analysis and interpretation must conclude. *Winterreise* ends in uncertainty with no resolution; in "Der Leiermann" the old man remains silent and does not answer the protagonist's queries. Likewise, any unequivocal assessment of the precise meaning of death in *Winterreise* is, in the end, impossible. From here on, interpretation of the cycle and its ending belongs to individual listeners, scholars, and performers.

Notes

1. Genesis and Narrative of *Winterreise*

1. This evolution has been set forth in numerous studies. See, for example, Feil (1988, 24–26); Georgiades (1967, 357–59); Lewis (1988, 58–62); Newcomb (1986, 165–66); and Youens (1991, 21–29). My account is based on these.

2. In the second column of table 1.1 (*Deutsche Blätter*), I have left empty spaces for those lines where the two poems not published in this collection ("Die Post" and "Täuschung") appear in Schubert's cycle. In the third column (*Waldhornisten II*), there is an empty line between poems 12 and 13. The two-part division is not found in Müller's cycle, but I have added it here in order to juxtapose these poems with Schubert's two-part cycle.

3. Schubert (1989, 42). I have not been able to study the engraver's copy; this information about the end of part 1 is given in Newcomb (1986, 165).

4. The order of the poems in Schubert's part 2 is close to that published in *Deutsche Blätter* (table 1.1). However, Schubert apparently did not know this publication.

5. The manuscript of *Winterreise* shows, furthermore, that Schubert did not always have a fixed idea about the key of a given song. In "Frühlingstraum" the right-hand part in the piano introduction was first drafted in G major and only later written in the final key of A major (Schubert 1989, 36).

6. In fact, these are the only songs transposed in the engraver's copy, since the copyist forgot to transpose "Rast." The publisher, Tobias Haslinger, added the transposition instructions into this copy; see Schubert (1989, xiii).

7. I am referring to the internal key relationships within the cycle, not to the more general topic of "key characteristics." This notion, still influential in Schubert's time, suggested that certain keys might be associated with certain emotions or topics. (For a thorough discussion of key characteristics, see Steblin 2002.) Walther Dürr (2004, 140) has suggested that Schubert's choice of keys in *Winterreise* depended on key characteristics. Richard Kramer (1994, 13–17) and Susan Youens (1991, 99–100), in turn, have spoken about a related view in which many keys have definite, recurring significance in Schubert's songs.

8. The reduced unity might actually be desirable here: in the final, two-part form of *Winterreise*, "Einsamkeit" no longer closes the cycle, as it did when Schubert finished part 1, so a strong impression of closure might interfere with the transition to part 2. For further discussion on the effect of "Einsamkeit," either in D minor as closing the original twelve-song cycle or in B minor as the end of the first part of *Winterreise*, see Kramer (1994, 166–71); and Youens (1991, 97).

9. Some writers also suggest that the outward action has certain functions; see, for example, Newcomb (1986, 166–67).

10. I do not deny, however, the significance of the thematic associations between non-contiguous poems, which are abundant in *Winterreise*. But since my focus here is on the overall narrative, I leave these aside. The thematic association created by those poems that contrast with others in the group can be clarified with Roland Barthes's idea that "units of a sequence, although forming a whole at the level of that very sequence, may be separated from one another by the insertion of units from other sequences" (1977, 118). Seymour Chatman (1978, 54–55) has further specified that narrative elements occurring outside their principal group can be either anticipatory or retrospective, depending on the temporal location of their primary group.

11. For a different interpretation of the division of the poems into thematically connected groups, see Lewis (1988, 62–66).

12. Anthony Newcomb (1986, 166–68) has suggested a narrative for part 1 that is primarily based on chronology and actions. His division of the poems into groups is somewhat different from what I have proposed above.

13. Historically, these differences between the view of death presented in "Der Lindenbaum" and "Irrlicht," on the one hand, and part 2, on the other, may arise from the fact that these two poems belong to the twelve that Müller apparently first considered to be an independent cycle (as discussed in section 1.1).

2. *Winterreise* in Context

1. The tradition of giving this date is mentioned (and challenged), for example, by Walther Dürr (1984, 7), who discusses the history of the Lied, and by Jane K. Brown (2004, 12), who charts the poetic background of the Lied. The date was first proposed by Oskar Bie in 1926.

2. Walther Dürr (1984, 8–10) has indicated that nineteenth-century writers also found it difficult to define the genre of the Lied precisely.

3. For further discussion on the poetic change at the end of the eighteenth century and its significance for the Lied, see Brown (2004); and Seelig (2010).

4. For a discussion on the significance of "folk literature" in late eighteenth-century and early nineteenth-century literature, see Lampart (2004).

5. Walther Dürr (1984, 7–35) discusses in detail the early commentaries on the Lied.

6. In the opening essay of his *Kreisleriana*, "The Kapellmeister's Musical Sorrows," E. T. A. Hoffmann (1996, 17–24) makes fun of the eagerness of amateurs with no talent to perform in social gatherings.

7. Hoffmann's observations on the Lied, which emphasize the significance of the text as the point of departure, differ greatly from his views on pure instrumental music, as stated, for example, in his well-known review of Beethoven's Fifth Symphony. Here he stresses the independence of music from all other media: "When music is spoken of as an independent art the term can properly apply only to instrumental music, which scorns all aid, all admixture of other arts" (Hoffmann 1989, 236). Here we can see a concrete shift in aesthetic orientation, which was taking place in the early nineteenth century: Hoffmann's opinions about the Lied, where text is considered primary, still retain eighteenth-century ideals, whereas his views on instrumental music rely on early Romantic, post-Kantian aesthetics.

8. The significance of private, amateur gatherings in the emergence of song cycles is discussed, for example, in Dürr (1984, 246–47); Peake (1982, 242–43); and Turchin (1981, 12–14).

9. For a discussion on the inconsistent use of these terms in the early nineteenth century, see Bingham (1993, 19–21).

10. For an English translation of von Dommer's definition, see Ferris (2000, 9).

11. In addition, Bingham discusses a fourth category, "musically constructed cycles," in which unity results from musical as well as from textual associations.

12. For a discussion of the use of the term *Roman* in connection with song cycles, see Turchin (1981, 19–37).

13. The requirement of unequivocally understood concepts was by no means a rule in the later eighteenth century, however. In the mid-eighteenth century, Edmund Burke, for example, in discussing the sublime in literature, observed that obscurity is an important aspect of poetry (Keach 1997, 133).

14. I do not intend to provide a comprehensive coverage of death at the turn of the eighteenth century to the nineteenth. For a more thorough discussion of this notion and its relationship to love, see Dye (2004, 16–40); and Saul (2009).

15. Sondrup (1990) discusses the literary and social influence of *Werther*.

16. Furst (1990) discusses the idea of the liberty of the self in *Werther*.

17. For a discussion of the early reception of *Werther*, see Duncan (2005, 7–28).

18. For a discussion of the novel's formal idiosyncrasies, see Behler (1993, 289–98); and Blackall (1983, 38–43).

19. Bauer (2000) is a thorough discussion of various aspects of death in *Lucinde*. Furthermore, he traces relationships and connections among the different views of this notion in the novel.

20. For a discussion of the pantheistic view of death, characteristic of Romantic aesthetics, see Dye (2004, 17–24).

21. A very similar view of death can be found in Novalis's *Hymnen an die Nacht* (Hymns to the night), published in 1800, a major poetic work from the first generation of Romantics (Novalis 1988). Bernadette Malinowski has remarked that in this work "art thus becomes the real place of spiritual resurrection, the place of Romantic suicide where the persona of the poet achieves idealistic-sentimental enhancement by the 'Annihilation' of his earthly, biographical self" (2004, 156).

22. In discussing the underlying narrative of *Winterreise* in chapter 13, I argue that this contradiction is only an apparent one.

23. For a biographical sketch of Müller's life that also describes his literary interests, see Baumann (1981, 1–34).

3. Text-Music Relationships

1. For another extensive, recent defense of music's nonrepresentational quality, see Kivy (2009). In the past few decades, the notion of music as an autonomous art has often been challenged. Coverage of the arguments of this at times heated discussion is beyond the scope of this study.

2. There are also writers who oppose this view and see music as a representational art form; see, for example, Kramer (1992); and Robinson (1994). For a brief exposition of the concept of representation viewed in a wider aesthetic context, see Lyas (1997, 37–58).

3. The addition of words, of course, also involves the sounds of the words themselves, so the same Lied sounds somewhat different when sung in German or Italian. This does not, however, affect the musical imitation, the topic at hand.

4. The imitation may also be quite indistinct in instrumental music in cases where the work's title or program provides a textual reference. The thematic fragmentation in the closing measures of Beethoven's *Coriolan* Overture, for example, and again in the second movement of the Third Symphony quite clearly imitates the last breaths of the dying hero or the final beats of his heart. But in both cases, this imitation is clarified by extramusical references: in the overture by Collin's play, and in the symphony by the title of the movement, Marcia funebre. So the vagueness of the imitation is clarified by a textual reference in a manner somewhat similar to that encountered in vocal music.

5. There are also philosophers who argue that music can express higher emotions. Jerrold Levinson (1990), for example, has discussed how the complex emotion of hope emerges in Mendelssohn's *Hebrides* Overture, while Jenefer Robinson (2005, 293–347) suggests more generally that music is capable of expressing full and nuanced emotions that can be approached through a virtual "persona" posited in music.

6. Kivy sums up the outlines of his theory on p. 83.

7. A clear instance in which a drop in the dynamic level signifies a high point can be found in Mendelssohn's *Elijah,* no. 34, the chorus "Behold, God the Lord." Here a fortissimo that culminates a long increase in tension in E minor is followed by an E-major chorale marked pianissimo (mm. 115 ff.). The musical high point aligns with the textual culmination, thus creating clear musico-poetic associations. The words of the chorus speak of vainly seeking the Lord in a tempest, an earthquake, and a fire. These violent options are set musically by a rising dynamic level and rhetorical intensity. Ultimately, God is found in a "still small voice," the words accompanied by the soft major-mode chorale, the music's high point.

8. The philosopher Jenefer Robinson has stressed the significance of a process-like course of sentiments for understanding music's emotional organization. In discussing Peter Kivy's theory of musical expression (which in its fundamentals is close to Stephen Davies's ideas outlined above), Robinson criticizes Kivy for ignoring or underemphasizing "the way in which musical expressiveness is a function of musical *process*" (2005, 303, emphasis in the original).

9. This possibility has also been suggested by Kofi Agawu (1992, 12) and Jerrold Levinson (1987, 290–93).

10. I am consciously disregarding many aspects of poetic structure, such as prosody, poetic meter, and grammar. Also, Robert Hatten (2008, 7) has suggested that lyric poems may have a "musically poetic language" of their own. Since my interpretations of Müller's poems will take the content as their starting point, I concentrate on content here as well.

11. Several scholars have noted the similarities between Schenkerian analysis and structuralist literary theory. Eero Tarasti, for example, has described Schenkerian theory as "structuralism before structuralism" (1994, 5).

12. Similarities between musical and textual structures have also been discussed without references to Schenkerian theory. Byron Almén, for example, has spoken about associations between musical and literary narrativity, referring to similarities (but not identities) between textual and musical structures: "Literature, drama, and music share a potential for meaningfully ordering events in time, but differ with respect to their degree of referential specificity" (2008, 14). Some scholars have even found it problematic that certain ideas of structuralist literary theory can be so closely associated with musical or-

ganization. Carolyn Abbate has argued that the likeness between the two is so great that the association between them becomes almost automatic and thus loses its explanatory power. She argues that the "application of structuralist categories to music thus involves a tautology" (Abbate 1991, 40).

13. Malin (2010) has done an extensive study on rhythmic and metric musico-poetic relationships in Lieder. For further examination of this topic, see, for example, Feil (1988); Georgiades (1967); and Jonas (1982, 149–61).

4. Musico-Poetic Associations

1. This description draws on Greimas (1983, 1987). For a thorough explication of Greimas's theories, see Schleifer (1987); and Budniakiewicz (1992). For a brief explanation that situates Greimassian theory in the wider field of structuralist and semiotic research, see Hawkes (1977, esp. 87–95).

2. The value of the very formal methodology of Greimassian semiotics has also been questioned by some literary theorists. Jonathan Culler, for instance, has asked, "What is gained . . . by attempting to derive the structure of an imaginative world from an analysis of discourse carried out in a supposedly formal and rigorous way rather than from the more intuitive consideration of sets of images?" (1975, 84).

3. Susan Youens has argued that Müller consciously intended the poems to be simple: "Müller wanted his poetry to speak directly to the heart, without the intervening obstacles of either poetic artifice . . . or other voices from within the poetry, such as a narrator or the poet himself" (1991, 53–54). Similarly, Cyrus Hamlin has spoken about "the norms of folksong which Müller was imitating, often with quite remarkable success" (1999, 130). Hence, the very nature of the poems, the intended formal and structural simplicity, justifies the use of only a few of Greimas's basic concepts. For a more thorough discussion of the relationships of Müller's poetry to folksongs, see Baumann (1981, 38–42).

4. Greimas gives a thorough explication of the actants in *Structural Semantics* (1966) (1983, 197–221). However, he changed his definition of the actants slightly in his subsequent writings, and the following outline respects the descriptions given in three of his articles: "A Problem of Narrative Semiotics: Objects of Value" (1973), "Actants, Actors, and Figures" (1973), and "Toward a Theory of Modalities" (1976) (Greimas 1987, 84–105, 106–120, and 121–39, respectively).

5. For a discussion of the changes in Greimas's definition of the object actant in his different writings, see Budniakiewicz (1992, 75–109).

6. In the three articles mentioned in note 4, Greimas uses two kinds of arrows (→ and ⇒) in a slightly inconsistent way. Here I will use the single arrow when describing a syntactical relation, the interdependence of elements; that is, "a → b" means "if *a*, then *b*." The double-line arrow will be used to describe a transformation or an action (temporal motion from one state to another); that is, "a ⇒ b" means "motion from state *a* to state *b*."

7. For a discussion on the changes in Greimas's definition of sender and receiver in his different writings, see Budniakiewicz (1992, 111–39).

8. The term *concealed repetition* is somewhat problematic; it implies that these connections would, by definition, remain hidden. However, if such connections are to be musically significant, then they must have an effect on one's perception of the music. Because of its problematic nature, I will not use Schenker's term *concealed repetition* but will refer to motivic connections instead.

9. However, in his analytical writings prior to *Free Composition*, Schenker was highly sensitive to motivic associations. In his 1930 analysis of Beethoven's "Eroica" Symphony, for example, he observed the importance of the C♯–D motion in mm. 7–9 of the first movement and the significance that this ascending step has for the entire movement: "This upward drive is, so to speak, the initial breath of the movement. Thereafter it continues to be of importance for the procurement of the content, no matter whether the ascent applies to a neighbour note . . . or a passing note" (1997, 11–12). He then gave instances of such upward motions in both the foreground and the middleground; see, for example, the arrows in Figur 3 (12–13) and Bild 1 (81). He did not, however, use the term *motive* to describe these motions. Nevertheless, he had used this term only a few years earlier, in 1926, to describe just such underlying repetitions; see, for example, Schenker (1996, 27).

10. The significance of seeking the origins of motivic associations in voice leading has also been emphasized by many more recent theorists: see, for example, Cadwallader and Pastille (1992, 132–34); and Rothgeb (1983, 40–42).

11. Cadwallader and Pastille (1992, 128) use the term *high-level motive* for more or less the same phenomenon.

12. For a thorough, partly Schenkerian-oriented discussion of the phenomenon of pitch-class motives and its elucidations in literature, see McCreless (2011). Because pitch-class motives are not outcomes of voice-leading processes, their foreground occurrences can, of course, be revealed without Schenkerian analysis. For a non-Schenkerian analysis of Schubert's Moment musical, op. 96, no. 6, in which a recurring pitch class is seen as a driving force of the musical drama, see Cone (1986).

13. I am referring to analyses that examine entire songs and their musico-poetic aspects. It is, of course, also possible to discuss excerpts of Lieder and their text-music associations. In such cases, there is naturally no need to examine the music of entire songs.

14. A clear instance of such nonalignment can be found in Schumann's song "Hör' ich das Liedchen klingen" (in *Dichterliebe*). Here both the poem and the music consist of a movement from the suppression of grief to its release, but the release does not occur in the music (mm. 24–27) at the same time as in the text (mm. 16–20). Nevertheless, the emotional arches of the poem and the music are similar, even though their culminations do not occur simultaneously. For further discussion of this aspect of the song, see Malin (2010, 131).

15. See Zbikowski (2002, esp. 77–95) for a more detailed discussion of CINs.

5. The Emergence of Death as a Positive Option

1. Such modulations do, however, occasionally occur. In Schubert's A-Minor Piano Sonata (D. 784), the second group of the opening movement's exposition is in E major (mm. 61 ff.). (For a discussion of the expressive effect of the major-mode secondary theme, see Hatten [2004, 190–92].) There are also instances, as in "Der greise Kopf," where the deep-level function of the tonicized major-mode dominant is uncertain. In the first movement of Mendelssohn's D-Minor Piano Trio, op. 49, the second group of the exposition (m. 119) starts in the dominant major (A major). But later in the exposition the music moves to A minor, and I do not take the A-major chord that opens the second group as the arrival at a deep-level *Stufe*.

2. Schenker (1979, 11) uses the term *diatony* when referring to the diatonic framework operating in the background, in practice, to the pitches of the tonic scale that also appear in the fundamental structure. In "Der greise Kopf," the emphasis on ♭3 and the

tonicization of G major thus imply an attempt to replace the C-minor diatony with a C-major framework.

3. In mm. 21–22 it would be possible to interpret two successive downbeats instead of the five-measure group shown in example 5.2b. (The metric interpretation of mm. 17–22 would then be 123411.) The interpretations are fundamentally similar: in both, the successive mm. 21 and 22 are strong measures on a hypermeasure level.

4. Walter Everett (1988, 203) reads the VI as more significant and interprets the E♭-major chord as a back-relating dominant.

5. Carl Schachter (1999b, 130–32) has discussed a somewhat similar situation in another song from *Winterreise,* "Auf dem Flusse," where the motivic design of the bass differs from the structural bass line.

6. A similar instance that features both mixture and the transference of the structural top-voice line to an inner voice occurs in Schubert's "Die liebe Farbe" (*Die schöne Müllerin*). For an analysis of this Lied, see Wen (1999, 279–80).

7. This idea is briefly mentioned at the end of "Irrlicht," but in the context of the first part of *Winterreise,* this reference to death remains isolated and thus receives no large-scale significance. For further discussion, see section 1.3.

8. Such a function has also been noted by Agawu (1984, 17–18).

6. Death Contemplated

1. The repetition follows the procedure Schenker calls "the freest form of interruption," whose "distinguishing feature is that the setting again takes up its initial position" (1979, 77). For another instance of this phenomenon in Schubert's music, see the opening movement of the *Unfinished* Symphony, mm. 31–37.

2. Felix Salzer (1982, 205) interprets the voice leading of the introduction differently, reading an octave-progression in the top voice. I consider the opening fourth of this descent (C–G) as a more local phenomenon than the concluding fifth (G–C); the fourth is supported by a contrapuntal prolongation of the tonic, whereas the G–C fifth has support from a more emphatic cadential progression and the significant 5–6 unfolding in the bass.

3. There are minor differences between the vocal part and the piano's left hand. Most important, at the end of mm. 7 and 11, Schubert adds to the piano part E♭s that, as the bass notes of a I⁶, prepare the predominant Fs of the ensuing measures, thus clarifying the bass line and harmony.

4. Marriage is a theme mentioned in the very first song, "Gute Nacht," in which the speaker tells the listener that "Das Mädchen sprach von Liebe / Die Mutter gar von Eh'" (the maiden spoke of love, the mother even of marriage). The reference to marriage here thus recalls a real possibility from the past.

7. From Hope for the Past to Hope for the Future

1. For a provocative commentary on the rhythmic complexities and unsettled aspects of meter in "Letzte Hoffnung," see Georgiades (1967, 370–75).

2. Richard Kramer (1994, 175) has also remarked on this association with the C minor of "Die Krähe."

3. Eytan Agmon (1987, 49–55) has discussed the role of the enharmonic pair C♭/B♮ in "Letzte Hoffnung." Mark Anson-Cartwright (2000) has argued that the C♭/B♮ pair is, in general, common in E♭-major works of the Classical and Romantic periods. He has

also noted the significance of the F♯/G♭ pair in this repertoire. Enharmonic pairs feature prominently in other Schubert songs as well. For an interesting examination of an F×/G♮ pair in "Nacht und Träume," see Schachter (1999b, 216–19).

4. A somewhat similar situation occurs in the second movement of Schubert's string quintet, where the B section of the E-major movement begins with an F-minor harmony. The top voice of this chord is an A♭, which functions as a neighbor note (♭4̂), despite being the enharmonic equivalent of the movement's *Kopfton*, G♯ (3̂). For a discussion of this movement, see Suurpää (2000, 455–65, esp. 460–61). Steven Laitz (1996, 140) has discussed a similar situation in the first song of Schubert's *Harfenspieler Gesänge*, in which the enharmonic pair ♯5̂/♭6̂ is prolonged. In "Aufenhalt" (in *Schwanengesang*) the foreground has two consecutive pitches forming an enharmonic pair with different structural functions. In mm. 123–29 there is a harmonic progression I–VI♭–V in which the VI♭ includes ♭1̂, while the V has ♯7̂.

5. See "Frühlingstraum" (*Winterreise*) and Impromptu, op. 90, no. 2. Unlike "Letzte Hoffnung," both of these works begin without minor allusions, however.

6. If the poem is read literally, the leaf does not actually fall: "Ach, und fällt das Blatt zu Boden" (Ah, and if the leaf were to fall to the ground). Nevertheless, in this phase of *Winterreise*, the context strongly suggests that hope is indeed gone, and the leaf falls.

7. Deborah Kessler follows similar lines when she writes about "the hero's resignation[, which] is conveyed by a poignant motion to E♭ major" (2006, 269). Such acceptance of a catastrophic outcome might be described with the term "abnegation," which, in Robert S. Hatten's words, is "willed resignation as spiritual acceptance of a (tragic) situation that leads to a positive inner state, implying transcendence" (1994, 287).

8. The possible influence of the music on the interpretation of the poem was discussed in proposition 5 in chapter 3.

8. Reflecting Lost Hope

1. Kofi Agawu (2009, 82–85) has discussed in some detail this deferral of the cadential arrival, as well as the cadential expansions in the A² section.

2. B♭ is also heard in m. 13, where it functions as a chromatic passing tone without significant tragic expressive references.

3. The interpretation of mm. 20–26, shown in example 8.1, requires a brief comment. I read the bass note D from m. 24 to the beginning of m. 26 as an anticipation; in the rhythmically normalized middleground, the D arrives only in the second half of m. 26. The situation is somewhat similar to that described by Schenker (1979, § 294 and fig. 145/2) in mm. 7–8 of Chopin's Mazurka, op. 24, no. 1. In Schubert's music an analogous situation can be found in mm. 6–7 of the opening movement of the B♭-major Piano Sonata (D. 960); here the dominant pitch, F, is heard as an anticipation in the second quarter of m. 6, while the dominant arrives as a *Stufe* only in the middle of m. 7.

4. Arnold Feil (1988, 33–37) makes a provocative metrical interpretation of the two cadential progressions: he argues that the second progression (mm. 43–45) consists of two complete triple ¹⁸/₈ measures (i.e., three ¹²/₈ measures), while in the first progression (mm. 38–39), the triple measures are left incomplete.

5. This association can be found, for example, in the article "pastorale" in Heinrich Christoph Koch's *Musikalisches Lexicon* (1802, cols. 1142–43).

6. Schenker (1979, 90) uses the concept of "addition of a root" to describe situations in which inner-voice tones are placed beneath the actual bass line. Carl Schachter

(1999b, 216–19) has discussed a somewhat similar situation to "Der stürmische Morgen" in Schubert's "Nacht und Träume," mm. 15–19.

7. In describing the sentence structure, I am following the terminology established by William Caplin (1998, 35–48).

8. Even though the *Kopfton* is supported in the foreground only by the predominant ♯IV, structurally, it belongs with the opening tonic; in other words, it has been rhythmically displaced. The process of shifting the arrival of the *Kopfton* from the opening tonic to a secondary harmony is shown clearly in Schenker's (1979, fig. 39/2) analysis of the second movement of Beethoven's Piano Sonata in D Major, op. 10, no. 3. For further discussion of this phenomenon, see Kamien (1998).

9. The positive associations created by the storm draw a connection between "Der stürmische Morgen" and "Einsamkeit."

10. The idea of the heart (the human emotions) freezing with the loss of love has already been suggested in "Erstarrung."

11. The right hand of the piano part in fact executes the top voice of the cadential figuration in mm. 37–38, but the harmony and vocal part cancel any sense of confirmation of the preceding cadential arrival.

12. Walter Everett (1988, 76–77) likewise does not interpret the A-minor triad of m. 22 as a minor-mode tonic. But instead of the auxiliary cadence, as shown in my example 8.3, he interprets the arrival as taking place at the structural dominant in m. 22, reading the A-minor chord as part of a $^{6-5}_{4-3}$ progression above an E in the bass, a pitch implied in mm. 22–23 and explicitly stated in m. 24. In my view, the E-major chord of m. 24 is so fleeting that I find it difficult to infer the arrival at the structural dominant here.

13. A similar situation occurs in mm. 27–33 of "Die Post." In this E♭-major song, the E♭-minor sonority that begins a new formal unit in m. 27 at first suggests the function of a minor-mode tonic. When seen in the larger context, however, it is better understood as a harmony beginning an auxiliary cadence VI–V–I tonicizing G♭ major (♭III in the main key), which arrives in m. 33.

9. Choosing Death

1. The length and significance of the coda might suggest an interpretation that reads the descent of the *Urlinie* only in the coda. Indeed, Walter Everett (1990, 167–73) reads the background descent only in mm. 79–81; his formal interpretation is somewhat different from mine, however, since he interprets mm. 57–83 as a C section in a formal ABAC construction rather than as a coda. Other analysts have suggested that when a ternary ABA scheme is followed by an extended coda, it may be plausible to interpret the descent of the *Urlinie* only in the coda; for an extended discussion of this topic, see Rink (1999), which examines Chopin's Nocturne in E♭ Major, op. 9, no 2. In "Der Wegweiser," however, I believe that the interpretation of the background top-voice descent as taking place only in the coda is not plausible. There are three cadential arrivals in the coda (mm. 66, 77, and 81), all of which secure the significance of î, a pitch reiterated, moreover, throughout much of the coda. This emphasis on G suggests that it governs the entire coda; therefore, it arrives before the onset of this final section.

2. Steven Laitz (1996) has written more generally about the significance of the relationships among 5̂, ♯5̂/♭6̂, and ♮6̂ in Schubert's songs.

3. Walter Everett (1990, 168–69) and Janet Schmalfeldt (1991, 262–64) read the voice-leading function of the F-minor chord tonicized in m. 15 differently; they both take it as a neighboring six-four chord above the C in m. 14. In my view, this interpreta-

tion disregards the significance given to the chord in the foreground, where it begins a new hypermeasure and is both prepared and confirmed by its own dominant.

4. My interpretation of the series of voice exchanges in mm. 57–64 is indebted to Aldwell and Schachter (1989, 540–41).

5. Similar accompanying figuration can be associated with walking in other parts of *Winterreise,* most clearly in the opening song, "Gute Nacht." Here Schubert (1989, 1) initially underlined this association: in the manuscript, the tempo indication was "Mäßig, in gehender Bewegung" (Moderate, in a walking tempo). The imitation of walking in "Gute Nacht" as well as in *Winterreise* more generally has been noted by several authors: see Everett (1988, 228–29); Feil (1988, 88–89); Rosen (1995, 123–24); and Youens (1991, 84–92; Youens uses the term "journeying figure").

6. Such an interpretation is suggested, at least indirectly, by the poem itself. Since in the first two lines the protagonist states that he avoids paths that other travelers take, he implies that he is not following the signs pointing to the towns mentioned in the third stanza. Hence, he must have another direction in mind, which is explicitly stated only in the poem's final stanza.

7. Such associations can be clearly heard, for example, in Dido's final scene ("When I am laid in earth") from Henry Purcell's opera *Dido and Aeneas* (first performed in 1689). Closer to Schubert's time, *passus duriusculus* can be found, for example, in mm. 5–11 of Mozart's overture to *Don Giovanni* (where it anticipates the arrival of the dead Commendatore at the end of the opera, an omen of Don Giovanni's death), as well as in mm. 166–72 in the opera's first scene where Don Giovanni and the Commendatore duel and the latter is killed. For a discussion of *passus duriusculus* as a rhetorical figure, see Bartel (1997, 357–58).

10. Death Eludes the Wanderer

1. Arnold Feil (1988, 121–22) has suggested that the religious associations are quite direct and that the thematic material of "Das Wirtshaus" is related to the Kyrie in the Gregorian *Requiem.*

2. In m. 11, which corresponds to m. 4, there is a straightforward V_{4-3}^{6-5} motion, which retrospectively enhances the view that m. 4 could also have functioned as the conclusion of a hypermeasure and as a half cadence ending a tonal progression.

3. It would be possible to interpret the arrival at the dominant only on the second quarter beat of m. 9, in which case the bass note C in m. 8 would be a passing tone within a third-progression Bb–C–D prolonging the IV. However, the significant motivic events would remain invariant in this reading.

4. A similar situation in which a new formal section begins with an apparent minor-mode tonic functioning at deeper levels as the initiation of an auxiliary cadence takes place in mm. 27–33 of "Die Post" and mm. 22–27 of "Täuschung."

5. For a general discussion of musical parenthesis, see Agawu (2009, 93–98); Bribitzer-Stull (2006); and Rothstein (1989, 87–92). The understanding of musical parentheses as an insertion within a unified structure is similar to the definition of parenthesis in classical rhetoric, where the concept is understood as "a word, phrase, or sentence inserted as an aside in a sentence complete in itself" (Lanham 1991, 108). The parenthesis in "Das Wirtshaus" differs from those discussed by Bribitzer-Stull and Rothstein in that it includes musical repetition rather than contrasting material.

6. For a clear instance of a situation like the one in "Das Wirtshaus," where only the second of the repeated arrivals at the tonic is structurally the primary one, see mm. 43–

47 of the opening movement of Beethoven's Piano Sonata, op. 14, no. 2. Here, the tonic in m. 45 can also be understood as parenthetical, with the cadential closure occurring only in m. 47. For a thorough discussion of this phenomenon, see Schmalfeldt (1992, esp. 35–42).

7. It is, of course, quite possible to hear the repetition of the music as again leading to the arrival at the tonic and still interpret the first tonic as the structurally conclusive harmony; an instance occurs, for example, in mm. 36–46 of the last song in part 1 of *Winterreise*, "Einsamkeit."

11. Reflecting on the Inability to Find Death

1. In the manuscript Schubert used repeat signs, while in the first edition the repetition is written out; see Schubert (1989, 67; 1828, 2:28–29).

2. The differences between the two phases of the second section justify interpreting them in example 11.1 as separate structural entities rather than as a repetition of only one voice-leading unit.

3. Walter Everett (1988, 92–93) interprets the A-minor chord in m. 16 as an apparent tonic, basically, a $^6_4$ sonority prolonging the dominant, which arrives as a $^5_3$ chord in the ensuing bar. In my view, the phrase structure of the B section speaks against this reading. The section consists of a sentence whose presentation (mm. 16–19) is subdivided into a basic idea (mm. 16–17) and its repetition (mm. 18–19). Thus, the dominants of mm. 17 and 19, which Everett reads as structural, are markedly embellishing and noncadential. The dominant that closes the entire sentence in m. 25, on the other hand, constitutes a strong half cadence, so I read the arrival at the structural dominant only there.

4. For my purposes, it is not important to assess concrete references to the three suns, since such specificity would not alter their function; it suffices to observe that they refer, in one way or another, to the beloved and to love more generally. For various concrete interpretations of the three suns (including the idea that the two extra suns are the beloved's eyes or that they are reflections of the one real sun seen through tears), see Feil (1988, 127); and Youens (1991, 290–92).

5. The second *ach* at the beginning of the seventh line is Schubert's. Müller's original has the word *ja* (yes).

6. In the manuscript Schubert (1989, 71–72) did not write out the repetition but used repeat signs instead.

12. The Song Cycle as a Genre

1. Since my approach in this study is music-theoretical, I have limited myself to studies by musical scholars. A different picture of the nature of the song cycle emerges if studies by literary critics are considered; see, for example, Bernhart (2001), Hamlin (1999), and Wolf (2001).

2. For a discussion relating McCreless's unordered and ordered relationships to Komar's seven qualities (discussed above), see Lodato (2001, 105–108).

3. In connection with Schumann's song cycles, Beate Julia Perrey (2002, 131–32) also addresses the significance of merging the past, present, and future in Romantic aesthetics, a phenomenon she calls "poetic time."

4. The notion of the fragment also plays a significant role in Rosen's *The Romantic Generation* (1995, 41–115), even though he does not explicitly use it in his discussion of the song cycle examined above.

5. By its very nature, the Romantic fragment is difficult to define in a precise manner. For a literary-historical discussion of this concept, see Lacoue-Labarthe and Nancy (1988, 39–58).

6. In his study on *Liederkreis,* op. 39, Leon Plantinga (2001, 152–58) too suggests that more significant cross-references can be found between the tenth song in the cycle ("Zwielicht") and a song outside the cycle ("Muttertraum," op. 40, no. 2) than among songs within the cycle.

7. This same argument is made in Plantinga (2001, 143–47). The early reviews, however, show that contemporaneous writers had no unanimous view on the issue of unity in song cycles; rather, individual commentators clearly had differing opinions on the topic (see, e.g., the reviews referred to in section 2.1, which, unlike those mentioned by Ferris, speak of unity). Indeed, in his review of Ferris's book, John Daverio has argued that Ferris's observations on the historical reception of song cycles are "based on selective—and at times tendentious—reading of the critical texts" (2002, 102).

13. *Winterreise* as a Cycle

1. As we saw in section 2.1, Ruth O. Bingham (1993, 2004) has divided the narrative cycles further into internal-plot and external-plot cycles. Since this chapter discusses only *Winterreise,* this distinction does not concern us here.

2. Yet there are also studies that do not consider the final song of *Winterreise* as a reference to death: we saw in section 2.3 that Susan Youens has suggested that the end of the cycle (thus including "Der Leiermann") refers to the protagonist becoming a musician and distancing himself from society.

3. Positive associations of death are already implied at the end of "Irrlicht." The notion of death had no immediate consequences on that part of the wanderer's journey, however, so the emergence of death as a positive option can be said to take place only in "Der greise Kopf." For further discussion, see section 1.3.

4. Literary critics are not, however, unanimous in their opinions about the function of causality in narrative. There are also theorists who do not consider causality a prerequisite for narrative. For a discussion of this topic, see Abbott (2002, 12).

5. Section 1.2 cites other studies that question the narrative quality of *Winterreise.*

6. Even though here I am again referring only to songs 14–24, I believe that this statement is valid for the entirety of *Winterreise.*

7. In referring to kernels and satellites, I am using Seymour Chatman's (1978, 53–54) English translation of Barthes's original terms *noyau* and *catalyse* rather than the translations given in Barthes (1977): "nucleus" and "catalyser."

8. Here I have replaced the terms "nucleus" and "catalyser" in the published translation with the terms "kernel" and "satellite."

9. Literary theorists occasionally make a distinction between the concepts of "closure" (the resolution of narrative tensions) and "end" (simply the ending of a narrative, where tensions may remain unresolved); see Abbott (2002, 51–61). In light of this distinction, "Der Leiermann" provides an end but no closure.

10. Even though Kramer (1994, 181) largely follows the keys in the manuscript, his overall graph has the closing song of part 1, "Einsamkeit," in the key of the first edition. Kramer (165–71) comments on this issue in detail.

11. For a discussion on "smooth" motion from one chord to another, whereby some pitches remain invariant while others move by step, see Cohn (2012), who provides a comprehensive introduction to neo-Riemannian ideas (even though Cohn here avoids

using the term "neo-Riemannian" for reasons explained on pp. xiii–xiv). For a thorough examination of the function of retained tones in nineteenth- and twentieth-century music theory, see Kopp (2002).

12. For a discussion of the relationships between neo-Riemannian (or, more generally, transformational) and Schenkerian theories as approaches to tonal music, see Rings (2011, esp. 9–38). Rings argues that, owing to the differences between the two approaches, "we should eye with caution any effort to unite these two styles of analytical thought into a grand *über*-method" (38). Because I am using the two approaches to discuss different musical elements and different kinds of harmonic connections (Schenkerian analysis for examining *Auskomponierung* in individual songs and some neo-Riemannian principles for elucidating relationships between the tonic triads of consecutive songs), I do not intend to suggest any kind of "*über*-method."

13. The present commentary follows the keys of the first edition. Example 13.1a indicates how the situation changes with the keys of the manuscript. Later in this section I will comment on these keys.

14. A close harmonic association between the beginning of "Letzte Hoffnung" and the end of the preceding song, "Die Krähe," is evident, despite the lack of common tones on the surface. The diminished seventh chord that begins "Letzte Hoffnung" initially sounds as if it were a VII^7 in the C minor of the preceding "Die Krähe"; for further discussion, see section 7.1.

15. This is the only instance of hierarchical connections in the harmonic organization shown in example 13.1. But even here the hierarchy differs considerably from the hierarchy in Schenkerian theory. The lower staff of example 13.1b does not suggest that the tonic chords of songs 17–19 prolong the tonic of song 16, as would be the case if the situation were described from a Schenkerian perspective. Rather, all that is maintained is that, if the tonic chords of songs 17–19 were removed—understood as parenthetical events, as it were—then the tonics of songs 16 and 20 could be connected. This hierarchy therefore contains only two levels, not a network of several intertwined layers, as in Schenkerian analysis.

16. A similar use of unison occurs in part 1 of *Winterreise*: see "Die Wetterfahne" (e.g., mm. 6–9), "Gefrorne Tränen" (mm. 21–28), and "Auf dem Flusse" (mm. 5–21).

17. The same kind of repeated closing cadential material, with similar poetic implications, occurs in part 1: see mm. 39–49 of "Gefrorne Tränen" and mm. 36–46 of "Einsamkeit."

18. Perrey in particular stresses the significance of Romantic literary ideals in discussing the disunity of song cycles. As a result, her view on discontinuity is based not only on the inner organization of the cycles but also on the historical context in which they were composed.

19. I refer here to discontinuity among adjacent songs, not incoherence within a given song. Instances of the latter also occur in *Winterreise* (most notably, in "Letzte Hoffnung") and have been examined in the analyses of individual songs.

14. Epilogue

1. This poem is given and analyzed in Malinowski (2004, 156–58).

2. The interpretation of these two stanzas is not straightforward, however. My reading relies on an association between two factors: on the one hand, the stilled sorrows (the fourth stanza) and the dead heart (the fifth stanza); on the other hand, the fact that no one speaks of the beloved (the fourth stanza) or her frozen image in the heart (the fifth

stanza). This association suggests, at least indirectly, that freezing the heart (which leads to its death) also signifies losing the thought of the beloved. But I concede that other interpretations of "Erstarrung" are possible.

3. Schubert's (1989, 16) manuscript shows that he first wrote *erfroren* (in light ink) and later changed it (with darker ink) into *erstorben*. One should remember, however, that when composing part 1 of *Winterreise,* Schubert was not aware of the poems that constitute the cycle's second part. So one cannot argue that, with this change, he consciously anticipated part 2 where death is spoken about.

4. Susan Youens has suggested that this poem is an "attempt to carve a makeshift tombstone for his [the protagonist's] love, a memorial to the past" (1991, 177). David Lewin, by contrast, has argued quite provocatively that the poem's final stanza should be taken "at face value, rather than rhetorically" (1986, 130).

References

Abbate, Carolyn. 1991. *Unsung Voices: Opera and Musical Narrative in the Nineteenth Century.* Princeton, N.J.: Princeton University Press.

Abbott, H. Porter. 2002. *The Cambridge Introduction to Narrative.* Cambridge: Cambridge University Press.

Abrams, M. H. 1953. *The Mirror and the Lamp: Romantic Theory and the Critical Tradition.* Oxford: Oxford University Press.

Agawu, V. Kofi. 1984. "On Schubert's 'Der greise Kopf.'" *In Theory Only* 8 (1): 3–22.

———. 1991. *Playing with Signs: A Semiotic Interpretation of Classic Music.* Princeton, N.J.: Princeton University Press.

———. 1992. "Theory and Practice in the Analysis of the Nineteenth-Century *Lied.*" *Music Analysis* 11 (1): 3–36.

———. 2009. *Music as Discourse: Semiotic Adventures in Romantic Music.* New York: Oxford University Press.

Agmon, Eytan. 1987. "Music and Text in Schubert Songs: The Role of Enharmonic Equivalence." *Israel Studies of Musicology* 4:49–58.

Aldwell, Edward, and Carl Schachter. 1989. *Harmony and Voice Leading.* 2nd ed. San Diego: Harcourt Brace Jovanovich.

Almén, Byron. 2008. *A Theory of Musical Narrative.* Bloomington: Indiana University Press.

Anson-Cartwright, Mark. 2000. "Chromatic Features of E♭-Major Works of the Classical Period." *Music Theory Spectrum* 22 (2): 177–204.

Barry, Barbara R. 2000. "'Sehnsucht' and Melancholy: Explorations of Time and Structure in Schubert's *Winterreise.*" In *The Philosopher's Stone: Essays in the Transformation of Musical Structure,* by Barbara R. Barry, 181–202. Hillsdale, N.Y.: Pendragon Press.

Bartel, Dietrich. 1997. *Musica Poetica: Musical-Rhetorical Figures in German Baroque Music.* Lincoln: University of Nebraska Press.

Barthes, Roland. 1977. "Introduction to the Structural Analysis of Narratives." In *Image, Music, Text,* translated by Stephen Heath, 79–124. New York: Hill and Wang. (French original, "Introduction à l'analyse structurale des récits," 1966.)

Bauer, Mark. 2000. "Der verborgene Mittelpunkt: Issues of Death and Awareness in Friedrich Schlegel's *Lucinde.*" *Monatshefte* 92 (2): 139–63.

Baumann, Cecilia. 1981. *Wilhelm Müller. The Poet of Schubert's Song Cycles: His Life and Works.* University Park: Pennsylvania State University Press.

Behler, Ernst. 1993. *German Romantic Literary Theory.* Cambridge: Cambridge University Press.

Beiser, Frederick C. 2003. *The Romantic Imperative: The Concept of Early German Romanticism.* Cambridge, Mass.: Harvard University Press.

Bernhardt, Walter. 2001. "Three Types of Song Cycles: The Variety of Britten's 'Charms.'" In *Word and Music Studies: Essays on the Song Cycle and on Defining the Field*, edited by Walter Bernhardt and Werner Wolf in collaboration with David Mosley, 211–26. Amsterdam: Rodopi.

Bingham, Ruth Otto. 1993. "The Song Cycle in German-Speaking Countries, 1790–1840: Approaches to a Changing Genre." PhD diss., Cornell University.

———. 2004. "The Early Nineteenth-Century Song Cycle." In *The Cambridge Companion to the Lied*, edited by James Parsons, 101–19. Cambridge: Cambridge University Press.

Bird, George, and Richard Stokes. 1991. *The Fischer-Dieskau Book of Lieder*. London: Victor Gollancz. (First published 1976.)

Blackall, Eric A. 1983. *The Novels of the German Romantics*. Ithaca, N.Y.: Cornell University Press.

Bohm, Arnd. 2004. "Goethe and the Romantics." In *The Literature of German Romanticism*, edited by Dennis F. Mahoney, 35–60. Camden House History of German Literature, vol. 8. Rochester, N.Y.: Camden House.

Bribitzer-Stull, Matthew. 2006. "The Cadenza as Parenthesis: An Analytical Approach." *Journal of Music Theory* 50 (2): 211–51.

Brown, Jane K. 2004. "In the Beginning Was Poetry." In *The Cambridge Companion to the Lied*, edited by James Parsons, 12–32. Cambridge: Cambridge University Press.

Budniakiewicz, Therese. 1992. *Fundamentals of Story Logic: Introduction to Greimassian Semiotics*. Amsterdam: John Benjamins Publishing Company.

Burkhart, Charles. 1978. "Schenker's 'Motivic Parallelisms.'" *Journal of Music Theory* 22 (2): 145–75.

———. 1990. "Departures from the Norm in Two Songs from Schumann's *Liederkreis*." In *Schenker Studies*, edited by Hedi Siegel, 146–64. Cambridge: Cambridge University Press.

Cadwallader, Allen. 1988. "Prolegomena to a General Description of Motivic Relationships in Tonal Music." *Intégral* 2:1–35.

Cadwallader, Allen, and William Pastille. 1992. "Schenker's High-Level Motives." *Journal of Music Theory* 36 (1): 119–48.

Caplin, William E. 1998. *Classical Form: A Theory of Formal Functions for the Instrumental Music of Haydn, Mozart, and Beethoven*. New York: Oxford University Press.

———. 2004. "The Classical Cadence: Conceptions and Misconceptions." *Journal of the American Musicological Society* 57 (1): 51–117.

Chatman, Seymour. 1978. *Story and Discourse: Narrative Structure in Fiction and Film*. Ithaca, N.Y.: Cornell University Press.

Cohn, Richard. 2012. *Audacious Euphony: Chromaticism and the Triad's Second Nature*. New York: Oxford University Press.

Cone, Edward T. 1974. *The Composer's Voice*. Berkeley: University of California Press.

———. 1986. "Schubert's Promissory Note: An Exercise in Musical Hermeneutics." In *Schubert: Critical and Analytical Studies*, edited by Walter Frisch, 13–30. Lincoln: University of Nebraska Press.

Cook, Nicholas. 2001. "Theorizing Musical Meaning." *Music Theory Spectrum* 23 (2): 170–95.

Culler, Jonathan. 1975. *Structuralist Poetics: Structuralism, Linguistics, and the Study of Literature*. Ithaca, N.Y.: Cornell University Press.

Dahlhaus, Carl. 1989. *Nineteenth-Century Music.* Translated by J. Bradford Robinson. Berkeley: University of California Press. (German original, *Die Musik des 19. Jahrhunderts,* 1980.)

Daverio, John. 2002. Untitled review of Ferris 2000. *19th-Century Music* 26 (1): 100–110.

———. 2010. "The Song Cycle: Journeys through a Romantic Landscape." In *German Lieder in the Nineteenth Century,* 2nd ed., edited by Rufus Hallmark, 363–404. New York: Schirmer Books. (1st ed., 1996.)

Davies, Stephen. 1994. *Musical Meaning and Expression.* Ithaca, N.Y.: Cornell University Press.

Duncan, Bruce. 2005. *Goethe's "Werther" and the Critics.* Rochester, N.Y.: Camden House.

Dürr, Walther. 1984. *Das deutsche Sololied im 19. Jahrhundert: Untersuchungen zu Sprache und Musik.* Wilhelmshaven: Heinrichshofen's Verlag.

———. 2004. "Winterreise: Gedanken zur Struktur des Zyklus." In *Meisterwerke neu gehört: Ein kleiner Kanon der Musik,* edited by Hans-Joachim Hinrichsen and Laurenz Lütteken, 131–55. Kassel: Bärenreiter.

Dye, Ellis. 2004. *Love and Death in Goethe: "One and Double."* Rochester, N.Y.: Camden House.

Eggebrecht, Hans Heinrich. 1970. "Prinzipen des Schubert-Liedes." *Archiv für Musikwissenschaft* 27 (2): 89–109.

Everett, Walter. 1988. "A Schenkerian View of Text-Painting in Schubert's Song Cycle 'Winterreise.'" PhD diss., University of Michigan.

———. 1990. "Grief in *Winterreise*: A Schenkerian Perspective." *Music Analysis* 9 (2): 157–75.

Feil, Arnold. 1988. *Franz Schubert: Die schöne Müllerin, Winterreise.* Translated by Ann C. Sherwin. Portland: Amadeus Press. (German original, *Franz Schubert: Die schöne Müllerin, Winterreise,* 1975.)

Ferris, David. 2000. *Schumann's Eichendorff "Liederkreis" and the Genre of the Romantic Cycle.* New York: Oxford University Press.

Furst, Lilian R. 1990. "The 'Imprisoning Self': Goethe's Werther and Rousseau's Solitary Walker." In *European Romanticism: Literary Cross-Currents, Modes, and Models,* edited by Gerhart Hoffmeister, 145–61. Detroit: Wayne State University Press.

Georgiades, Thrasybulos G. 1967. *Schubert: Musik und Lyrik.* Göttingen: Vandenhoeck & Ruprecht.

Goethe, Johann Wolfgang von. 1989. *The Sorrows of Young Werther.* Translated by Michael Hulse. London: Penguin Books. (German original, *Die Leiden des jungen Werthers,* 1774.)

Greimas, Algirdas Julien. 1983. *Structural Semantics: An Attempt at a Method.* Translated by Daniele McDowell, Ronald Schleifer, and Alan Velie. Lincoln: University of Nebraska Press. (French original, *Sémantique structurale: Recherche de méthode,* 1966.)

———. 1987. *On Meaning: Selected Writings in Semiotic Theory.* Translated by Paul J. Perron and Frank H. Collins. Minneapolis: University of Minnesota Press. (Original essays first published in French, 1963–83.)

Hamlin, Cyrus. 1999. "The Romantic Song Cycle as Literary Genre." In *Word and Music Studies: Defining the Field,* edited by Walter Bernhart, Steven Paul Scher, and Werner Wolf, 113–34. Amsterdam: Rodopi.

———. 2005. "German Classical Poetry." In *The Literature of Weimar Classicism,* edited by Simon Richter, 169–99. Camden House History of German Literature, vol. 7. Rochester, N.Y.: Camden House.

Hatten, Robert S. 1994. *Musical Meaning in Beethoven: Markedness, Correlation, and Interpretation.* Bloomington: Indiana University Press.

——. 2004. *Interpreting Musical Gestures, Topics, and Tropes: Mozart, Beethoven, Schubert.* Bloomington: Indiana University Press.

——. 2008. "A Surfeit of Musics: What Goethe's Lyrics Concede When Set to Schubert's Music." *Nineteenth-Century Music Review* 5 (2): 7–18.

Hawkes, Terence. 1977. *Structuralism and Semiotics.* Berkeley: University of California Press.

Hoeckner, Berthold. 2006. "Paths through *Dichterliebe.*" *19th-Century Music* 30 (1): 65–80.

Hoffmann, E. T. A. 1989. *E. T. A. Hoffmann's Musical Writings: "Kreisleriana," "The Poet and the Composer," Music Criticism.* Edited by David Charlton, translated by Martyn Clarke. Cambridge: Cambridge University Press.

——. 1996. *Fantasy Pieces in Callot's Manner.* Translated by Joseph M. Hayse. Schenectady, N.Y.: Union College Press. (German original, *Fantasiestücke in Callots Manier,* 1814.)

Hudson, Nicholas. 1997. "Theories of Language." In *The Eighteenth Century,* edited by H. B. Nisbet and Claude Rawson, 335–48. Vol. 4 of *The Cambridge History of Literary Criticism.* Cambridge: Cambridge University Press.

Jonas, Oswald. 1982. *Introduction to the Theory of Heinrich Schenker.* Translated and edited by John Rothgeb. New York: Longman. (German original, *Das Wesen des musikalischen Kunstwerks: Eine Einführung in die Lehre Heinrich Schenkers,* 1934; rev. ed., 1972.)

Kamien, Roger. 1998. "Non-tonic Settings of the Primary Tone in Beethoven's Piano Sonatas." *Journal of Musicology* 16 (3): 379–93.

Keach, William. 1997. "Poetry, after 1740." In *The Eighteenth Century,* edited by H. B. Nisbet and Claude Rawson, 117–66. Vol. 4 of *The Cambridge History of Literary Criticism.* Cambridge: Cambridge University Press.

Kessler, Deborah. 2006. "Motive and Motivation in Schubert's Three-Key Expositions." In *Structure and Meaning in Tonal Music: Festschrift in Honor of Carl Schachter,* edited by L. Poundie Burstein and David Gagné, 259–76. Hillsdale, N.Y.: Pendragon Press.

Kinderman, William. 1986. "Schubert's Tragic Perspective." In *Schubert: Critical and Analytical Studies,* edited by Walter Frisch, 65–83. Lincoln: University of Nebraska Press.

Kivy, Peter. 1989. *Sound Sentiment: An Essay on the Musical Emotions, Including the Complete Text of "The Corded Shell."* Philadelphia: Temple University Press.

——. 2009. *Antithetical Arts: On the Ancient Quarrel between Literature and Music.* Oxford: Clarendon Press.

Koch, Heinrich Christoph. 1802. *Musikalisches Lexikon.* Frankfurt am Main: August Hermann dem Jüngern. Facsimile reprint, Kassel: Bärenreiter, 2001.

Komar, Arthur. 1971. "The Music of *Dichterliebe:* The Whole and Its Parts." In *Dichterliebe,* edited by Arthur Komar, 63–94. New York: W. W. Norton.

Kopp, David. 2002. *Chromatic Transformations in Nineteenth-Century Music.* Cambridge: Cambridge University Press.

Kramer, Lawrence. 1986. "The Schubert Lied: Romantic Form and Romantic Consciousness." In *Schubert: Critical and Analytical Studies,* edited by Walter Frisch, 200–236. Lincoln: University of Nebraska Press.

———. 1992. "Music and Representation: The Instance of Haydn's *Creation.*" In *Music and Text: Critical Inquiries,* edited by Steven Paul Scher, 139–62. Cambridge: Cambridge University Press.

Kramer, Richard. 1994. *Distant Cycles: Schubert and the Conceiving of Song.* Chicago: University of Chicago Press.

Lacoue-Labarthe, Philippe, and Jean-Luc Nancy. 1988. *The Literary Absolute: The Theory of Literature in German Romanticism.* Translated by Philip Barnard and Cheryl Lester. Albany: State University of New York Press. (French original, *L'absolu littéraire,* 1978.)

Laitz, Steven. 1996. "The Submediant Complex: Its Musical and Poetic Roles in Schubert's Songs." *Theory and Practice* 21:123–65.

Lampart, Fabian. 2004. "The Turn to History and the *Volk:* Brentano, Arnim, and the Grimm Brothers." In *The Literature of German Romanticism,* edited by Dennis F. Mahoney, 171–89. Camden House History of German Literature, vol. 8. Rochester, N.Y.: Camden House.

Lanham, Richard A. 1991. *A Handlist of Rhetorical Terms.* 2nd ed. Berkeley: University of California Press.

Latham, Edward D. 2009. *"Drei Nebensonnen:* Forte's Linear-Motivic Analysis, Korngold's *Die tote Stadt,* and Schubert's *Winterreise* as Visions of Closure." *Gamut* 2 (1): 299–346. Accessed August 11, 2009. http://dlc.lib.utk.edu/web/ojs/index.php/first/issue/current.

Laufer, Edward. 1977. "A Schenkerian Approach [to Brahms's op. 105, no. 1]." In *Readings in Schenker Analysis and Other Approaches,* edited by Maury Yeston, 254–72. New Haven, Conn.: Yale University Press. (First published 1971.)

———. 1988. "On the Fantasy." *Intégral* 2:99–133.

Levinson, Jerrold. 1987. "Song and Music Drama." In *What Is Music: An Introduction to the Philosophy of Music,* edited by Philip Alperson, 283–301. University Park: Pennsylvania State University Press.

———. 1990. "Hope in the Hebrides." In *Music, Art, and Metaphysics: Essays in Philosophical Aesthetics,* 336–75. Ithaca, N.Y.: Cornell University Press.

Lewin, David. 1986. *"Auf dem Flusse:* Image and Background in a Schubert Song." In *Schubert: Critical and Analytical Studies,* edited by Walter Frisch, 126–52. Lincoln: University of Nebraska Press. (First published 1982.)

———. 2006. *Studies in Music with Text.* New York: Oxford University Press.

Lewis, Christopher. 1988. "Text, Time, and Tonic: Aspects of Patterning in the Romantic Cycle." *Intégral* 2:37–73.

Lodato, Suzanne M. 2001. "Problems in Song Cycle Analysis and the Case of *Mädchenblumen.*" In *Word and Music Studies: Essays on the Song Cycle and on Defining the Field,* edited by Walter Bernhardt and Werner Wolf in collaboration with David Mosley, 103–20. Amsterdam: Rodopi.

Lyas, Colin. 1997. *Aesthetics.* London: UCL Press.

Malin, Yonatan. 2010. *Songs in Motion: Rhythm and Meter in the German Lied.* New York: Oxford University Press.

Malinowski, Bernadette. 2004. "German Romantic Poetry in Theory and Practice: The Schlegel Brothers, Schelling, Tieck, Novalis, Eichendorff, and Heine." In *The Literature of German Romanticism,* edited by Dennis F. Mahoney, 147–69. Camden House History of German Literature, vol. 8. Rochester, N.Y.: Camden House.

McCreless, Patrick. 1986. "Song Order in the Song Cycle: Schumann's *Liederkreis,* Op. 39." *Music Analysis* 5 (1): 5–28.

———. 2011. "Pitch-Class Motive in Tonal Analysis: Some Historical and Critical Observations." *Res Musica*, no. 3:52–66.

Nägeli, Hans Georg. 1817. "Die Liederkunst." *Allgemeine musikalische Zeitung* 19 (45): cols. 761–67.

Neumeyer, David. 1982. "Organic Structure and the Song Cycle: Another Look at Schumann's *Dichterliebe*." *Music Theory Spectrum* 4:92–105.

Newcomb, Anthony. 1986. "Structure and Expression in a Schubert Song: *Noch einmal 'Auf dem Flusse' zu hören*." In *Schubert: Critical and Analytical Studies*, edited by Walter Frisch, 153–74. Lincoln: University of Nebraska Press.

Novalis. 1988. *Hymns to the Night*, 3rd ed. Translated by Dick Higgins. Kingston, N.Y.: McPherson & Company. (German original, *Hymnen an die Nacht*, 1800.)

———. 1997. *Philosophical Writings*. Translated and edited by Margaret Mahony Stojar. Albany: State University of New York Press.

Peake, Luise Eitel. 1982. "The Antecedents of Beethoven's *Liederkreis*." *Music & Letters* 63 (3–4): 242–60.

Perrey, Beate Julia. 2002. *Schumann's "Dichterliebe" and Early Romantic Poetics: Fragmentation of Desire*. Cambridge: Cambridge University Press.

Phillips, Lois. 1996. *Lieder Line by Line, and Word for Word*. Oxford: Clarendon Press. (First published 1979.)

Plantinga, Leon. 2001. "Design and Unity in Schumann's *Liederkreis*, Op. 39?." In *Word and Music Studies: Essays on the Song Cycle and on Defining the Field*, edited by Walter Bernhardt and Werner Wolf in collaboration with David Mosley, 141–63. Amsterdam: Rodopi.

Propp, Vladimir. 1968. *Morphology of the Folktale*. 2nd ed. Translated by Laurence Scott. Austin: University of Texas Press. (Russian original, *Morgologija skazki*, 1928.)

Ratner, Leonard G. 1980. *Classic Music: Expression, Form, and Style*. New York: Schirmer Books.

Rings, Steven. 2011. *Tonality and Transformation*. New York: Oxford University Press.

Rink, John. 1999. "'Structural Momentum' and Closure in Chopin's Nocturne Op. 9, No. 2." In *Schenker Studies* 2, edited by Carl Schachter and Hedi Siegel, 109–26. Cambridge: Cambridge University Press.

Robinson, Jenefer. 1994. "Music as a Representational Art." In *What Is Music: An Introduction to the Philosophy of Music*, edited by Philip Alperson, 167–92. University Park: Pennsylvania State University Press.

———. 2005. *Deeper than Reason: Emotion and Its Role in Literature, Music, and Art*. Oxford: Clarendon Press.

Rosen, Charles. 1995. *The Romantic Generation*. Cambridge, Mass.: Harvard University Press.

Rothgeb, John. 1983. "Thematic Content: A Schenkerian View." In *Aspects of Schenkerian Theory*, edited by David Beach, 39–60. New Haven, Conn.: Yale University Press.

Rothstein, William. 1989. *Phrase Rhythm in Tonal Music*. New York: Schirmer Books.

Salzer, Felix. 1982. *Structural Hearing: Tonal Coherence in Music*. New York: Dover. (First published 1952.)

Saul, Nicholas. 2009. "Love, Death and *Liebestod* in German Romanticism." In *The Cambridge Companion to German Romanticism*, edited by Nicholas Saul, 163–74. Cambridge: Cambridge University Press.

Schachter, Carl. 1994. "The Prelude from Bach's Suite No. 4 for Violoncello Solo: The Submerged Urlinie." *Current Musicology* 56:54–71.

———. 1999a. "Structure as Foreground: 'Das Drama des Ursatzes.'" In *Schenker Studies 2*, edited by Carl Schachter and Hedi Siegel, 298–314. Cambridge: Cambridge University Press.

———. 1999b. *Unfoldings: Essays in Schenkerian Theory and Analysis*. Edited by Joseph N. Straus. New York: Oxford University Press. (Original essays first published 1973–95.)

Schenker, Heinrich. 1979. *Free Composition*. Edited and translated by Ernst Oster. New York: Longman. (German original, *Der freie Satz*, 1935; rev. ed., 1956.)

———. 1996. *The Masterwork in Music: A Yearbook, Volume 2 (1926)*. Edited by William Drabkin, translated by Ian Bent, William Drabkin, John Rothgeb, and Hedi Siegel. Cambridge: Cambridge University Press. (German original, *Das Meisterwerk in der Musik* II, 1926.)

———. 1997. *The Masterwork in Music: A Yearbook, Volume 3 (1930)*. Edited by William Drabkin, translated by Ian Bent, Alfred Clayton, and Derrick Puffett. Cambridge: Cambridge University Press. (German original, *Das Meisterwerk in der Musik* III, 1930.)

Scher, Steven Paul. 1990. "The German Lied: A Genre and Its European Reception." In *European Romanticism: Literary Cross-Currents, Modes, and Models*, edited by Gerhart Hoffmeister, 127–41. Detroit: Wayne State University Press.

Schlegel, Friedrich. 1971. *"Lucinde" and the Fragments*. Translated by Peter Firchow. Minneapolis: University of Minnesota Press.

Schleifer, Ronald. 1987. *A. J. Greimas and the Nature of Meaning: Linguistics, Semiotics and Discourse Theory*. Lincoln: University of Nebraska Press.

Schmalfeldt, Janet. 1991. "Towards a Reconciliation of Schenkerian Concepts with Traditional and Recent Theories of Form." *Music Analysis* 10 (3): 233–87.

———. 1992. "Cadential Processes: The Evaded Cadence and the 'One More Time' Technique." *Journal of Musicological Research* 12 (1–2): 1–52.

Schubert, Franz. 1828. *Winterreise*. Vienna: Tobias Haslinger. Published in two separate volumes.

———. 1989. *Winterreise: The Autograph Score*. With an introduction by Susan Youens. New York: Dover.

Schumann, Robert. 1983. *On Music and Musicians*. Edited by Konrad Wolff, translated by Paul Rosenfeld. Berkeley: University of California Press. (First published 1946.)

Scruton, Roger. 1997. *The Aesthetics of Music*. Oxford: Oxford University Press.

Seelig, Harry. 2010. "The Literary Context: Goethe as Source and Catalyst." In *German Lieder in the Nineteenth Century*, 2nd ed., edited by Rufus Hallmark, 1–34. New York: Routledge. (1st ed., 1996.)

Sondrup, Steven P. 1990. "Wertherism and *Die Leiden des jungen Werthers*." In *European Romanticism: Literary Cross-Currents, Modes, and Models*, edited by Gerhart Hoffmeister, 163–79. Detroit: Wayne State University Press.

Steblin, Rita. 2002. *A History of Key Characteristics in the Eighteenth and Early Nineteenth Centuries*. 2nd ed. Rochester, N.Y.: University of Rochester Press.

Suurpää, Lauri. 2000. "The Path from Tonic to Dominant in the Second Movement of Schubert's String Quintet and in Chopin's Fourth Ballade." *Journal of Music Theory* 44 (2): 451–79.

———. 2003. "Loss of Love in Two Sibelius Songs." In *Sibelius Forum II*, edited by Matti Huttunen, Kari Kilpeläinen, and Veijo Murtomäki, 278–86. Helsinki: Sibelius Academy.

Tarasti, Eero. 1994. *A Theory of Musical Semiotics*. Bloomington: Indiana University Press.

Tunbridge, Laura. 2010. *The Song Cycle*. Cambridge: Cambridge University Press.

Turchin, Barbara. 1981. "Robert Schumann's Song Cycles in the Context of the Early Nineteenth-Century *Liederkreis*." PhD diss., Columbia University.

———. 1987. "The Nineteenth-Century *Wanderlieder* Cycle." *Journal of Musicology* 5 (4): 498–525.

Wen, Eric. 1999. "Bass-Line Articulations of the *Urlinie*." In *Schenker Studies 2*, edited by Carl Schachter and Hedi Siegel, 276–97. Cambridge: Cambridge University Press.

Wigmore, Richard. 1988. *Schubert: The Complete Song Texts*. New York: Schirmer Books.

Winter, Robert. 1982. "Paper Studies and the Future of Schubert Research." In *Schubert Studies: Problems of Style and Chronology,* edited by Eva Badura-Skoda and Peter Branscombe, 209–75. Cambridge: Cambridge University Press.

Wolf, Werner. 2001. "'Willst zu meinen Liedern deine Leier drehn?' Intermedial Metatextuality in Schubert's 'Der Leiermann' as a Motivation for Song and Accompaniment and a Contribution to the Unity of *Die Winterreise*." In *Word and Music Studies: Essays on the Song Cycle and on Defining the Field,* edited by Walter Bernhardt and Werner Wolf in collaboration with David Mosley, 121–40. Amsterdam: Rodopi.

Youens, Susan. 1987. "*Wegweiser* in *Winterreise*." *Journal of Musicology* 5 (3): 357–79.

———. 1991. *Retracing a Winter's Journey: Schubert's "Winterreise."* Ithaca, N.Y.: Cornell University Press.

———. 2006. *Schubert's Late Lieder: Beyond the Song Cycles*. Cambridge: Cambridge University Press.

Zbikowski, Lawrence M. 1999. "The Blossoms of 'Trockne Blumen': Music and Text in the Early Nineteenth Century." *Music Analysis* 18 (3): 307–45.

———. 2002. *Conceptualizing Music: Cognitive Structure, Theory, and Analysis*. New York: Oxford University Press.

Index

dramatic peak, 52; in "Der greise Kopf," 63; in "Der Wegweiser," 115, 122; in "Im Dorfe," 102, 105; in "Letzte Hoffnung," 86
Duncan, Bruce, 199n17
Dürr, Walther, 179, 197n7, 198n1, 198n2, 198n5, 199n8
Dye, Ellis, 199n14, 199n20

Eggebrecht, Hans Heinrich, 180–181
Eichendorff, Joseph von, 162; "Die zwei Gesellen," 192, 209n1
emotions: emotion characteristics in appearances, 33; higher emotions, 33, 51. *See also* musico-poetic associations, emotions
end vs. closure, 172, 208n9
enharmonic relationships: in "Der greise Kopf," 64–65, 67–68, 71–73, 185–186; in "Der Wegweiser," 118–119, 124, 126, 185–186; in "Die Krähe," 79, 185–186; in "Letzte Hoffnung," 87–88, 90, 92, 94–96, 99, 185–186, 203n3; as a musical cross-reference, 185–186; in "Täuschung," 111, 113
Everett, Walter, 56–58, 174, 179–180, 203n4, 205n12, 205n1, 205n3, 206n5 (chap9), 207n3 (chap11)
expression. *See* joyful expression; tragic expression
expressive genre, 34–35, 51; in "Das Wirtshaus," 136; in "Der greise Kopf," 63, 71; in "Der Wegweiser," 124; in "Die Krähe," 75, 82–83; in "Die Nebensonnen," 146; in "Letzte Hoffnung," 85–86; in "Mut," 143
expressive qualities, 36, 51; confirming, 36, 65–66, 68, 73, 88, 95, 145, 146; contemplative, 122, 127; declamatory, 36, 63–64, 71, 78, 83, 90–91, 95, 101, 117, 122, 125, 127, 132, 138–139, 143, 146–147, 150, 186; depressed, 133; dreamy, 102; frustrated, 80, 84; hollow, 66–67, 72; horrified, 119, 122, 126–127; inward, 36, 64–65, 71, 77–80, 83–84, 116–117, 122, 127; lamenting, 111, 146, 149–150; numb, 151; pastoral, 101, 104; pious, 102, 129–130, 132–134, 146–147, 149–150, 172, 186; playful, 111; pleading, 90; pompous, 105, 107, 109; rejoicing, 143; relaxed, 117, 125; relieved, 134; resigned, 67, 72, 119, 122, 127; searching, 65, 72, 87–88, 92, 95, 98–99; settled, 86; surprised, 129, 137; tentatively confirming, 68, 73; uncertain, 36, 143, 145; undecided, 133; unsettled, 85–86; yearning, 118–119, 126, 151
extroversive vs. introversive semioses, 38–39

Feil, Arnold, 197n1, 201n13, 204n4 (chap8), 206n5 (chap9), 206n1, 207n4 (chap11)

Ferris, David, 163–166, 187–188, 208n7 (chap12)
Fichte, Johann Gottlieb, 22
fictional world. *See* Scruton, Roger: fictional world
Fischer, Kurt von, 5
fragment, 25, 27, 164–166, 187–188, 207n4 (chap12), 208n5 (chap12)
Franz, Robert, 159–160
freer associations, 48–50, 179–180; pitch-class motives as, 49, 202n12
Froberger, Johann Jacob: *Tombeau de M. Blancrocher,* 32
Furst, Lilian R., 199n16

Gadamer, Hans-Georg, 164
Georgiades, Thrasybulos G., 7, 167, 197n1, 201n13, 203n1 (chap7)
Goethe, Johann Wolfgang von, 15–16, 22, 24–28, 58; *Die Leiden des jungen Werthers,* 24–28, 191, 199nn15–17; "Erlkönig," 16, 40; *Wilhelm Meister,* 20
Greimas, A. J., 42, 201n1, 201nn4–7
Greimassian semiotics, x, 37–40, 42–48, 50, 55, 59–60, 201nn1–7; actants, 44, 48, 59, 169, 201n4; actors, 44, 48, 82, 169; conjunction, 45–47, 70, 93–94, 97–98, 112, 123, 144; disjunction, 45–47, 70, 94, 97, 112, 123, 136, 144, 153–154, 189; helper, 44; interdependence (arrow), 44–45, 201n6; narrative transformation (double-line arrow), 45–47, 70–71, 103, 123, 125, 136, 138, 169, 201n6; object, 44–47, 59–60, 70, 82–83, 93–94, 97–98, 108–109, 112, 123–127, 136–137, 144, 148, 153–155, 167, 169–170, 173, 176–178, 184–186, 189, 201n5; opponent, 44; receiver, 44, 47–48, 70, 153, 201n7; semiotic square, 42; sender, 44, 47–48, 70, 81, 83–84, 94, 108–109, 112, 123–124, 136, 148–149, 153, 201n7; subject, 44–47, 70, 93–94, 97, 99, 112, 123, 136–137, 144, 153–155, 167, 169–170, 178

Hamlin, Cyrus, 7, 15, 187, 201n3, 207n1 (chap12)
Haslinger, Tobias, 5–6, 197n6
Hatten, Robert S., 34–36, 51, 58, 200n10, 202n1, 204n7 (chap7)
Hawkes, Terence, 201n1
Heine, Heinrich, 164, 192; "Ihr Bild," 57–58
Herder, Johann Gottfried, 22
high point, 35–36, 52, 200n7; in "Das Wirtshaus," 129, 133, 139; in "Der greise Kopf," 63, 66, 72; in "Der stürmische Morgen," 107, 109; in "Der Wegweiser," 115, 122, 127; in "Die Krähe," 75, 80, 84; in "Die Nebenson-

musico-poetic associations, imitation, x, 31–32, 39, 41, 51–53, 179; in "Das Wirtshaus," 137; in "Der Leiermann," 154; in "Der stürmische Morgen," 108; in "Der Wegweiser," 123–124; in "Die Krähe," 82; in "Die Nebensonnen," 150; in "Gute Nacht," 206n5 (chap9); in "Letzte Hoffnung," 96; less specific, 32, 200n4

musico-poetic associations, interpretation, 39–41; effect of analytical methodologies on, 39–41, 50–51, 55; effect of the music on the interpretation of the text, 40–41, 51, 53, 59, 82–83, 97–99, 103–105, 125, 139, 169, 172, 186, 194–195

musico-poetic associations, representation, 30–31, 41

musico-poetic associations, structural, x, 37–39, 41, 42, 51–58, 161–162; freer associations, 48; independent interpretation of musical and poetic structures, x, 37–38, 50, 58–59; motives as referential signs (extroversive semiosis), 38–39, 48, 52–53, 56–58, 182–183, 185; Schenkerian and Greimassian theories, x, 37–39, 50–51, 55

Nägeli, Hans Georg, 18
Nancy, Jean-Luc, 208n5 (chap12)
narrative, 45–47, 170–171, 208n4
neo-Riemannian theory, xi, 167, 175–176, 208n11, 209n12, 209n15
Neumeyer, David, 161
Newcomb, Anthony, 5, 197n1, 197n3, 198n9, 198n12
Nicolai, Friedrich, 25
Novalis, 24, 27, 29, 164, 191, 195; *Hymnen an die Nacht,* 199n21; *Monologue,* 23–24

paradigmatic. See syntagmatic vs. paradigmatic
parenthesis, 134, 206n5 (chap10); in "Das Wirtshaus," 134, 139, 184, 206n5 (chap10); in "Der stürmische Morgen," 106–107; in "Die Krähe," 75, 134
parsimonious voice leading. See smooth voice leading
passus duriusculus, 206n7; in "Der Wegweiser," 127
Pastille, William, 202nn10–11
Peake, Luise Eitel, 199n8
Perrey, Beate Julia, 163–166, 187–188, 207n3 (chap12), 209n18
Plantinga, Leon, 163, 166, 187, 208nn6–7 (chap12)
poetic self, 15–16, 22, 24
Propp, Vladimir, 43–44

Purcell, Henry: *Dido and Aeneas,* 206n7
purple patch, 102

Ratner, Leonard G., 126
reaching-over: in "Der stürmische Morgen," 107
representation. See musico-poetic associations, representation
Riem, Wilhelm Friedrich, 16–17
Rings, Steven, 209n12
Rink, John, 205n1
Robinson, Jenefer, 199n2, 200n5, 200n8
Romantic poetry, 22–23, 26
Rosen, Charles, 7, 27–28, 162–163, 165, 174, 187–188, 206n5 (chap9), 207n4 (chap12)
Rothgeb, John, 202n10
Rothstein, William, 206n5 (chap10)

Salzer, Felix, 203n2 (chap6)
satellites. See kernels and satellites
Saul, Nicholas, 27, 199n14
Saussure, Ferdinand de, 22
Schachter, Carl, 50, 56–58, 181, 203n5, 204n6, 206n4 (chap9)
Schenker, Heinrich, 48–49, 201n8, 202n9, 202n2, 203n1 (chap6), 204n3, 204n6, 205n8
Schenkerian analysis, x–xi, 37–40, 48–50, 53–58, 160, 173–174, 176, 179, 200n11, 209n12, 209n15
Scher, Steven Paul, 16
Schlegel, Friedrich, 22–23, 164–165, 191; *Lucinde,* 24–27, 29, 191, 199nn18–19
Schleifer, Ronald, 201n1
Schmalfeldt, Janet, 205n3, 206n6
Schober, Franz von, 21
Schoenberg, Arnold: *Erwartung,* 7
Schubert, Franz: "Aufenhalt" (*Schwanengesang*), 204n4 (chap7); as a composer of Lieder, 15, 18; "Die liebe Farbe" (*Die schöne Müllerin*), 203n6; *Die schöne Müllerin,* 6, 28; "Erlkönig," 40; "Gretchen am Spinnrade," 15–16; *Harfenspieler Gesänge,* 204n4 (chap7); "Ihr Bild" (*Schwanengesang*), 57–58, 181; Impromptu, op. 90, no. 2, 204n5 (chap7); Moment musical, op. 96, no. 6, 202n12; "Nacht und Träume," 56–57, 203n3, 204n6; Piano Sonata, D. 784, I, 202n1; Piano Sonata, D. 960, I, 204n3; String Quintet, II, 204n4 (chap7); "Trockne Blumen" (*Die schöne Müllerin*), 55; *Unfinished* Symphony, I, 203n1 (chap6). See also *Winterreise*
Schumann, Robert, 159–166, 187–188; "Am leuchtenden Sommermorgen" (*Dichterliebe*), 192; "Der schwere Abend," op. 90, no. 6, 164; *Dichterliebe,* 160–161, 163–165, 190,

192; "Die alten, bösen Lieder" (Dichterliebe), 192; "Hör' ich das Liedchen klingen" (Dichterliebe), 202n14; "Ich hab' im Traum geweinet" (Dichterliebe), 164; "Im wunderschönen Monat Mai" (Dichterliebe), 187; Liederkreis, op. 39, 162–163, 165, 208n6 (chap12); "Muttertraum," op. 40, no. 2, 208n6 (chap12); "Schöne Fremde" (Liederkreis, op. 39), 56; "Zwielicht" (Liederkreis, op. 39), 208n6 (chap12)

Scruton, Roger, 30–31, 34; fictional world, 30–32

Seelig, Harry, 198n3

Sehnsucht. See longing

sentence, 205n7; in "Der stürmische Morgen," 106–107

Sibelius, Jean: "Den första kyssen," op. 37, no. 1, 41

signified. See signifier vs. signified

signifier vs. signified, 22–23, 25–27, 191

smooth voice leading, 175–179, 189, 208n11. See also neo-Riemannian theory

Sondrup, Steven P., 199n15

song cycle: analytical views on, 159–166; discontinuity in, xi, 163–166, 187–188, 209n18; early performances of, 21; harmonic unity in, xi, 159–163, 165; historical views on, 18–21, 159, 165, 208n7 (chap12); individual songs as the analytical starting point, 163, 165; merging of past and present in, 162–163, 207n3 (chap12); musical cross-references in, xi, 19, 159–163, 165; musical unity in, 19–20, 159–163, 165, 199n11; ordered vs. unordered motivic connections in, 162, 165, 207n2 (chap12); textual unity in, x, 19, 59–60, 159, 161–162, 165; topical vs. narrative unity in, 20, 162, 165, 167; turning point in, 161–162, 165

Spaun, Joseph, 21

Steblin, Rita, 197n7

sublime, 199n13

Sulzer, Johann Georg, 21–22

Suurpää, Lauri, 41, 204n4 (chap7)

syntagmatic vs. paradigmatic, 8

Tarasti, Eero, 200n11

topics, 38–39, 48; ombra in "Der Wegweiser," 126–127; sarabande in "Die Nebensonnen," 146

Tovey, Donald Francis, 102

tragic expression, 36, 51, 179; in "Das Wirtshaus," 129–134, 137–139; in "Der greise Kopf," 63–67, 69, 72; in "Der Leiermann," 151; in "Der stürmische Morgen," 105, 107,

109; in "Der Wegweiser," 115–116, 119, 124, 126; in "Die Krähe," 77–79, 82–83; in "Die Nebensonnen," 146, 149; in "Im Dorfe," 100–105; in "Letzte Hoffnung," 85–86, 88, 90, 95–96; in "Mut," 141, 143–145; in "Täsuchung," 110–113

Tunbridge, Laura, 21

Turchin, Barbara, 18–19, 159, 174, 199n8, 199n12

unfolding: in "Der greise Kopf," 66; in "Die Krähe," 75, 77, 79–80, 83; in "Letzte Hoffnung," 184

unison: in "Der greise Kopf," 66–67, 72, 183–184; in "Der stürmische Morgen," 108–109, 183; in "Die Krähe," 75–77, 82, 184; in "Letzte Hoffnung," 88, 184; as a musical cross-reference, 183–184

Urlinie, 49–50, 57, 182–183; as a musical cross-reference, 182–183; in "Der greise Kopf," 73, 183–184; in "Der Leiermann," 152, 183; in "Der stürmische Morgen," 101, 105, 107, 109, 183; in "Der Wegweiser," 205n1; in "Die Krähe," 76, 79, 84, 183; in "Im Dorfe," 113, 183; in "Mut," 142; in "Täuschung," 110

Ursatz, 49, 176; in "Der Wegweiser," 126; in "Täuschung," 113

Wagner, Richard, 120

Weber, Gottfried, 161

Wen, Eric, 203n6

Winter, Robert, 3, 5

Winterreise: cyclical organization of, x–xi, 167–190; death in, ix, xi, 7–8, 11–14, 27–29, 43, 47–48, 52, 59–60, 69–70, 73–74, 81–84, 97–100, 105, 108–109, 114, 123–128, 135–138, 140–141, 144, 148–150, 153, 155, 167, 169–170, 172–173, 176–178, 182–195, 203n7, 208nn2–3 (see also death); discontinuity in, 167, 187–190, 209n19; genesis of, 3–6; harmonic organization of, 167, 173–180, 190; keys of the manuscript vs. keys of the first publication in, 5–6, 173–174, 179, 189, 208n10, 209n13; longing in, ix–x, 7–8, 11, 59–60, 123, 125–126, 150, 167, 169–170 (see also longing); lost love in, ix, 7–13, 43, 47–48, 52, 59, 82, 84, 97–99, 105, 108–109, 112–114, 123, 148, 167, 169–170, 172–173, 176–178, 182–186, 192–195; musical cross-references in, 167, 179–187, 190, 195; narrative of, ix–x, 6–13, 59–60, 123, 148, 170–174, 176–183, 185–190, 193–195; order of songs in, 3–5; ordered and unordered musical cross-references in, 180–187, 195; reality and illusion in, ix, 7–13, 43, 46–

48, 52, 69–74, 81–84, 94, 97–98, 103, 112–113, 136–140, 144–146, 155, 180–182, 184–185, 195; textual unity in, 167–173, 190; topical vs. narrative structure in, 167, 169–173, 179–181, 190; turning points in, 11, 59–60, 84, 97, 99, 123, 135, 178, 182, 187; views on narrative unity in, 6–7, 171

Winterreise, songs: "Auf dem Flusse," 7, 193, 203n5, 209n16, 210n4; "Das Wirtshaus," 12, 28, 128–141, 144, 146, 149, 153–155, 170, 172, 178–179, 181–182, 184, 186, 189–190, 194–195, 206n1, 206n5 (chap10), 206n6; "Der greise Kopf," 11, 13–14, 63–75, 79, 84, 97, 109, 123, 125, 169, 176, 182–187, 189, 191, 193, 202n1, 202n2, 208n3; "Der Leiermann," 7, 12, 115, 119, 150–155, 169, 172, 178–180, 183, 188, 190, 194–195, 208n2, 208n9; "Der Linden-baum," ix, 9, 10, 13–14, 21, 84, 198n13; "Der stürmische Morgen," 7, 12, 99–100, 105–110, 113, 169–170, 180, 183, 188–189, 193–195, 205n9; "Der Wegweiser," 12–13, 28, 114, 129–131, 135–137, 140–141, 170, 172, 177–178, 185–186, 189, 191, 194, 205n1; "Die Krähe," 11, 74–84, 87, 97, 134, 169, 176–177, 182–187, 193, 203n2 (chap7), 209n14; "Die Neben-sonnen," 5, 12, 146–150, 155, 172, 179, 181–182, 186, 194–195; "Die Post," 3, 7, 10–11, 27, 41, 63, 169, 176, 178, 182, 205n13, 206n4 (chap10); "Die Wetterfahne," 8, 97, 209n16; "Einsamkeit," 6, 10–12, 43, 45–48, 59–60, 205n9, 207n7, 208n10, 209n17; "Erstarrung," 9, 12, 84, 193, 205n10, 209n2; "Frühling-straum," 10, 86, 197n5, 204n5 (chap7); "Ge-frorne Tränen," 9, 12, 31–32, 34, 209nn16–17; "Gute Nacht," 8, 179, 203n4 (chap6), 206n5 (chap9); "Im Dorfe," 11, 99–105, 109, 113–114, 169, 177, 183–184, 186, 188; "Irrlicht," 9–10, 13–14, 198n13, 203n7, 208n3; "Letzte Hoff-nung," 11, 84–100, 102–105, 109, 112–114, 169, 172, 176–178, 182–184, 186–189, 193–194, 203n1 (chap7), 203n3, 204n5, 209n14, 209n19; "Mut," 5, 12, 141–146, 155, 172, 179, 186, 189–190; "Rast," 5–6, 10, 197n6; "Rück-blick," 3, 9–10, 12; "Täuschung," 3, 11, 99–100, 110–114, 177, 181–182, 188–189, 194, 206n4 (chap10); "Wasserflut," 6, 9, 174

Wolf, Hugo, 120
Wolf, Werner, 207n1 (chap12)

Youens, Susan, 3, 5–7, 28, 54, 82, 93, 96, 167, 174, 179–180, 197n1, 197nn7–8, 201n3, 206n5 (chap9), 207n4 (chap11), 208n2, 210n4

Zbikowski, Lawrence M., 40–41, 54–55, 58, 202n15

LAURI SUURPÄÄ is Professor of Music Theory at the Sibelius Academy, University of the Arts, Helsinki, Finland. His main research interest is analysis of tonal music. In his research and publications he has often combined Schenkerian analysis with issues such as musical form, programmatic aspects, narrativity, musico-poetic associations in vocal music, eighteenth-century rhetoric, and Romantic literary theory and aesthetics.